3D Studio

David Carter
Eric Chadwick
Rick Daniels
Tim Forcade
Terry Locke
Brandon MacDougall
Kyle McKisic
George Maestri
Kirk Nash
Eric Peterson
Greg Phillips
Ken Robertson
Richard Sher
Paul Taylor

HOLLYWOOD & GAMING EFFECTS

New Riders Publishing, Indianapolis, Indiana

3D Studio Hollywood and Gaming Effects

By David Carter, Eric Chadwick, Rick Daniels, Tim Forcade, Terry Locke, Brandon MacDougall, Kyle McKisic, George Maestri, Kirk Nash, Eric Peterson, Greg Phillips, Ken Robertson, Richard Sher, and Paul Taylor

Published by:
New Riders Publishing
201 West 103rd Street
Indianapolis, IN 46290 USA

All rights reserved. No part of this book may be reproduced or transmitted in any form or by any means, electronic or mechanical, including photocopying, recording, or by any information storage and retrieval system, without written permission from the publisher, except for the inclusion of brief quotations in a review.

Copyright © 1996 by New Riders Publishing

Printed in the United States of America 1 2 3 4 5 6 7 8 9 0

```
***CIP data available upon request***
```

Warning and Disclaimer

This book is designed to provide information about the 3D Studio computer program. Every effort has been made to make this book as complete and as accurate as possible, but no warranty or fitness is implied.

The information is provided on an "as is" basis. The author(s) and New Riders Publishing shall have neither liability nor responsibility to any person or entity with respect to any loss or damages arising from the information contained in this book or from the use of the disks or programs that may accompany it.

Publisher	Don Fowley
Publishing Manager	David Dwyer
Marketing Manager	Ray Robinson
Managing Editor	Tad Ringo

Trademark Acknowledgments

All terms mentioned in this book that are known to be trademarks or service marks have been appropriately capitalized. New Riders Publishing cannot attest to the accuracy of this information. Use of a term in this book should not be regarded as affecting the validity of any trademark or service mark.

Development Editor
John Kane

Production Editor
Amy Bezek

Copy Editor
Phil Worthington

Technical Editor
Eric Peterson

Associate Marketing Manager
Tamara Apple

Acquisitions Coordinator
Stacey Beheler

Publisher's Assistant
Karen Opal

Cover Designer
Karen Ruggles

Cover Illustrator
Greg Phillips

Book Designer
Paula Carroll

Manufacturing Coordinator
Paul Gilchrist

Production Manager
Kelly Dobbs

Production Team Supervisor
Laurie Casey

Graphics Image Specialists
Clint Lahnen
Laura Robbins
Todd Wente

Production Analysts
Jason Hand
Bobbi Satterfield

Production Team
Heather Butler
Dan Caparo
Kim Cofer
Jennifer Eberhardt
David Garratt
Aleata Howard
Joe Millay
Erika Millen
Beth Rago
Regina Rexrode
Erich Richter
Christine Tyner
Karen Walsh

Indexer
Jeanne Clark

Contents at a Glance

	Introduction, 1
Effect 1	Solar Flares from *The Daedalus Encounter*, 5
Effect 2	Muscle Bot, 27
Effect 3	Gizmo Lightning, 59
Effect 4	Time Machine, 71
Effect 5	The Tail of the Comet, 81
Effect 6	Tornado!, 99
Effect 7	Interaction between Human and Computer Characters, 113
Effect 8	Warp Tube, 149
Effect 9	Warp Star Field, 163
Effect 10	Particle Cannon, 175
Effect 11	Search Light, 185
Effect 12	The KPT Gradient Designer, 201
Effect 13	Organic Modeling with Metaballs, 211
Appendix	Textures on the CD-ROM—Maps and AniMaps, 229
	Index, 251

Table of Contents

Introduction 1

Effect 1
Solar Flares from *The Daedalus Encounter*   5

- Use opacity masking and subtractive and additive transparencies to simulate flames, heat, and gaseous effects.
- Animate endlessly—and without taking up valuable RAM—with SMOKE_I.SXP.
- Create complex transparencies by using the 3D Studio Materials Editor's opacity channel in combination with its mask channel.

Effect 2
Muscle Bot   27

- Create and animate a bone-like skeleton, which you then use to morph a seamless organic mesh.
- Use this effect to simulate the natural bulge and flex of muscles.
- Conquer the problems of continuous polygon intersection and no stretching or contracting of fleshy/muscular areas inherent in multi-object characters by using the Bones Pro IPAS routine.

Effect 3
Gizmo Lightning   59

- Animate an image modeled and rendered in 3D Studio using the Layers feature in Adobe Photoshop 3.0.
- Produce powerful results using a scene created in 3D Studio as a background for animating.
- Develop a working knowledge of 3D Studio to create artistic images, valued in the fast-growing gaming industry.

Effect 4
Time Machine 71

- Use 3D Studio to create exciting lighting effects and animated texture maps.
- Use AVI video files to create animated texture maps for the Time Machine effect of people walking in a city.
- Animate color strobe lighting effects created from the holes in geometry.

Effect 5
The Tail of the Comet 81

- Use particle animation and image processing to create a comet traveling across the screen with pieces of the tail joining to form words.
- Captivate your viewers with an eye-catching particalization that draws them into seeing what will be created.
- Create and modify a Video Post Queue to control the image processing.

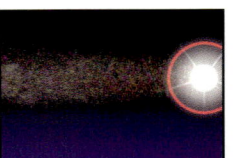

Effect 6
Tornado! 99

- Create a realistic spinning, animatable tornado.
- Use animated texture and opacity maps to achieve a particle-like effect.
- Although 3D Studio does have a tornado IPAS particle system, you can't control the shape of the particles, nor can you reshape the system; this method gives you such control and renders much faster.

3D Studio Hollywood and Gaming Effects

Effect 7

Interaction between Human and Computer Characters　　113

- Make a 3D computer-generated character revolve around and interact with a human actor.
- Use the Bones Pro IPAS routine to give life to the object. (If you don't have Bones Pro, you can use morphing targets or move the object without deforming it.)
- Use Fractal Design Painter to make the appropriate parts of the object disappear behind the actor.
- When you finish this effect, you will have a final animation with a fully composited, computer-generated object and video background/foreground.

Effect 8

Warp Tube　　149

- A light bursts from empty space, stretching out to engulf the cosmic traveler in a dance of plasma and propel the traveler through the cosmos.
- Enhance the illusion of speed by moving energy toward the camera.
- Customize the plasma material to be much more unusual than a standard fire.

Effect 9

Warp Star Field　　163

- Create a variation of the tube type of warp (seen in Effect 8): the streaking stars warp.
- Use the Scatter IPAS routine for the scatter procedural modeling process.

Effect 10
Particle Cannon   175

- Create a particle cannon in space that fires purple blasts of energy.
- Simulate a particle blast from the cannon.
- Determine the particle's color and trail color for each frame using the SPURT_I.AXP plug-in.

Effect 11
Search Light   185

- Use controlled transparency to merge computer-generated elements over other images.
- Provide the illusion of a projected light beam intersecting either smoke or dust.
- Employ animated procedural surface textures, gradient opacity maps, both mesh and material morphs, and camera motion to achieve the final result.

Effect 12
The KPT Gradient Designer   201

- Work with HSC's Gradient Designer for 3D Studio, a powerful tool for making complex lighting effects.
- Use Gradient Designer to add color and lighting effects to a somewhat dull looking image by building up *.GRD files, loading the files as a new backdrop, and adding to this by changing colors and settings.
- Composite a lightning bolt onto the image to add more dramatic effect.

Effect 13
Organic Modeling with Metaballs   211

- Construct two different characters that are modeled with metaballs, employing a slightly different method for each.

- Use metaballs technology to create a single, static mesh that you can scale, rotate, and squash just like a regular mesh object.
- Use the Smooth IPAS plug-in to process your mesh object so that it works better with Bones Pro deformation, eliminating hard edges and keeping the polygons in the mesh uniform.

Appendix
Textures on the CD-ROM—Maps and AniMaps   229

- Unusual images.
- Animation clips.

- Use for direct application as any of 3D Studio's maps or masks.
- Use as points of departure to create your own custom effects.

Index   251

Introduction

Have you ever seen a computer animation special effect in a hot new video game or Hollywood movie and said to yourself, "How'd they do that? I want to do that in my animations!" *3D Studio Hollywood and Gaming Effects* shows you how.

3D Studio Hollywood and Gaming Effects is a collection of special effects and techniques from some of the world's most creative 3D Studio artists. Each special effect is described, step-by-step, by the artist and is illustrated with full-color screen shots and renderings.

The effects in this book cover all areas of 3D Studio, including modeling, materials and maps, keyframing, and IPAS. All types of animators can benefit from these special effects. Whether you produce animations for network broadcast, multimedia presentations, games, 3D design, or just for fun, you will find this book is an excellent idea resource for spicing up your animations. Even veteran 3D Studio users will benefit from the techniques in this book.

Getting the Most from This Book

3D Studio Hollywood and Gaming Effects is written at a level for intermediate through advanced 3D Studio users. This is not to say that beginning 3D Studio users won't find useful information in this book. If nothing else, this book will inspire the beginner to dive deeper into 3D Studio. However, this book doesn't focus on teaching 3D Studio; it concentrates on teaching the artists' special effects. Each effect is written to reflect the procedure that the author/animator used to create it, even though it might not be the quickest way. So if you know quick key commands that work faster, use them.

You should have a general, well-rounded knowledge of 3D Studio in order to get the most out of the effects in this book. You should have completed the 3D Studio tutorials and should now thoroughly understand the concepts presented in them. You also should be familiar with the 3D Studio reference manuals or New Riders' *Inside 3D Studio*, and know where to find needed information. Last, but not least, you should have created several animations of your own ideas and designs.

What You Need to Use This Book

Some of the special effects in this book only require 3D Studio itself. However, to do all the effects you will need several other applications as well. These other applications are standard parts to a 3D Studio animator's toolkit and are noted in the specific effects.

Other Reference Materials

Besides 3D Studio's reference manuals, there are other books that can help you produce better animations. *Inside 3D Studio* from New Riders Publishing is an excellent and highly recommended extension to the 3D Studio manuals. *3D Studio IPAS Plug-In Reference* and *3D Studio Special Effects*, both from New Riders Publishing, will help maximize your creativity and proficiency with 3D Studio.

Using the CD-ROM

Included in the back of this book is a CD-ROM that contains the project files, maps, and meshes to create most of the special effects in this book. Some could not be included due to the proprietary nature of the actual materials. There is also a completed FLIC animation for most of the animated effects. Several of the effects also have still renderings on the CD-ROM. Each effect's files are in a separate directory on the CD-ROM. The project files are not only useful for creating the specific special effects, but, when analyzed, provide clues beyond the steps in the text about how the effects are created.

You do not need to install the project files from the SF/X CD-ROM onto your hard drive. You can load the project files directly into 3D Studio. 3D Studio will automatically add the CD-ROM directory to the Map Paths list.

Also on the SF/X CD-ROM is a bonus collection of original still and animated maps that you can use in your own animations. You may not resell or otherwise distribute them. This book's appendix includes all the maps, as well as instructions and tips on how to use them.

Notes, Tips, and Warnings

3D Studio Hollywood and Gaming Effects features special sidebars, which are set apart from the normal text by icons. Three different types of sidebars are used: Notes, Tips, and Warnings.

> **Notes include extra information that you should find useful, but which complements the discussion at hand instead of being a part of it.**
>
> **Notes might describe special situations that result from unusual circumstances. These sidebars tell you what to expect or what steps to take when such situations occur. Notes also might tell you how to avoid problems with your software and hardware.**

Tips provide you with quick instructions for getting the most from your system. A Tip might show you how to conserve memory in some setups, how to speed up a procedure, or how to perform one of many time-saving and system-enhancing techniques.

Warnings inform you when a procedure might be dangerous; that is, when you run the risk of losing data, locking your system, or even damaging your hardware. Warnings generally tell you how to avoid such losses or describe the steps you can take to remedy them.

These sidebars enhance the possibility that *3D Studio Hollywood and Gaming Effects* will be able to answer questions about 3D Studio use and performance. Although Notes, Tips, and Warnings do not condense an entire section into a few steps, these snippets will point you in new directions for solutions to your needs and problems.

Using CompuServe

The Autodesk Software Forum (GO ASOFT) on CompuServe is the best source for 3D Studio information and help. In fact, being a part of the forum is just as important as any software application or piece of hardware for the 3D Studio user. If you need help with creating your own special effect, this is the place to go. In addition to other 3D Studio animators, the programmers of 3D Studio also hang out on the forum to answer your deepest and darkest technical questions.

New Riders Publishing

The staff of New Riders Publishing is committed to bringing you the very best in computer reference material. Each New Riders book is the result of months of work by authors and staff who research and refine the information contained within its covers. Updates and other 3D Studio information can also be accessed through our World Wide Web site at http://www.mcp.com/newriders/.

As part of this commitment to you, the NRP reader, New Riders invites your input. Please let us know if you enjoy this book, if you have trouble with the information and examples presented, or if you have a suggestion for the next edition.

Please note, though: New Riders staff cannot serve as a technical resource for 3D Studio or for related questions about software- or hardware-related problems. Please refer to the documentation that accompanies 3D Studio or to the applications' Help systems.

If you have a question or comment about any New Riders book, there are several ways to contact New Riders Publishing. We will respond to as many readers as we can. Your name, address, and phone number will never become part of a mailing list or be used for any purpose other than to help us continue to bring you the best books possible. You can write to us at the following address:

> New Riders Publishing
> Attn: Publishing Manager—Graphics
> 201 W. 103rd Street
> Indianapolis, IN 46290

If you prefer, you can fax New Riders Publishing at (317) 581-4670.

To send mail from the Internet, use the following address:

`ddwyer@mcp.com`

New Riders Publishing is an imprint of Macmillan Computer Publishing. To obtain a catalog or information, or to purchase any Macmillan Computer Publishing book, call (800) 428-5331.

Thank you for selecting *3D Studio Hollywood and Gaming Effects*!

Bonus Effect On the New Riders Website

New Riders has placed a bonus effect on our World Wide Web homepage at

`http://www.mcp.com/newriders`

The special project file—the equivalent of an entire chapter from this book—is entitled "Ghost in the Tunnel" and was created by Rick Daniels and Terry Locke, with further development from Eric Peterson.

In this effect, you can learn how to create one of the most common computer graphics effects for games and movies—movement through a tunnel—then project an animation rendered separately onto an element in the main scheme.

The project files for "Ghost" are on the CD-ROM inside this book; all of the explanatory text and accompanying figures can be accessed by pointing your Web browser to this URL:

`http://www.mcp.com/newriders/gm/index.html`

Check it out!

Solar Flares from *The Daedalus Encounter*

Effect 1

by Eric Chadwick
San Francisco, California

Equipment and Software Used

- 60 MHz Pentium PC with 64 MB RAM
- 24-bit color graphics card (ATI Ultra XLR)
- 3D Studio Release 4
- Adobe Photoshop 3.0 (Windows)
- Yost Group's DSPLAC_I.PXP, SMOKE_I.SXP and STARS3_I.IXP IPAS applications

Artist Biography

Eric Chadwick is a senior artist at Mechadeus, focusing on 3D computer graphics and animation. Eric received his BFA in Illustration from Rhode Island School of Design. He then joined Mondo Media in 1991, working on interactive multimedia for corporate clients.

Mechadeus spun off from Mondo Media in 1993 in order to create original, interactive entertainment titles. Eric recently finished work on the company's latest CD-ROM game *The Daedalus Encounter*, and also provided artwork and 3D animation for their first game title, *Critical Path*.

Eric enjoys living in San Francisco with two rambunctious cats and his surprisingly calm girlfriend. Currently, Eric is exploring the next step in 3D animation technologies to be used in future Mechadeus products.

Effect Overview

The Solar Flares effect presented here is a study in transparencies and layering—subtractive transparency versus additive transparency, the opacity channel and its mask, and transparency falloff. By layering semi-opaque materials, this effect takes full advantage of 3D Studio's additive and subtractive transparency rendering methods. The goal of this effect is to create a glowing, searing-hot fireball of a sun, animated and surrounded by a cloud of spiraling incandescent dust. Study the animation included on the CD. Although the effect does lose some of its subtleties when you reduce it to 256 colors, you still can see clearly the strengths of the effect.

Traditionally, animated mapping has been done with memory-intensive sequential bitmaps, such as video of bubbling water or a raging fire. A great deal of the Solar Flares effect is created mathematically (without bitmaps) by the SMOKE_I.SXP—it animates in a natural way that is impossible to duplicate by hand, yet is difficult and time-consuming to achieve with particle systems. The sun spots illustrate this clearly as they evolve and grow over time, appearing and disappearing in a natural pattern.

With experimentation, SMOKE_I.SXP can be used for a great variety of natural effects. By using it as a mask for an opacity map, it can simulate fires, billowing clouds, and other gaseous phenomena. If you use SMOKE_I.SXP as a texture and bump map, it can simulate liquids such as bubbling mud, lava flows, toxic waste, or boiling water.

The key to SMOKE_I.SXP is to take advantage of its naturalistic animation, which will billow endlessly and never repeat itself, yet always retains its essential character. The ability to animate endlessly, and do so without taking up valuable RAM, makes SMOKE_I.SXP a great alternative to sequential bitmaps. By combining SMOKE_I.SXP with another opacity map, a great deal of animated effects can be created, a few of which are illustrated here.

STOP: Ownership of the Yost Group's IPAS Disk1, Disk2, and Disk7 is required for this effect. Specifically, you need to own STARS3_I.IXP, SMOKE_I.SXP, and DSPLAC_I.PXP.

Procedure

Before you get started, you need to be sure to set NEW-SUBTRACTIVE-TRANSPARENCY = OFF in your 3DS.SET file, using any DOS text editor. Note that OFF is the default setting, so you only need to change your 3DS.SET if you have previously turned the setting ON. 3D Studio's version 2 subtractive algorithm is used by the Renderer to correctly calculate the transparencies for the Solar Flares effect.

This exercise assumes the reader has the default 3D Studio left-hand coordinate system. When seen in the Front view, this orientation shows Y as the height vector, X as the width vector and Z as the depth vector. Users of CAD systems frequently alter their 3DS.SET files to reflect a right-hand coordinate system, which when viewed from the Front view shows Z as the height vector, Y as the width vector, and X as the depth vector. The distinction between left-hand and right-hand coordinates is important in this exercise because I refer to axis-specific actions in certain steps. The left-hand system is the default 3D Studio setting, so like the transparency setting mentioned above, you do not need to alter your SET file unless you have previously altered the setting Sets axis labeling. The correct setting for this exercise is:

H-LABEL = Y

W-LABEL = X

D-LABEL = Z

After altering your 3DS.SET, start 3D Studio. Choose **Views/Unit Setup** and set it to Metric with a Denominator of **100** and 1 Unit = **1.0 M.**

Table 1.1   The Project, Material Library, Bitmap, Flic, and Video Post Files for the Solar Flares Effect

File Name	Description
SUN.PRJ	Final Solar Flares project.
SUN.MLI	Project materials library.
CLD_OPAC.GIF	Custom bitmap for CLOUD opacity.
CLDSPLAC.GIF	Custom bitmap for CLOUD displacement.
FLARE01.GIF	Custom bitmap for FLARE1 and FLARE2 opacity.
FLARE03.GIF	Custom bitmap for FLARELOW and FLARE3 opacity.
NEBULAO.GIF	Custom bitmap for NEBULA opacity.
NEBULAO.TGA	Custom bitmap for NEBULA texture.
SUN.FLC	Rendered animation of the effect.
SUN.VP	Video Post file for using STARS3_I.IXP.

The Sun Surfaces

Now create some mesh with which to work. The sun is a series of nested spheres with varying transparencies.

1. Choose **Display/Const/Show** to show the construction planes.

2. In the Front view, choose **Create/Gsphere** to make a smoothed Gsphere with **2500** faces. Put its center on the construction crosshairs and give it a radius of about **1800** meters, then name it **SURFACE**.

3. Choose **Modify/Object/3D Scale**. While holding down the Shift key, click on SURFACE. Scale SURFACE up the smallest increment possible. While using Shift+3D Scale, you will see the scale percentage displayed at the top of the screen. This should be adjusted to read **100.25%**. A .25% increase in size is the smallest scale possible in 3D Studio. Name the new sphere **SPOTS**.

4. To create the last concentric sphere, you need to use the Window Zoom icon to zoom in close to the top edge of SURFACE and SPOTS, so that the two objects are distinctly pickable. Choose **Modify/Object/3D Scale**, hold down the Shift key and click on SPOTS. Scale it to **100.25%**, and name the new sphere **BRIGHT**.

These objects and their names might not seem to make sense right now, but they do later, as you create materials for them.

The Spiraling Cloud

Now that you have created the basic sun meshes, you need a flat grid for the spiraling cloud around the sun. Use GRIDS_I.PXP to create two grids of the same size—one at full resolution for the actual displacement and the other at low resolution as a render stand-in for the reference map. From the **Program** menu, choose **PXP Loader** to load GRIDS.

Use the following settings for the displacement grid, then name the object **CLOUD**:

Length :	**20000**	Grids :	**100**
Width :	**20000**	Grids :	**100**
Height :	**0**	Grids :	**1**

Use the following settings for the stand-in grid, then name the object **CLOUDBOX**:

Length :	**20000**	Grids :	**1**
Width :	**20000**	Grids :	**1**
Height :	**0**	Grids :	**1**

1. Select both grids and arrange them in the Top view to center them on the spheres. Watch the display at the top of your screen, and move the grids as close as possible to Selected Offsets: X:-10000.000m Y:0.000 Z:-10000.000m. You don't need to be exact, just close. When finished, deselect the grids by pressing ALT+N.

2. Now you need to render the Top view as a reference for when you paint the displacement map for CLOUD. In the Front view, create an Omni Light just inside the top edge of SURFACE, set Luminance to **255** and use a Multiplier of **1.5**. Hide CLOUD, SPOTS, and SURFACE. Choose **Renderer/Setup/Configure**, enter a Width of **500**, a Height of **500**, and an Aspect Ratio of **1.0**. Then, in the Top View, press ALT+E to activate the Safe Frame. Click on the Window Zoom icon to create a window along the edges of CLOUDBOX. Don't worry when it doesn't zoom to fit exactly within the Safe Frame—that's impossible, but also, that's all right. Render as follows:

   Render View

   Shading Limit: **Phong**

   Anti-aliasing: **On**

   (All other settings turn off)

   Output: **Display**

   Render

3. Render to disk as **CLOUDREF.TGA**. This render creates an image of a gray box that contains a black circle surrounded by a white radial gradient (see fig. 1.1), which forms the basis of the displacement map for the CLOUD object. Delete CLOUDBOX, so it doesn't get in the way later.

Figure 1.1
The reference rendering for the displacement map.

4. Save the project and exit 3D Studio, so you can paint the displacement map. Use the reference render as a guideline for painting a spiraling grayscale map in a 24-bit paint program.

> **STOP:** Do not change the size of the black circle in the center; you need it to prevent displacing the center of the CLOUD. You do, however, need to blur the edges of the circle so you can displace without hard edges. The edges of the map also need to fade to solid black, to avoid displacing the edges of the CLOUD object.

Convert the finished map from 24-bit to 8-bit (grayscale) and save as **CLDSPLAC.GIF** (see fig. 1.2).

Figure 1.2
The finished displacement map.

5. After you finish painting, start 3D Studio and load the project file you saved. Unhide the CLOUD object. In the Top view, create mapping coordinates for CLOUD by choosing **Surface/Mapping/Type/Planar**. Choose **Surface/Mapping/Adjust/Scale**. Make sure the Safe Frame is off, then press and hold the Alt key and click on CLOUD. This action scales the coordinates to fit the dimensions of the CLOUD mesh. Apply the coordinates to CLOUD.

Displacing the Cloud

Now it is time to use the Yost Group's DSPLAC_I.PXP. Choose it from the PXP Loader.

1. In DSPLAC, choose Pick Object, then pick the CLOUD object. Choose Pick Image, then pick CLDSPLAC.PCX. Under Map:, pick Plane, and use Fit To: Image. Be sure to enable Render On, which helps you visualize

the deformation as the settings change. This is especially important when you optimize, so you can decrease optimization if you see missing faces. Set Displacement Strength to around **750**. This varies according to the map you use. An Object Optimize Angle of **2.000** works well—but again, this varies. Click on Optimize, then choose Apply and OK to edit. Figure 1.3 shows the desired result.

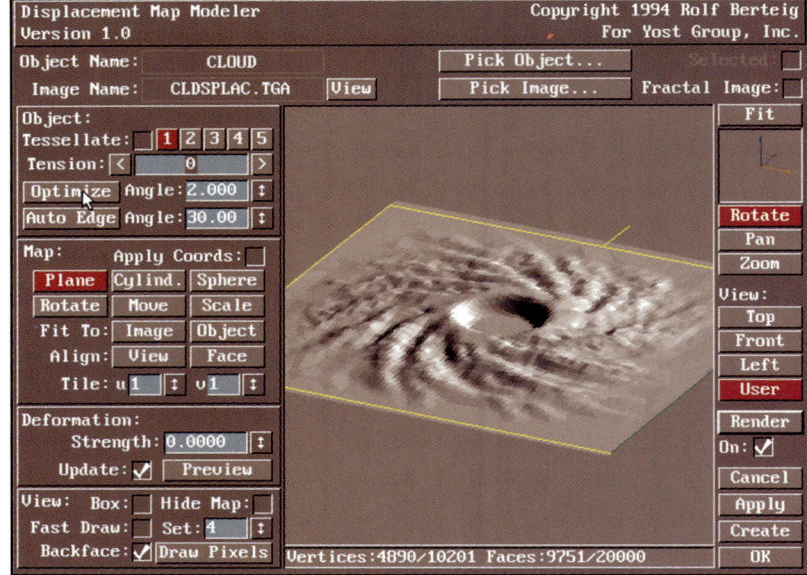

Figure 1.3
The CLOUD mesh in DSPLAC__I.PXP, displaced and optimized.

TIP: Work with the Optimize settings in DSPLAC_I.PXP to get the best result for the needs of your particular project—the more optimizing you can do without sacrificing render quality, the less you have to wait for screen redraws and the faster your renders run.

However, the use of OPTIMIZE can be problematic. Careless adjustment of the settings can result in massive disruption of the objects to which the process is applied. I recommend liberal use of the HOLD button prior to using the OPTIMIZE command in DSPLAC_I.PXP.

2. At this point, set up a test rendering to examine the displacement. In the Front view create a camera, placing it at about 10000 meters on both the X and Y axes. Place the target at the center of the construction crosshairs. Accept the default Camera Definition by clicking on Create. The camera should now be looking at the spheres from the upper right area of the screen. In the Left view, move the Omni light from just inside the top of the spheres to about 5000 meters on the Y axis, and

about **–7000** meters on the Z axis. Adjust the Omni light back down to a Luminance value of **180** and a Multiplier of **1.0**. The light should now be directly in front and above the spheres. Choose **Renderer/ Setup/Configure** and set the Width to **640**, the Height to **480**, and the Aspect Ratio to **1.0**. Activate the camera as your viewport and choose **Renderer/Render View**. Set up Render Still Image as Phong, with Anti-aliasing On, and Output to Display.

3. The resulting view (see fig. 1.4) shows the CLOUD covering too much of the sun. In the Front view, choose **Modify/Object/Move** and reposition CLOUD about 350.000 meters lower on the Y axis. Notice also that the dip in the CLOUD displacement is too constricting—the sun's flare objects, which will project out from the surface, must not intersect with the inner edge of the CLOUD, or it will call attention to the intersecting geometry and ruin the effect.

4. In the Top view, choose **Modify/Object/3D Scale** and click on CLOUD, scaling it to **175.00%**.

5. You will use two layers of cloud mesh to create the cloud effect. In the Front view, you create the second CLOUD by using the Zoom Window icon to zoom in close to CLOUD, close enough to see only about five of the grid units across the view. Choose **Modify/Object/Move**, hold down the Shift key and click on CLOUD. Move it about 10 meters up, and name the new mesh **CLOUD2**.

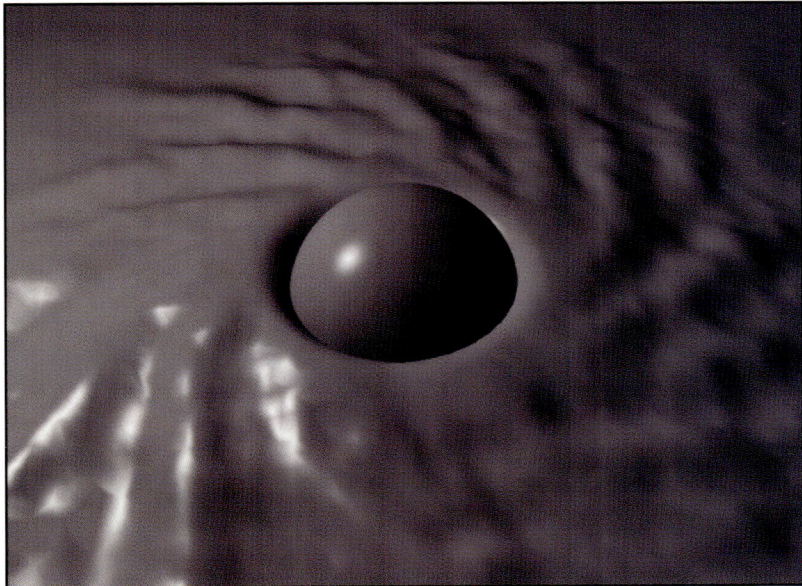

Figure 1.4
The displacement rendered with the sun mesh and default materials.

Creating the Solar Flares

To make the solar flares that shoot off around the sun, you use four nested self-illuminated disks, animated to always face the camera. Because you can see the flare effect only at the edges of the sun, you need not use a flare mesh except at those edges. These disks simulate flames coming off the entire surface, without increasing render time with unnecessary (and unseen) work.

1. Create the flare objects by first hiding everything but SURFACE. In the 2D Shaper, choose **Display/3D Display/Choose** and pick SURFACE. Choose **Display/3D Display/On**. Use the Zoom Out icon to zoom out the view until SURFACE is contained within the view window. Choose **Create/N-gon/# Sides** and set it to **60** Sides. Choose **Create/N-gon/Circular**, center the N-gon on the origin, and use a radius of about **3000** meters. In the 3D Editor, activate the Front view and choose **Create/Object/Get Shape**. In the Get Shape dialog box, name the shape **FLARE3**, set Shape Detail to Low, set Cap Shape to On, and click OK.

Because the flare disk uses SMOKE_I.SXP, you need to correct the disk's SXP animation direction. SXPs derive their mapping coordinates from the world space rather than local coordinates, so you don't need traditional mapping coordinates. SXPs animate upwardly relative to the viewport from which you create the mesh object. If you make a box in the Top view, for example, the SXP moves through the box and along the world Z-axis in a positive direction (that is, backwards). If you make another box in the Front view, the SXP moves along the world Y-axis in a positive direction (that is, upward). This orientation is fixed with the mesh throughout the duration of the animation, unless the mesh is re-created at render time, as during morphing or with AXPs.

2. You need to reset the SXP direction before you create the other disks. At this point, if you were to assign an SXP to FLARE3 and render an animation, the SXP would appear to move upwards across the disk. To change FLARE3's SXP direction, choose **Views/Angle Snap**. In the Left view, choose **Modify/Object/Rotate**, click on FLARE3 and rotate it **90.00** degrees. Choose **Modify/Object/Reset Xform**, click on FLARE3, and pick OK at the prompt. Choose **Modify/Object/Rotate**, click on FLARE3 and rotate it back upright **–90.00** degrees. Now the disk has the SXP moving through it, not upwards across it.

3. Although SXPs do not require mapping coordinates, you do need coordinates for the bitmaps used in the disk materials. In the Front view choose **Surface/Mapping/Type/Planar**, then **Surface/Mapping/Adjust/Scale**. Hold down the Alt key and click on FLARE3, then use **Apply Obj**. to apply the coordinates.

4. Choose **Modify/Object/2D Scale**, hold down the Shift key and click on FLARE3. Reduce its scale to **80.00%** and name the new disk **FLARE2**.

5. Hold down the Shift key and click on FLARE3 again. Reduce it to **67.00%** and name this disk **FLARE1**.

6. Hold down the Shift key and click on FLARE3 once more. Reduce it to **75.00%** and name this last disk **FLARELOW**.

7. In the Right view, use the Zoom Window icon to zoom in tight on the disks. Figure 1.5 shows how close you should be. Choose **Modify/Object/Move**, then press the H key to pick the disks by name. Move each of the disks so they are in a closely layered order as shown in figure 1.5, with FLARELOW in front, FLARE1 behind it, FLARE2 behind FLARE1, and FLARE3 unmoved in the rear. You order the disks in this way so that you create a complex layering effect using several partially transparent materials.

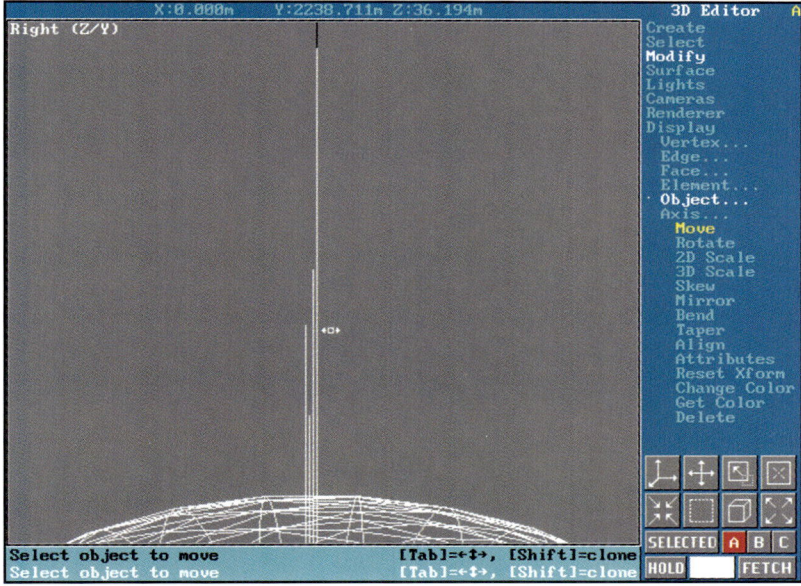

Figure 1.5
Moving the FLARE disks into their layered positions.

Creating the Nebula

Now that the sun, spiral clouds, and flares are in place, you need to add an encircling nebula cloud. You tie together the whole effect of the system by creating a translucent cloud between the system and the stars beyond.

1. Hide everything but CLOUD, then in the Top view, create a smoothed Lsphere with **30** segments, centered on the construction crosshairs, with a radius of about **30000** meters—enough to fully enclose CLOUD. Name it **NEBULA**.

> **NOTE:** Create the NEBULA with a larger radius if you plan any far-away shots—this sphere must always fully enclose the system, including the camera, for its effect to work.

2. In the Front view, choose **Surface/Mapping/Type/Spherical**, then choose **Surface/Mapping/Adjust/Scale.** Hold down the Alt key and click on NEBULA, then Apply the coordinates.

3. Choose **Surface/Normals/Object Flip** and click on NEBULA. You flipped the surface normals because NEBULA encloses the scene, and you thus view it only from the inside.

Rendering Setup

Now that you have created and placed the mesh, you need to set up the scene so you can test the materials.

1. In the Left view of the 3D Editor, hide everything but SURFACE and move the Omni Light to the center of the construction crosshairs.

2. Next you need to link the FLARE disks in a hierarchy, so when you animate the camera you can easily rotate the disks to always face it. Go to the Keyframer, hide all but the four FLARE objects and SURFACE. Choose **Hierarchy/Center Pivot** and click on each of the flares to reset the flares' pivots, choose **Hierarchy/Link** to link FLARELOW, FLARE1, and FLARE2 to FLARE3.

> **TIP:** Animating this effect starting at Frame 1 is easier because if you need to redo the animation with the flares rotated on Frame 0, resetting them to their original starting orientation—facing forward—is difficult. Leaving Frame 0 alone makes it simple to store objects' original keyframes for easy retrieval.
>
> It is essential that keys for your objects at Frame 0 never be modified. Any changes made to an object at Frame 0 in the Keyframer are immediately reflected in the Editor the next time the scene is saved. Rotate an object in the Keyframer at Frame 0, and it rotates in the Editor. This complicates the revision of complex geometry subsequent to keyframing if the construction or maintenance of the geometry in *any way* relies on any sort of orthogonal relationship with the construction axes. In the Keyframer, right-click on the Tracks button

from the icon panel. Once in the Tracks screen, copy the All Tracks indicator from Frame 0 to Frame 1. Click on OK and using **Time/Define Segment** select a segment from Frame 1 to the last frame. Your keys at Frame 0 are protected, and you still have the convenience of fully defined keys at the beginning of your active segment.

3. In the Camera view make sure Angle Snap is off then choose **Modify/Object/Rotate** and click on FLARE3. Rotate FLARE3 first along the Z axis, then around the X axis, so that the edges of the bounding boxes end up parallel to the edges of the Camera view (as shown in figure 1.6). Do not rotate on the Y axis—doing so causes the disks to arc around the sun and ruins the effect of flames emanating from particular areas on the surface.

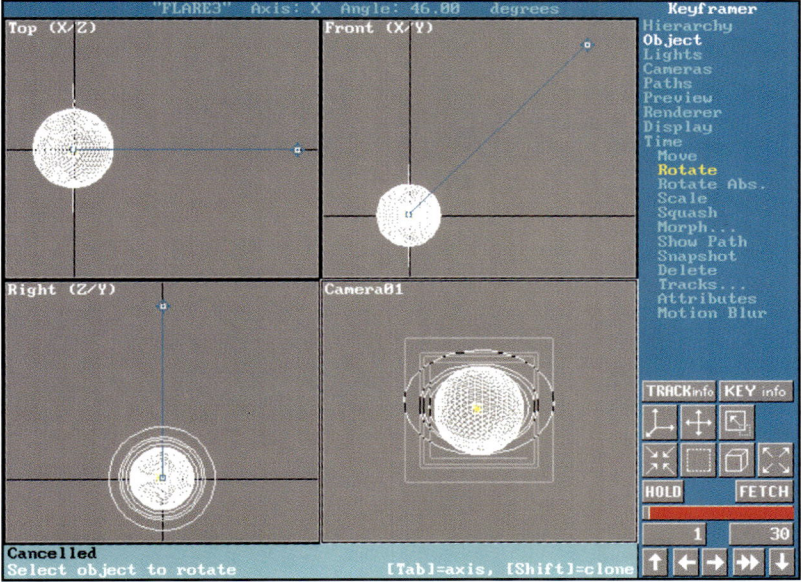

Figure 1.6
Using bounding boxes to align FLARE objects to the camera.

TIP: To constrain FLARE3 to rotate only on the X and Z axes, go to the Key Info dialog box for FLARE3 and activate the Rotate Y axis Lock button.

4. Unhide everything. This is a good time to save your scene. When done saving, go to the Materials Editor.

The Materials

Earlier you altered FLARE disks so that the SXP direction is perpendicular to their surfaces. This made the SXP run *through* the disks, which does not exactly create the effect of the smoke moving out from the center of the sun, but rather a "boiling" effect—the tendrils of flame seem to sometimes leave the surface, and other times to fall back towards it, which works fine for this effect.

Because you use SMOKE_I.SXP several times here, each with different settings, rendering times can slow tremendously. As it turns out, this happens only when you use different Exponent settings. In the materials used here, only five unique Exponent settings exist, so you need five copies of the smoke SXP.

1. Choose **Program/DOS Window** to go to DOS.

2. Go to your 3D Studio MAPS directory, and copy SMOKE_I.SXP four times. Name each copy with a number after the E in SMOKE. You should end up with five files named **SMOKE_I.SXP**, **SMOKE2_I.SXP**, **SMOKE3_I.SXP**, **SMOKE4_I.SXP**, and **SMOKE5_I.SXP**.

3. Type **EXIT** to return to the Materials Editor.

You really create the focus of this whole effect here in the Materials Editor using a combination of transparency settings (see fig. 1.7). Choose **Info/Configure/Map Paths** and add the CD maps directory for the Solar Flares effect to your map paths. Choose **Library/Load Library** to load the SUN.MLI material library from the CD-ROM, and examine the materials (see figs. 1.8 through 1.12).

Figure 1.7
A view of the Materials Editor showing some of the materials used.

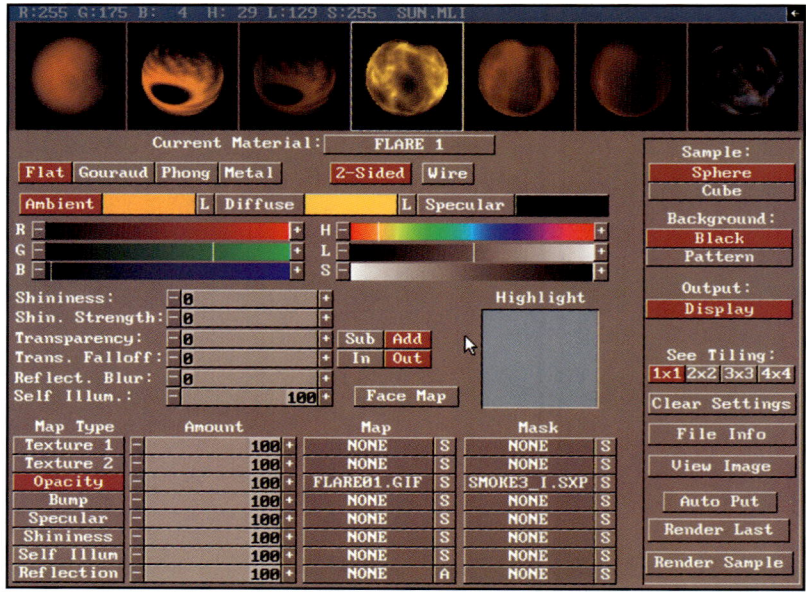

Figure 1.8
The CLOUD opacity map.

Figure 1.9
The opacity map for FLARE1 and FLARE2.

Figure 1.10
The opacity map for FLARELOW and FLARE3.

Figure 1.11
The NEBULA opacity map.

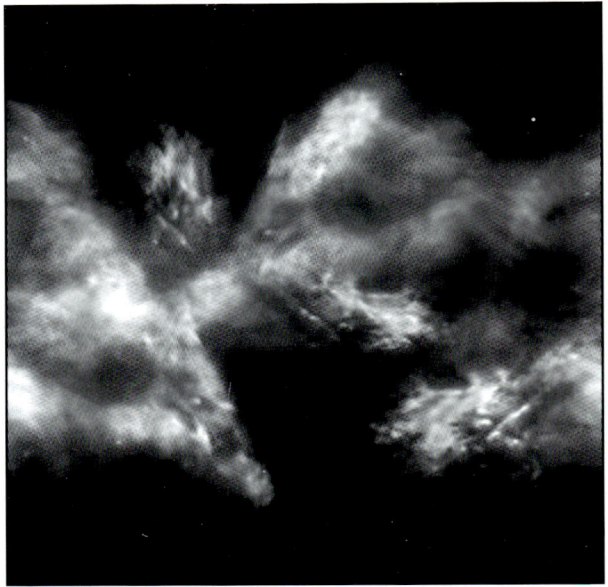

Figure 1.12
The NEBULA texture map.

* **BRIGHT.** The only material with Phong Shading—transparency falloff doesn't work correctly with Flat or Gouraud. Also, Additive, with SMOKE as its opacity. You get a layer of brightness on top of the underlying SURFACE and SPOTS, so the surface appears hotter in the center and undulations of heat move across the sun.

* **CLOUD.** Set as Subtractive, so it reinforces the density of the spiraling cloud and occludes the sun where it passes through the cloud. CLOUD uses a variation of CLDSPLAC.GIF, painted to include star spots texturing its surface; SMOKE is used in the Texture channel to add some motion and texture as well.

* **CLOUD2.** Essentially, the same as CLOUD except that it uses Additive transparency to add heat to the cloud.

* **FLARE 1.** Two-sided, so it doesn't matter which side faces the camera. The diffuse color is the lightest of the flares, because it's closest to the sun's surface. Click and drag the Opacity channel map FLARE01.GIF to View Image. It shows a white circle on black with a radial gradation from white to black at the edges. The width of this gradated edge determines the opacity falloff of the flare material at the edge of the disk. Think of the solid white part of the circle as the surface of the sun, where the flare is densest. The black at the edges of the map represents where the flare

has dissipated already. The arc of gradation between the white and the black determines how the flare material fades out as it leaves the sun. With the SXP in the Opacity Mask channel, only the smoke tendrils are opaque, while the spaces between them are transparent.

★ **FLARE 2.** Basically the same as FLARE 1, with a slightly warmer diffuse color. This material uses subtractive transparency to increase the contrast between the flares.

★ **FLARE 3.** Much darker, with a different Opacity map. FLARE03.GIF has a larger falloff, which gives it more of a burning-off-into-space look.

> **TIP:** Try combining the circle-gradation map with some type of cycling grayscale animation to replace FLARE03.GIF with an IFL in the Opacity channel, which would disperse the edge of the SMOKE more randomly.

★ **FLARELOW.** Uses the FLARE03.GIF opacity map to add an overall additive brightness and softness to the other flares.

★ **NEBULA.** Uses a texture I found on the Internet, from NASA's Hubble telescope archives, altered to tile around the NEBULA sphere. Here, I've halved its U Scale so I could put more of the texture within the camera's view. The material uses a contrast-increased grayscale version of the texture map for its opacity, and I left it Subtractive to obscure the stars behind it as would a murky gas.

★ **SPOTS.** Uses a high SMOKE exponent value to produce dark clumps of smoke, and although you can't see the effect in the Materials Editor, it animates in and out of existence much like real sun spots do. With the SURFACE sphere underneath it and the BRIGHT sphere over it, SPOTS simulates one of the more interesting effects seen on the sun's surface.

★ **SURFACE.** The base material for the sun—a completely opaque texture, with a slight animation, providing a base for the other effects in the scene.

You can subtly adjust SXP speeds for a wide range of effects—experiment with them, as well as the colors and iterations, to get a unique effect. I found that FLARE3 needs to animate slower because it expands out from the faster FLARE1 and FLARE2, and SPOTS needs a slower speed so the spots don't disappear too fast.

Because the sun is a source of light, each material's Self Illumination is set at **100%**. Shading is set to Flat because the materials are completely self-illuminated, which means that no light is reflected, thus you don't need highlighting or smoothing. Use Flat to optimize the rendering speed.

Choose Render View and render as follows:

Render Animation

Shading Limit: **Phong**

Anti-aliasing: **On**

Filter Maps: **On**

Mapping: **On**

Figure 1.13
A closeup view of the finished Solar Flares effect.

Animation and Rendering

The versatile and well-designed SMOKE_I.SXP generates a lot of the animation for you. If the camera moves, however, remember that the flare disks must continually face it, or the flare effect falls apart. To animate the disks, it works well to rotate the disks on the same keyframes that the camera uses. To help you see the bounding boxes better, convert the Camera view to a User view by pressing the U key and use the Zoom Out icon to scale the view back.

The flare effect does have its drawbacks—moving in a steady arc around the sun is problematic because the disks seem to slide across the surface of the sun, ruining the illusion of the flares' connection to the sun. This can be avoided, however, by flying the camera by at a slower speed, or by carefully matching the SMOKE_I.SXP speed to that of the camera. The speeds of the various SMOKE materials should be altered to reflect whichever playback speed your animation is rendered at. The SUN.MLI materials are set for **15** frames per second playback, which performs well on most PCs.

As a final addition, add stars behind the scene using STARS3_I.IXP. Choose **Renderer/Video Post** and click on the Camera view. Choose Load to load SUN.VP from the CD. You might need to alter STARS3's setup to match your camera's field of view—the longer the lens, the less stars will appear, and vice versa. The setup used in SUN.VP works well with the default Camera.

Conclusion

The Solar Flares effect presents a look at how attentive use of opacity masking, and subtractive and additive transparencies can simulate flames, heat, and gaseous effects. By using SXPs as shown here, you can create complex animation with a minimum of hassle, and avoid some of the difficulties associated with sequential bitmapping.

Because 3D Studio's Materials Editor gives you powerful channel masking tools, complex transparencies can be created by using the opacity channel in combination with its mask channel. The various transparency functions—additive and subtractive transparency, transparency falloff, the opacity channel and its mask—give you the flexibility to create a multitude of different possibilities.

In addition, IXPs can be used to enhance the effect. I suggest adding refraction effects on top of the sun surface using Digimation's Lumina, which would increase the appearance of heat shimmering across the sun. Try adding glows, motion blur, or contrast and saturation to heighten the effects.

Because SMOKE_I.SXP doesn't have distance-based map filtering, like the Filter Maps setting used with bitmaps, the SXP might start to shimmer if you view the sun system from a distance. If you run into this problem, try post-processing the shimmer with a blur IXP. Better yet, write your own SXP with filtering built right in. In any case, be aware that shimmering might occur, and it may require an alteration of your design.

I used the solar effect in a number of scenes in Mechadeus' CD game title *The Daedalus Encounter*, using a variation of this effect—a binary solar system with a large yellow sun and a smaller blue one. The cloud swirl was a swirling mass pulled between the two, and I used GLOW_I.IXP to further process the sun surface. There are a few images from the game in this book's gallery section and even more on the CD. The game's 3D graphics and animation were created almost exclusively with 3D Studio.

For one of the death scenes in *The Daedalus Encounter*, I used glow, rain, and explode IPASs to show a ship burning up in the sun's heat. Use the effect as a backdrop for some spectacular spaceship flybys, or create your own lavish death scenes. Experiment with the settings and layout to find new combinations or better ways of representing what you need. What comes out is always a surprise.

Muscle Bot

Effect 2

By David Carter
Aurora, Illinois

Equipment and Software Used

- LANtastic network of two IBM PC-compatibles: Pentium 90 with 32 MB RAM, 486/66 with 64 MB RAM
- 3D-Studio 4.0
- Digimation Bones Pro IPAS
- No Fluff

Artist Biography

David Carter is a 3D artist/animator and the owner of ImagiCAD in Aurora, Illinois. He currently is working as a full-time staff artist/animator for Epic MegaGames of Rockville, Maryland. Carter's works have been exhibited in the U.S., across Europe, and recently during network news broadcasts in Russia. He was recently involved in the production of the Imagination Pilots game *Blown Away*, based loosely on the movie of the same name. He has created extensive animation for reference products released by MindScape, previously known as The Software Toolworks, and has created several animated works for clients such as McDonalds Corp., Turtle Wax, and Dow Chemical.

Effect Overview

This chapter defines the basic steps necessary for creating and animating a bone-like skeleton, which you then use, in turn, to morph a seamless organic mesh. The odds are quite high you've experienced this effect first hand. The skeletal deformation effect is used quite often in today's entertainment, in film and television. One of the most recent and memorable examples occurs in the movie, *Jurassic Park*. After you create the seamless organic mesh, you contruct a bone-like skeleton inside the mesh. You then give this skeleton control over a range of points or vertices in the mesh. After you assign the bone control, you can animate the bones. The seamless mesh moves as though it possesses a natural skeleton. You also can use this effect to simulate the natural bulge and flex of muscles. Until recently, animating a seamless mesh, in particular humanoid or animal, in 3D Studio has been a labor-intensive activity. It typically involved moving and rotating vertices and faces to achieve morph targets for the primary keys. This type of animation is very time consuming and unrewarding. Using the Bones Pro IPAS Routine, by Digimation Inc., provides a quick and easy way to build and animate a skeleton within a seamless organic mesh. I find this to be a most useful tool for 3D Studio character animation. My current work in the gaming industry demands a high level of realism and fluidity. It also requires that my work be done in a timely fashion. Bones Pro is fast and quite easy to use, and the results are, well, to quote the president of Epic MegaGames, "AWESOME!".

Procedure

Table 2.1 describes the files used for the Muscle Bot effect.

Table 2.1   Files Used in this Project

File Name	Description
MUSC-A.PRJ	Base project for tutorial work
MUSC-ALL.PRJ	Complete project with all bones and animation
SKEL-A.PRJ	Example of skeleton for MUSC-A.RPJ
MUSC-A.FLI	Animated example of bones-type animation

Start 3D Studio and load the project file, MUSC-A.PRJ. Familiarize yourself with the geometry (see fig. 2.1). I created the musculature from scratch using lspheres, bolleans, and the Smooth IPAS, Digimation Inc. I cannibalized the helmet, hands, and feet from a motocross rider (ViewPoint).

Figure 2.1
A shot of the camera preview window from MUSC-A.PRJ.

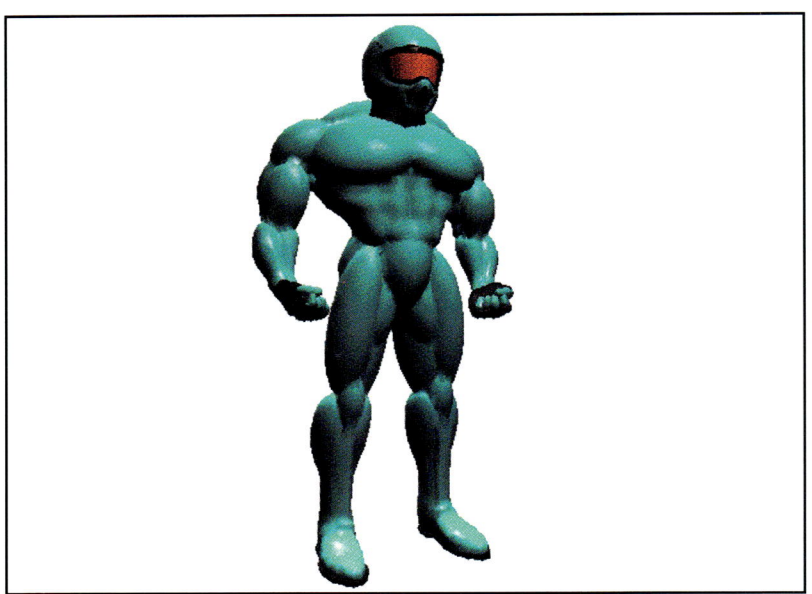

 **TIP:** Bones uses bounding boxes to calculate the influence a bone has over the mesh. Thus, your bones don't have to be boxes, but having them so is a good idea for visualization purposes. You also must be careful when you modify the bones. If you create one half of the skeleton with some of the bones rotated, for example, and then mirror those bones while holding down the Shift key, the bounding boxes on the mirrored copies change because the mirrored copies are newly created geometry. When geometry is created in the 3D Editor, via cloning or otherwise, the bounding box for that geometry is aligned with the world axes. Hence, when a rotated bone is cloned, the bounding box for that clone will no longer be rotated (see fig. 2.2). The bounding box will be aligned with the world axes. You can use the **Display/Geometry/Box** command to check for changes in your bones' bounding boxes. You also can use the shortcut ALT+B to activate box mode.

Figure 2.2 shows an example of the problem with a change in bounding boxes associated with cloning rotated bones. In the first screen, a rotated rectangular box has been mirrored with the cloning option. The boxes look identical. In the second screen, the same rectangular boxes are viewed in box mode. Their bounding boxes are quite different.

The Body

Use the rendered bone diagrams DIAG.1 and DIAG.2 as guidelines for your bone placement and rotation.

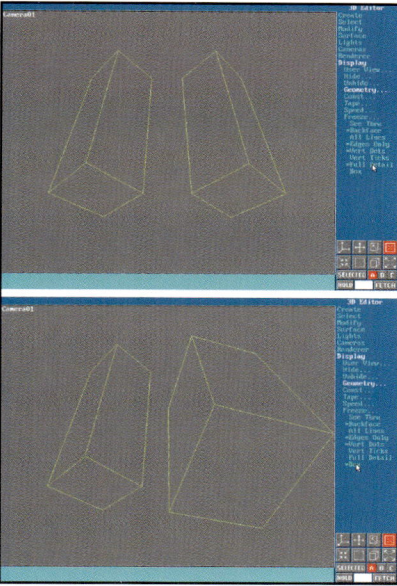

Figure 2.2
An example of the problem with a change in bounding boxes associated with cloning rotated bones.

1. Freeze the main mesh object so you don't accidentally modify it, in this case, BODY. Be sure that snap mode is enabled. Start with the bone you expect to have the most influence over your mesh, here, the pelvis. Activate the Front viewport. Construct a box, X=4.50,Y=3.00,Z=3.00, and center it roughly in the pelvic area. Name the pelvic bone **BODY01** (see fig. 2.3).

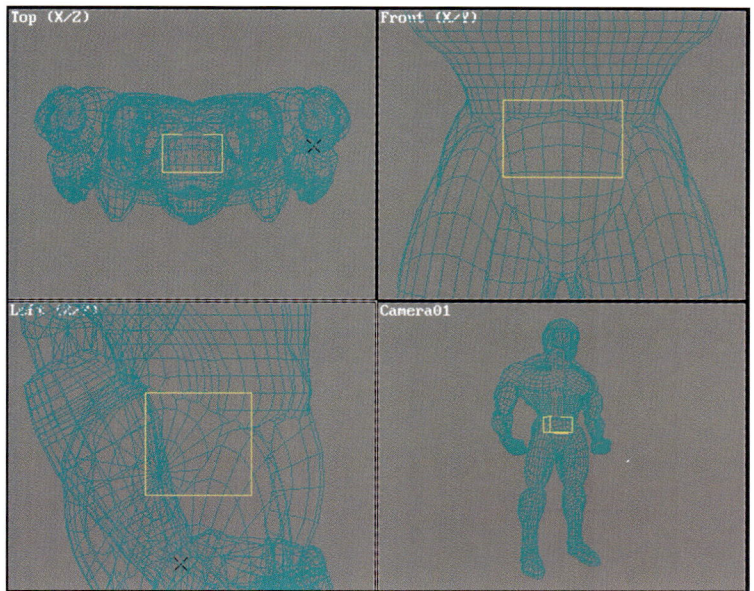

Figure 2.3
The location of the first bone of the skeleton, BODY01.

NOTE: The main mesh object in this case is BODY. A minor limitation of the Bones Pro IPAS is that the corresponding bones must have a name common with the main mesh object, such as BODY01, BODY02, BODY03, and so on.

2. Next, create the spine. For this exercise, you don't have to create a bone for every vertebrae. Create a box, X=1.50,Y=4.00,Z=1.50, and name it **BODY02**. Place it directly on top of the pelvic bone then move it Y=.25,Z=-.25. This bone represents the base of the spine. Create a copy of BODY02, Y=4.25,Z=-.50, and name it **BODY03**, the middle of the spine. Create another copy of BODY02, Y=9.50,Z=.25, and name it **BODY04**. This bone represents the spine at the shoulders and the neck (see fig. 2.4).

TIP: By pressing the Shift key while using the more basic editing commands (i.e. move, rotate, mirror), you can create "clones" or copies of your geometry. Use of this cloning function will make the bone creation process a great deal easier.

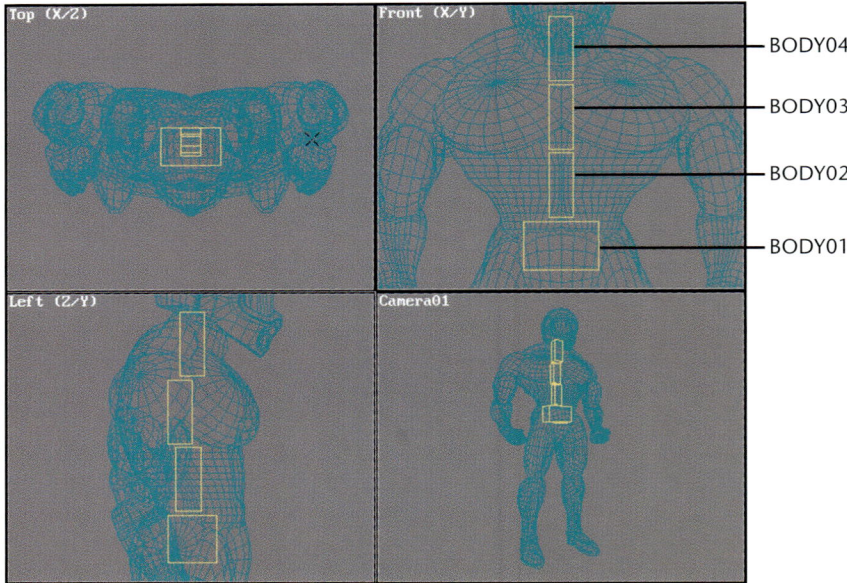

Figure 2.4
Location of the three spine bones—BODY02, BODY03, and BODY04—in relation to the Main Mesh Object and BODY01.

3. Next, create support bones for the shoulders and arms. Create a box, X=6.00,Y=1.50,Z=1.50, and name it **BODY05**. Place this bone so that the upper-right corner lines up with the top center of BODY03. Then

move it X=–.25,Y=–.25,Z=–1.75. This bone controls the uppermost portion of the back, and serves as a visual reference to the arm bones. Create a copy of this bone for the other side of the spine and name it **BODY06** (see fig. 2.5).

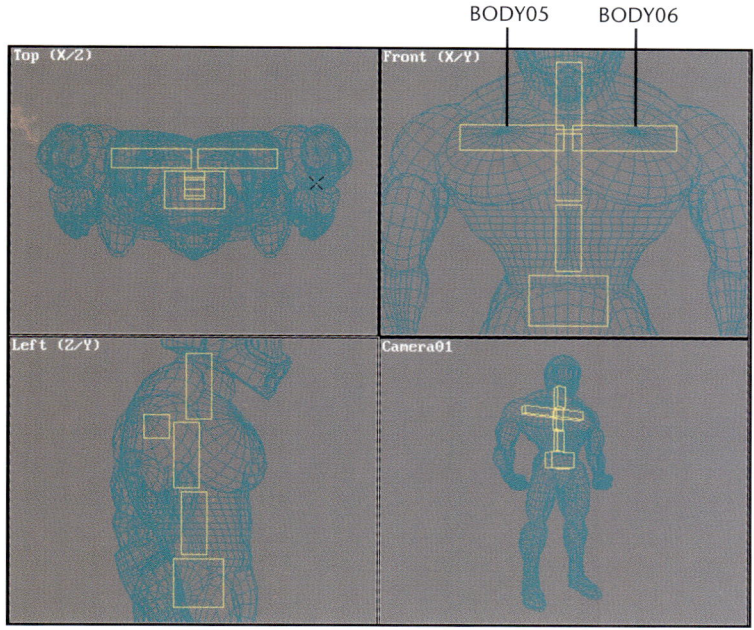

Figure 2.5
Placement of the shoulder/clavical bones—BODY05 and BODY06—in relation to the spine bones.

TIP: Remember, you don't have to place a bone for every bone in the human skeleton. Feel free to use the supplied skeleton in SKEL-A.PRJ as a guideline.

The Legs

1. Next, create the leg bones, starting with the right thigh. In the Front viewport, create a box, X=1.50,Y=11.00,Z=1.50, and name it **BODY07**. Place it within the right thigh so that it is centered front to back on the pelvic bone. Then move this bone to a position that places it X=–.50,Y=.50 from the pelvic bone. Create an identical copy for the left thigh, and place it similarly. Name this bone **BODY08** (see fig. 2.6).

2. Create a box, X=1.50,Y=12.00,Z=1.50, and name it **BODY09**. Place it within the right lower leg, and center it X=–.25 below BODY07. Move it from this location to X=–1.00,Z=–1.00. Make a copy of this bone for the left lower leg, placing it in a similar fashion, and name it **BODY10**. Turn on the local axes icon and activate the Left view, then rotate the lower leg bones –8°. This action places these bones in a good position for the knee joint and aligns them with the shins.

Figure 2.6
Location of the leg bones—BODY07 through BODY12—in relation to the Main Mesh Object.

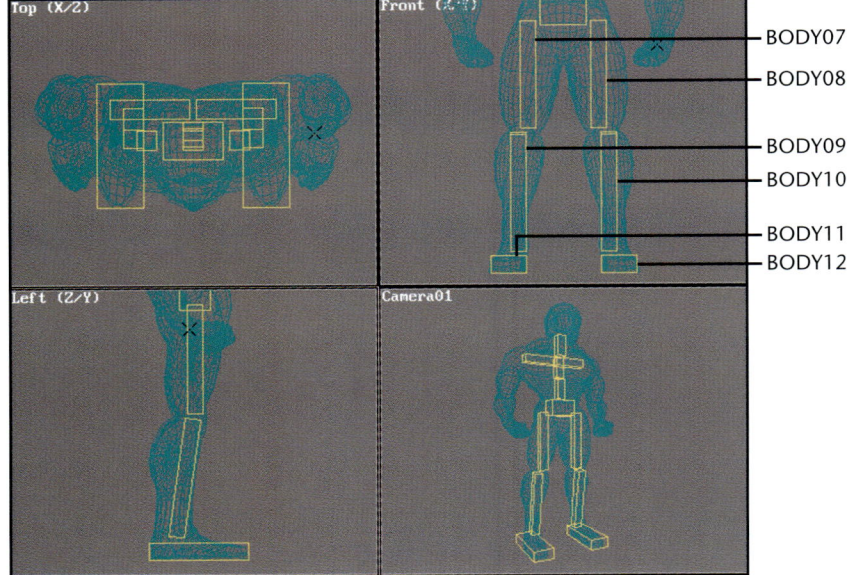

3. Now generate bones for the feet. Create a box X=3.50, Y=1.75, Z=9.75, and name it **BODY11**. Align it with the sole of the right foot. Create a copy named **BODY12**, and align it with the sole of the left foot.

The Upper Arms

1. Start by creating the shoulder bones. Create a box X=2.00, Y=3.50, Z=3.00 and name it **BODY13**. Center it .25 off the end of BODY05 (the right arm support). Now, move the bone Y=–.50, Z=–.25. Create a copy of this bone for the left shoulder and name it **BODY14** (see fig. 2.7).

2. Next, create a box, X=1.50, Y=6.00, Z=1.50, and name it **BODY15**. Place this bone in the right upper arm so that the upper inside edge is centered on the lower outside edge of BODY13. Then move this bone X=–.25, Y=.75, Z=1.00. Create a copy of this bone for the left side and name it **BODY16**.

The Lower Arms

1. Create a copy of BODY15 at X=–.25, Y=–6.00, Z=–1.00 and name it **BODY17**. Create a copy of this bone for the left side and call it **BODY18** (see fig. 2.8). Turn on the local axes icon. Rotate BODY17 and BODY18 30°, so that they line up with the lengths of the forearms.

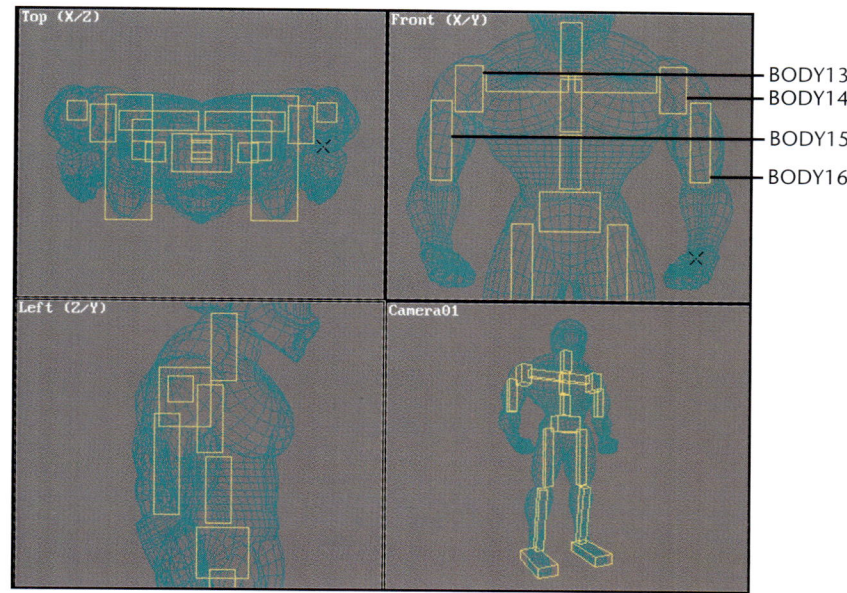

Figure 2.7
Placement of the upper arm bones—BODY13 through BODY16—in relation to the Main Mesh Object.

For this exercise, you do not need to move the fingers. Hence, you use only one bone for the entire hand. Placing bones for the hands is a little tricky nonetheless. The hands are not in a position that allows you to use a bone that is aligned with any viewport. You must rotate the hand bones on all axes.

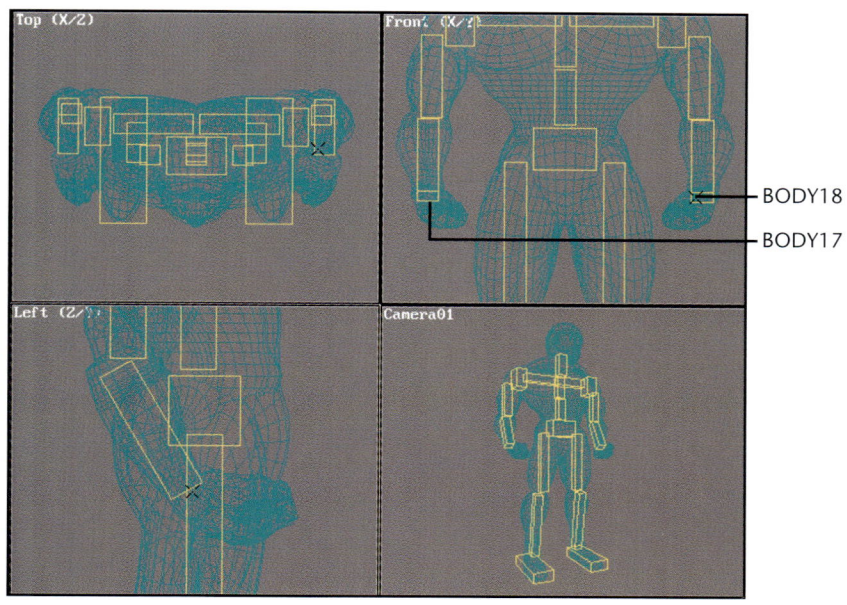

Figure 2.8
Location and rotation of the lower arm bones—BODY17 and BODY18.

2. Start by creating a box, X=3.50,Y=2.50,Z=4.00, and name it **BODY19**. Center this bone against the end of BODY17 in the Front view. In the left view, move it so that the back side roughly lines up with the end of BODY17. Create a copy for the left side, name it **BODY20**, and place it similarly.

3. Choose **Modify/Axes/Place** to place the World Axes at X=–9.50,Y=–13.00,Z=1.75, which should place the axes at the end of BODY17, slightly off center. Be sure to turn off the Local Axes icon. In the Front view, rotate BODY19 (the right hand bone) –20°. In the Top view, rotate BODY19 15°. In the Left view, rotate BODY19 –20°. BODY19 should, at this point, roughly encompass the right hand of the main mesh object (see fig. 2.9).

4. Again, choose **Modify/Axes/Place** to place the World Axes at X=9.00,Y=–13.00,Z=1.75. This time, the axes should lie at the end of BODY18 (the left forearm bone). In the Front view, rotate BODY20 (the left hand bone) 20°. In the Top view, rotate BODY20 –15°. In the Left view, rotate BODY20 –20°. Now BODY20 should roughly encompass the left hand of the main mesh object (see fig. 2.10).

Figure 2.9
Placement and rotation of the right hand bone, BODY19, in relation to the right hand of the Main Mesh Object.

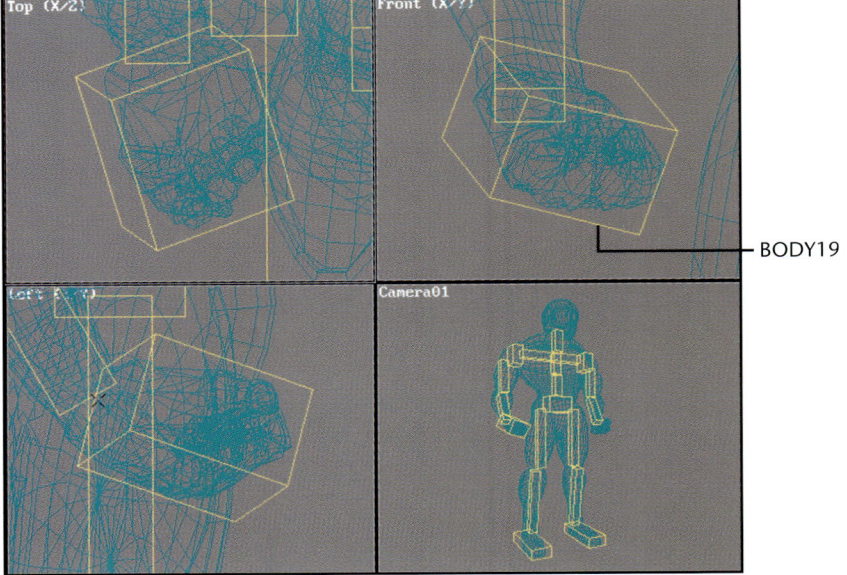

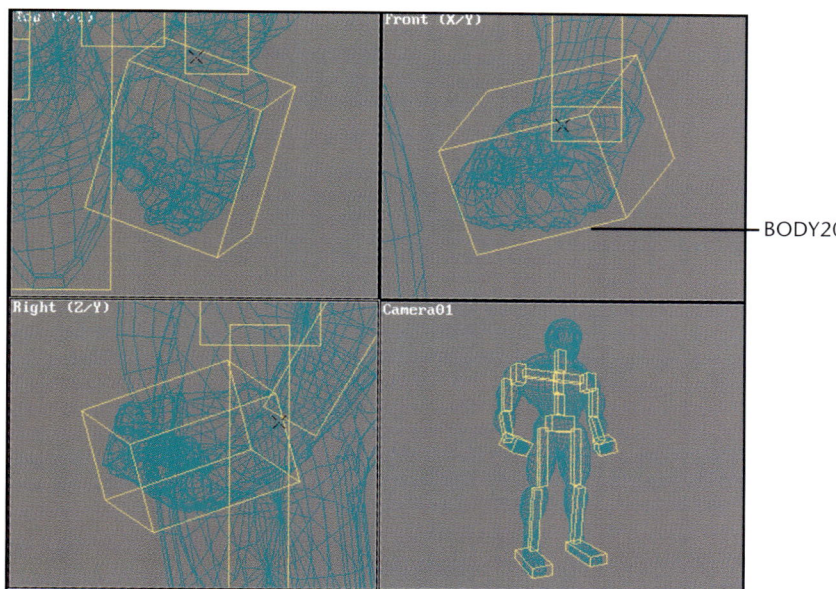

Figure 2.10
Placement and rotation of the left hand bone, BODY20, in relation to the left hand of the Main Mesh Object.

The Head

1. The head of the main mesh object is wearing a helmet. Therefore, you want more rigid control over the helmet vertices. By making the bone as large, or larger than, the vertices it controls, you easily affect more rigid control. Make a box, X=6.00, Y=6.25, Z=8.00, and name it **BODY21**. In the Front view, roughly center this bone on the helmet of the main mesh object. In the Left view, move the bone so that it is roughly Z=.75 off center of the helmet. Turn on the local axes icon. Rotate BODY21 –20°. At this point, BODY21 should just cover the lower rim and front vents of the helmet (see fig. 2.11). If not, turn off Snap and perform minor adjustments. Remember to turn Snap back on, once you have finished your adjustments.

> **NOTE:** A few of the bones in SKEL-A.PRJ are larger than the corresponding area of the mesh. Notice that the main mesh object in MUSC-A.PRJ is wearing a helmet. Helmets typically do not bend, twist, or flex. The bone for the head, BODY21, is larger to allow more rigid control over the helmet vertices. Similar control is required for both the hands and the soles of the feet.

Figure 2.11
Location and rotation of the head/helmet bone. BODY21.

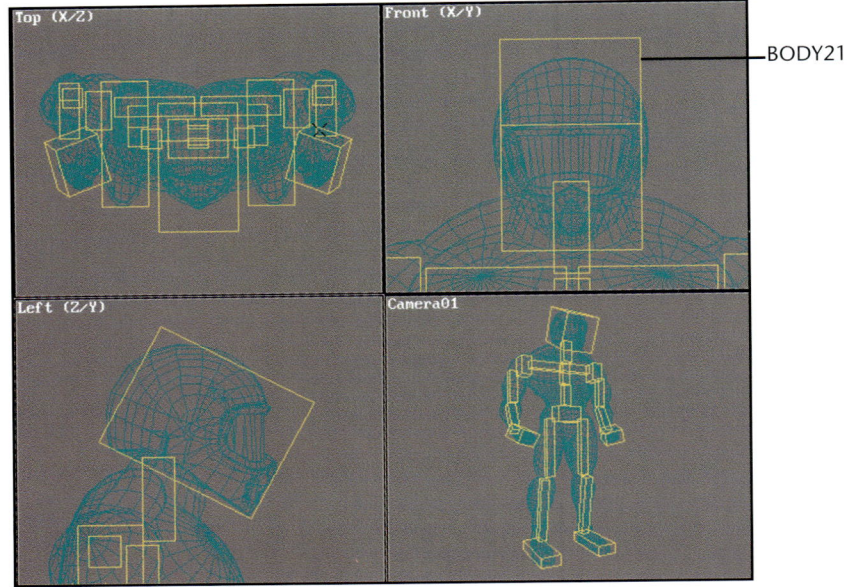

The Muscles

The next step is to place "Muscle" bones, that is, if your mesh is muscular and you want to be able to flex those muscles. In MUSC-A.PRJ, the biceps and pectorals are good muscles for flexing.

1. Create a "bicep" bone by placing a box X=2.00,Y=2.50,Z=1.00 roughly at the center of the right bicep, lying it directly on the front of the upper arm bone. Name this bone **BODY22**. Create a similar bone for the left bicep and call it **BODY23** (see fig. 2.12).

2. Next, place the right "pectoral" bone. Create a box, X=6.00,Y=4.25, Z=2.00, and name it **BODY24**. Place this muscle bone in the right side of the chest, slightly to the right of center. Make sure that this muscle bone is far enough forward to lie within the chest muscles without overlapping BODY13. Create a duplicate bone for the pectoral and name it **BODY25** (see fig. 2.13).

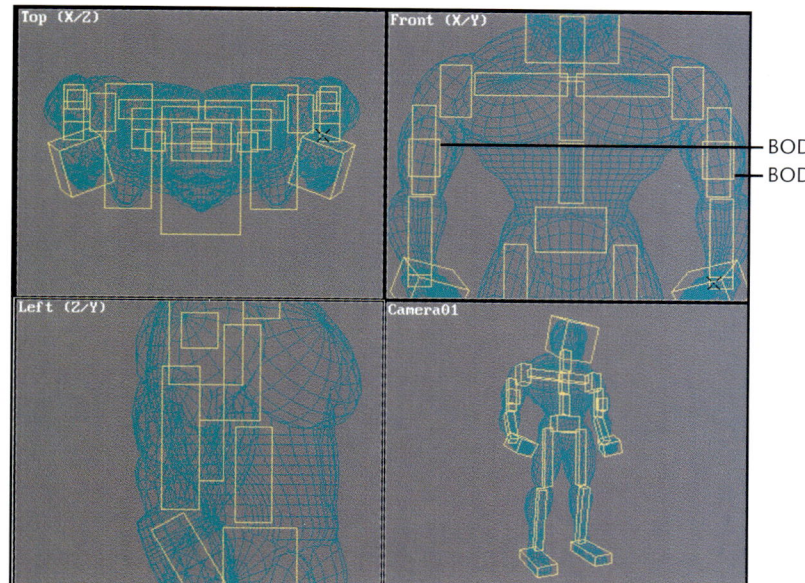

Figure 2.12
The bicep bones—BODY22 and BODY23—are placed directly on the front of the upper arm bones.

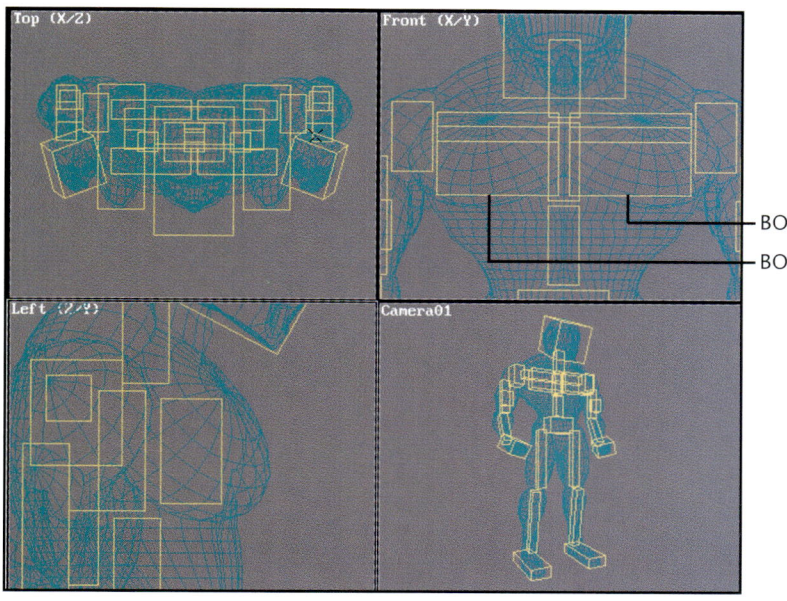

Figure 2.13
The pectoral bones—BODY24 and BODY25—placed within the chest muscles without overlapping other bones.

The Retaining Bones

Now you need a few retaining bones—the bones that help prevent the undesirable flattening and folding of faces. In other words, certain areas in the mesh don't require bone-like animation, yet the vertices in these areas must retain their position relative to the rest of the mesh, including the upper thighs, groin, buttocks, and torso.

1. Create a box, X=2.50,Y=2.00,Z=2.50, and name it **BODY26**. Center it under the pelvic bone, then move it Z=.25 so that it lines up with the front of the pelvis bone (see fig. 2.14). This bone helps prevent exaggerated skewing of the groin area when the upper leg bones are scissored, for example, if you wanted to create an animation of the mesh running or walking.

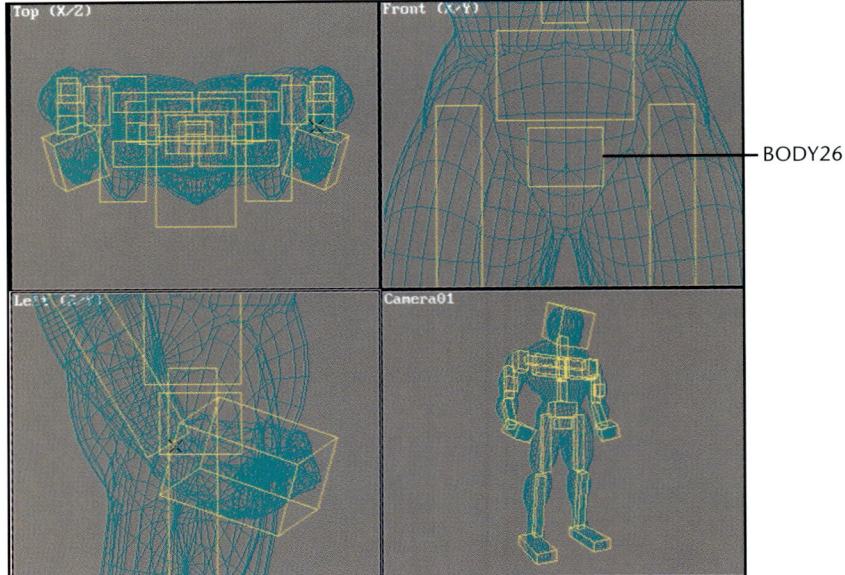

Figure 2.14
Placing a retaining bone, BODY26, in the groin area helps to maintain rigidity in the pelvic region.

2. Create a box, X=1.00,Y=5.25,Z=2.00, and name it **BODY27**. Place it inside and slightly to the rear of the right thigh, to prevent the flattening of the thigh that occurs when the upper leg bone bends up toward the chest. Create a similar bone for the left thigh and name it **BODY28**. (see fig. 2.15).

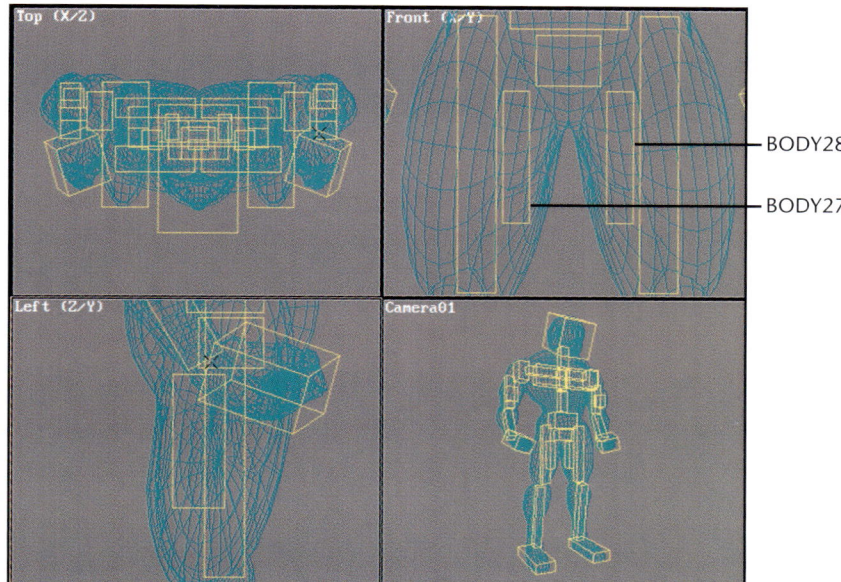

Figure 2.15
Adding retaining thigh bones—BODY27 and BODY28—helps to maintain the shape of the thighs when the leg bones are rotated to extremes.

3. On to the buttocks. Create a box, X=2.00,Y=3.25,Z=1.50, and name it **BODY29**. Place this bone just about in the center of the right cheek and to the rear of BODY01 (the pelvic bone). Avoid overlapping the pelvic bone, if possible. Create a duplicate bone for the left cheek and name it **BODY30** (see fig. 2.16). These bones have an effect similar to the retaining bones created for the thighs. As the upper legs bend forward (as in running or walking), the buttocks tends to flatten out. Although a slight flattening does occur in nature, the effect would be quite exaggerated without the retaining buttocks bones.

4. Owing to the desire to dramatically move the arm bones, you need a simulated rib structure. This rib structure prevents the torso from collapsing and creasing as the arm bones move toward their extents. Create a box, X=3.75,Y=2.75,Z=1.50, and name it **BODY31**. Place it .50 under the right pectoral "muscle" bone. This bone simulates the right front rib cage. Place another rib cage bone for the left side and name it **BODY32**. Next, create a box, X=5.00,Y=4.00,Z=1.50, and name it **BODY33**. Center this bone in the upper-right region of the back. Create another box, X=3.00,Y=4.25,Z=1.50, and name it **BODY34**. Place this bone in the lower right portion of the back under the previously created bone. These bones simulate the right rear section of the rib cage. Continue by creating matching bones for the left rear area of the rib cage. Name these bones **BODY35** and **BODY36**, respectively (see fig. 2.17).

Figure 2.16
Buttocks bones—BODY29 and BODY30—maintain the shape of the buttocks of the Main Mesh Object when the leg bones are rotated to extremes.

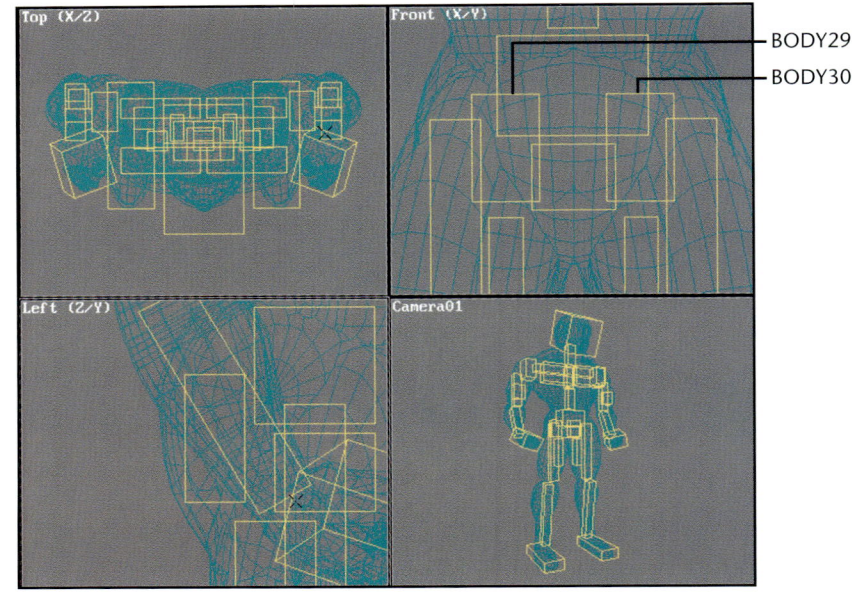

Figure 2.17
Location of the rib bones—BODY31 through BODY36—correctly placed within the torso of the Main Mesh Object.

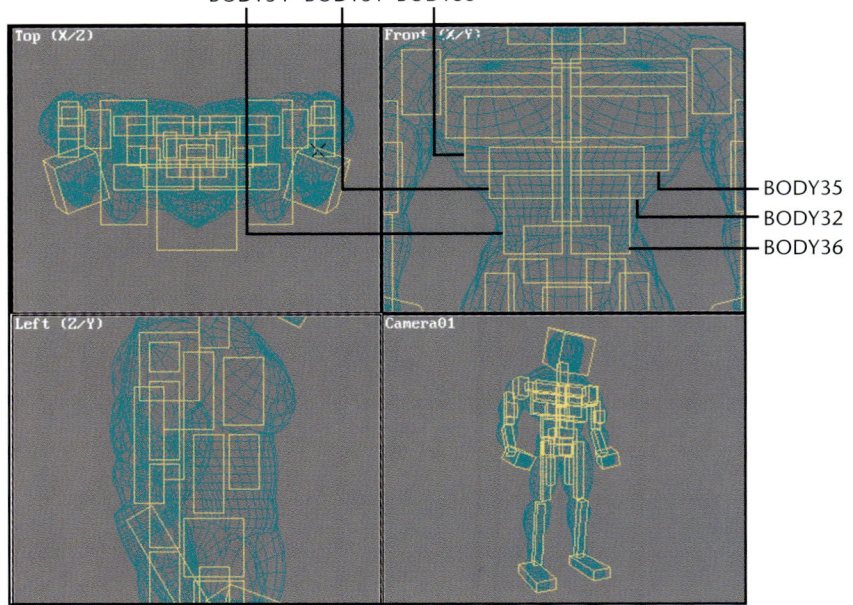

Linking the Bones

First, switch over to the Keyframer by pressing the F4 function key. Make sure that the main mesh object, BODY, is frozen (see fig. 2.18). Here, link your bones together and set their logical pivot points. Set the pivot points in relation to both the bones and the mesh; usually this would be the logical intersection points of the bones. Link the retaining and muscle bones to their logical primary bones, as described in the following instructions.

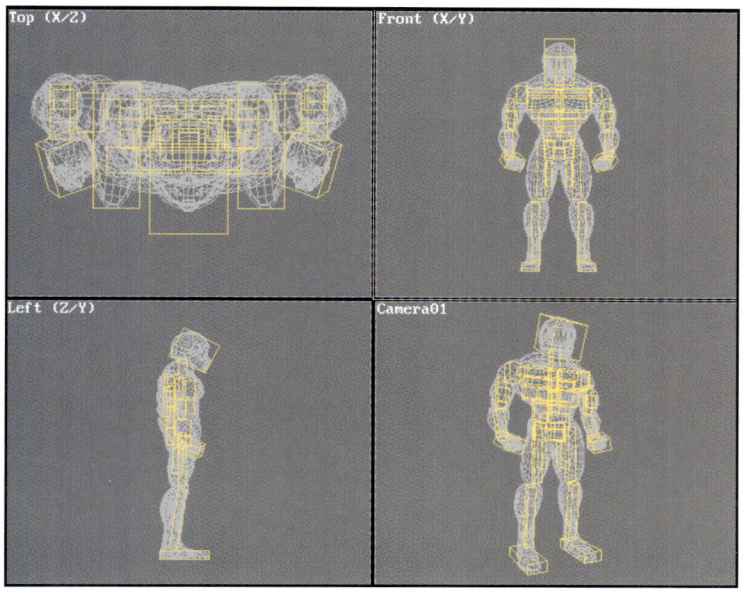

Figure 2.18
The completed skeleton in the Keyframer with the Main Mesh Object, BODY, frozen.

1. Begin by linking the pelvic retaining bone, BODY26, to BODY01 (the primary pelvic bone). The pivot point is irrelevant.

2. Link the thigh retaining bones, BODY27 and BODY28, to the upper leg bones, BODY07 and BODY08, respectively. Again, the pivot points are irrelevant.

3. Link the buttocks retaining bones, BODY29 and BODY30, to BODY01 (the primary pelvic bone). Set the pivot points for the buttocks bones to the top center and pelvic side.

4. Link the rib cage retaining bones, BODY31 through BODY36, to the nearest of the spine bones, BODY02 or BODY03, respectively.

5. Link the chest muscle bones, BODY24 and BODY25, to the clavicle arm support bones, BODY05 and BODY06, respectively. Set the pivot points to the top, rear, and inside corner of the chest muscle bones.

6. Link the bicep muscle bones, BODY22 and BODY23, to the upper arm bones, BODY15 and BODY16, respectively. Set the pivot points at the top, rear, and center of the bicep muscle bones.

7. Your completed hierarchy should look something like the following:

BODY01
  BODY08
    BODY10
      BODY12
    BODY28
  BODY07
    BODY09
      BODY11
    BODY27
  BODY26
  BODY02
    BODY03
      BODY04
        BODY21
      BODY06
        BODY14
          BODY16
            BODY18
              BODY20
          BODY23
      BODY25
      BODY35
    BODY05
      BODY13
        BODY15
          BODY17
            BODY19
          BODY22
      BODY24
      BODY33
  BODY31
  BODY32
  BODY36
  BODY34
BODY30
BODY29

Keyframing a Test Animation

Keyframing a short test animation before you enter the "Bones Pro" interface often is a good idea—doing so allows you to easily check the influence the bones have over the main mesh object.

1. If you currently aren't in the Keyframer, switch to it by pressing F4. Hide the main mesh object, BODY. Set the total frames number, in the lower-right corner, to 60.

2. Create two dummy objects, by choosing **Hierarchy/Create Dummy** from the right side menu, to use as follow objects for the feet. Name the dummies **L-FOLLOW** and **R-FOLLOW**, respectively. These should roughly match the size of the feet, and should line up with the soles (see fig. 2.19). You will use these dummies to hold the feet in place while the rest of the skeleton moves.

3. Use the frame slider to set the current frame to 30. Switch to the front view. Move BODY01 (the primary pelvic bone) X=2.00,Y=–1.00. Rotate BODY02 (the bottom spine bone) 15° around the Y axis. Then rotate BODY03 (the middle spine bone) 10° around the Y axis and 10° around the Z axis. Rotate BODY21 (the head bone) –45° around the Y axis and –10° around the X axis (see fig. 2.20).

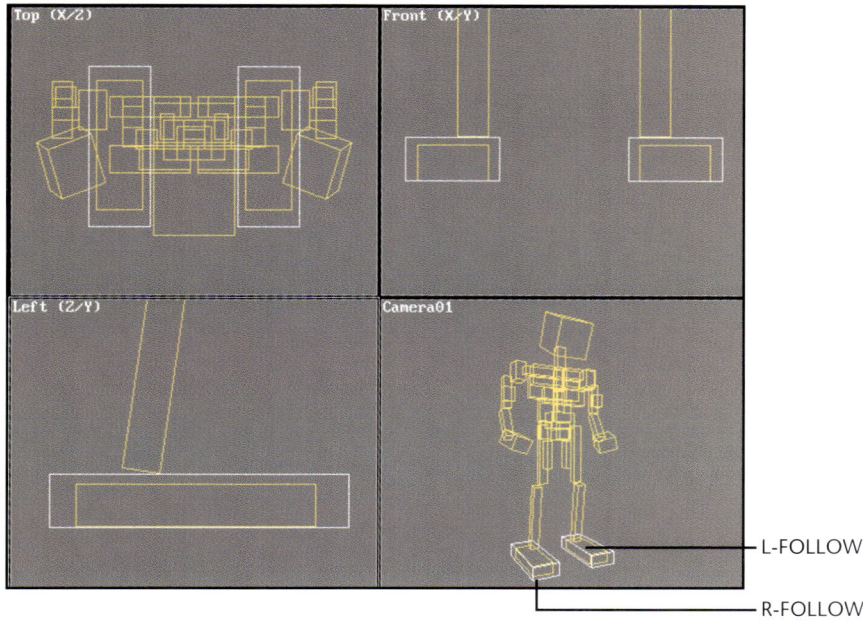

Figure 2.19
Placement of the dummy objects, L-FOLLOW and R-FOLLOW, in relation to the foot bones.

Figure 2.20
The first rotation keys, set at frame 30.

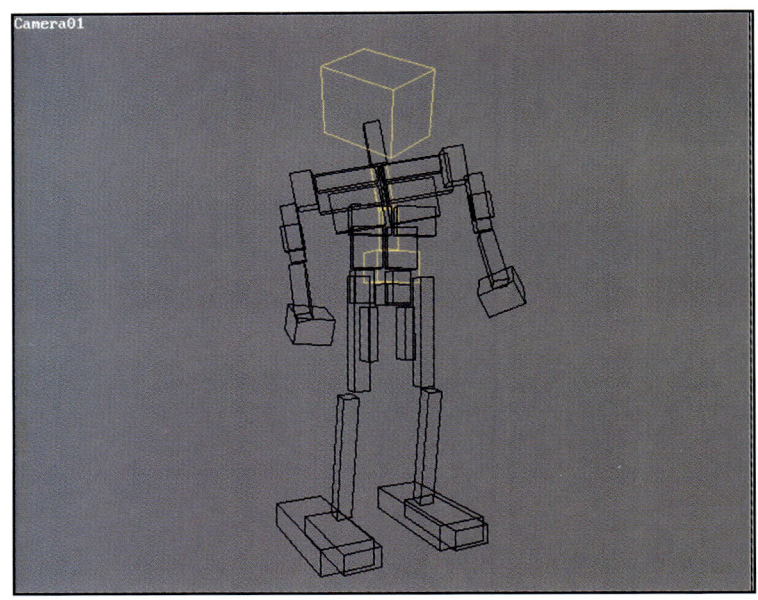

4. Use the frame slider to set the current frame to 25. Rotate BODY13 (the right shoulder bone) –30° around the Z axis and 30° around the X axis. Similarly rotate BODY14 30° around the Z axis and 30° around the X axis. Next, rotate BODY15 (the right upper arm bone) –45° around the Z axis, and rotate BODY16 (the left upper arm bone) 45° around the Z axis. Rotate BODY17 (the lower right arm bone) 30° around the X axis and rotate BODY18 (the lower left arm bone) 30° around the X axis. Rotate BODY19 (the right hand bone) –30° around the Z axis and rotate BODY20 (the left hand bone) 30° around the Z axis (see fig. 2.21).

5. Use the frame slider to set the current frame back to 30. Rotate BODY17 an additional 45° around the X axis. Do the same to BODY18. Then rotate BODY19 back 45° around the Z axis and rotate BODY20 back –45° around the X axis. Now you want to flex those biceps. Scale BODY 22 (the right bicep muscle bone) 200% on the Z axis only. Scale BODY23 in the same fashion (see fig. 2.22).

6. Next you need to copy a few tracks. Select the TRACK info button in the lower-right section of the screen, and pick BODY13 (the right shoulder bone). Check the Object slider window, to verify that the active object is BODY13. Be sure to set the scope to Self. Copy the rotate track at frame 25 to frame 40. Click on the right or left arrow on the object slider until it reads BODY14 (the left shoulder bone). Copy the rotate tracks as you did for BODY13.

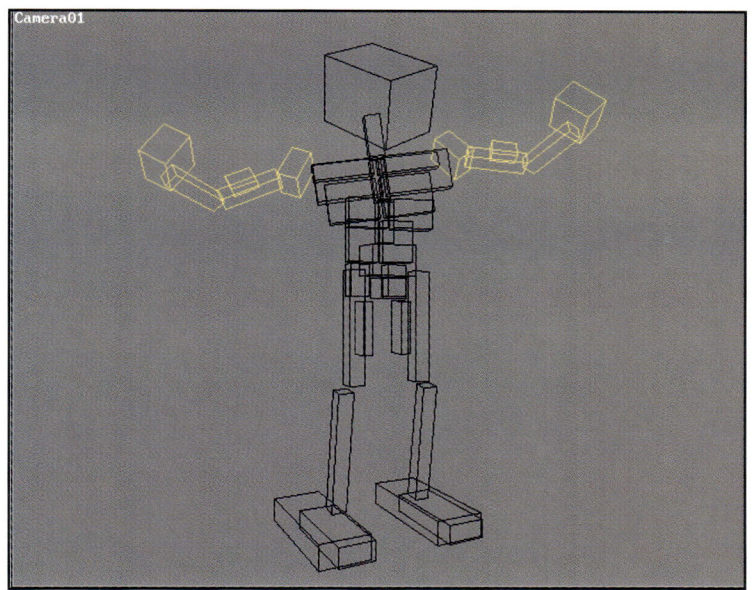

Figure 2.21
Assigning rotation keys in preparation of flexing the biceps.

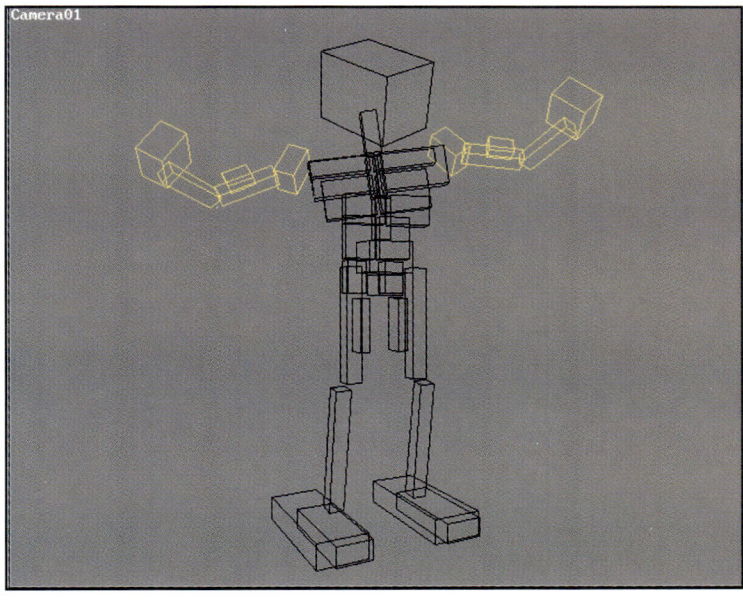

Figure 2.22
Scaling the bicep bones will cause a bulging of the biceps on the Main Mesh Object.

7. Click on the right or left arrow on the object slider until it reads BODY15 (the right upper arm bone). Copy the rotate track at frame 25 to frame 40. Click on the right or left arrow on the object slider until it reads BODY16 (the left upper arm bone). Copy the rotate keys as you did for BODY15.

8. Click on the right or left arrow on the object slider until it reads BODY17 (the lower right arm bone). Set the scope to Sub-Tree. Copy the rotate track at frame 30 to frame 35. Copy the rotate track at frame 25 to frame 45. Click on the right or left arrow on the object slider until it reads BODY18 (the lower left arm bone). Copy the rotate tracks as you did for BODY17.

9. Set the scope back to Self. Click the right or left arrow on the object slider until it reads BODY22 (the right bicep muscle bone). Copy the scale track at frame 0 to frame 25. Copy the scale track at frame 30 to frame 35. Copy the scale track at frame 25 to frame 40. Click on the right or left arrow on the object slider until it reads BODY23 (the left bicep muscle bone). Copy the scale tracks as you did for BODY22.

10. Click on the right or left arrow on the object slider until it reads BODY02 (the bottom spine bone). Copy the rotate track at frame 30 to frame 35. Click on the right or left arrow on the object slider until it reads BODY03 (the middle spine bone). Copy the rotate track as you did for BODY02. Click on the right or left arrow on the object slider until it reads BODY21 (the head bone). Copy the rotate track as you did for BODY03.

    Click on the OK button in the lower-right corner of the TRACK info window.

11. Click on the double-right arrow button at the lower-right corner of the screen. Check your animation. If everything looks fine, click the right mouse button to stop the preview and save your work. Give it a name, something like **PUMPED1.PRJ**. After you save your project, choose **Object/Tracks/Loop** and select BODY01 (the primary pelvic bone). Loop the subtree also. Click on the double-right arrow button again. You now should have a smoothly looping animation.

IK Animation of the Legs

Press F8 on the keyboard to activate Inverse Kinematics. Click on the Pick Objects... button in the upper-left corner of the screen. Select any bone in the skeleton. You should now see a hierarchical list of all the bones (see fig. 2.23).

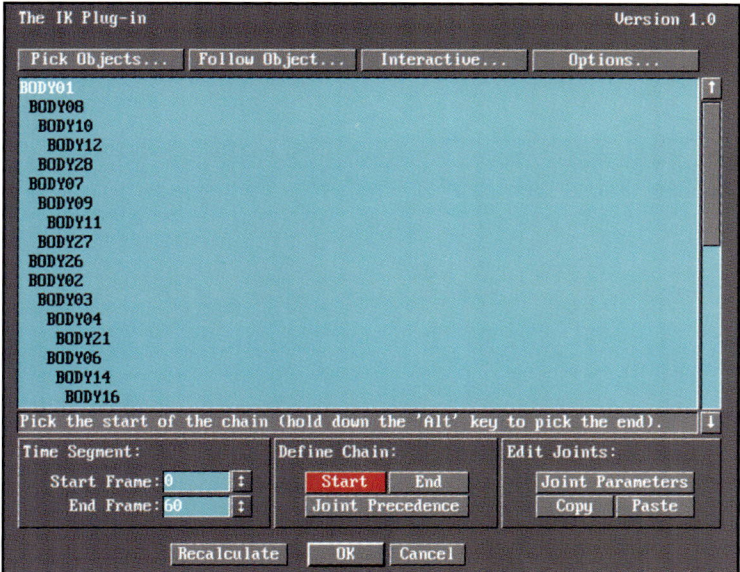

Figure 2.23
The Bones hierarchy, once loaded in the IK interface.

1. Click on the Joint Parameters button in the Edit Joints area in the lower-right corner. Select BODY12 (the left foot bone) from the list. Make sure that all the Axis icons are red (see fig. 2.24). Red indicates that the axes are active. Click in the Limit Joint area for all three axes. A check mark should appear in all three boxes. Set the joint limits as follows: **X—From: 15.00, To: -15.00**, **Y—From: 105.00, To: 75.00**, **Z—From: 30.00, To: -30**.

2. Click on the Prev. button in the lower-right corner. The Edit Object text box now should read "BODY10" (the lower left leg bone). Activate the X axis only and click in its Limit Joint check box. Set the X limits as follows: **X—From: –8.00, To: –105.00**.

3. Click on the Prev. button again. The Edit Object text box now should read "BODY08" (the upper left leg bone). Activate all three axes. Check all three Limit Joint check boxes. Set the limits as follows: **X—From: 115.00, To: –45.00, Y—From: –45.00, To: 0, Z—From: 45.00, To: –10.00**.

4. Click in the Edit Object text box and select BODY11 (the right foot bone) from the list. Set all the Axis parameters the same as for BODY12. Click on the Prev. button and "BODY09" (the lower right leg bone) should appear in the Edit Object text box. Set all the Axis parameters the same as for BODY10. Click on the Prev. button again and the Edit Object text box should read "BODY07" (the upper right leg bone). Set all the

Axis parameters, except for the Z axis, the same as for BODY08. Set the joint limits for the Z axis as follows: Z—From: –45.00, To: 10.00. This is the only variance. Click on the OK button in the lower-right corner.

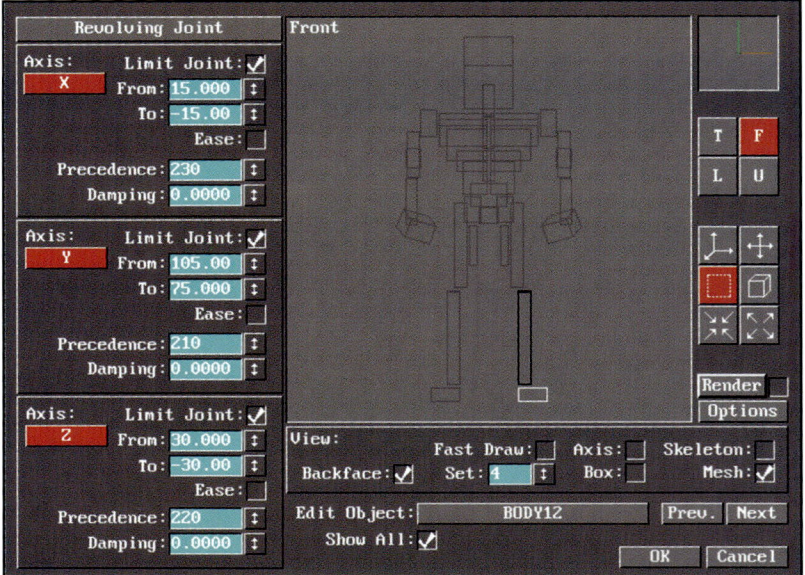

Figure 2.24
The Joint Parameters window. Here you will set the rotations and limits for your kinematic chains.

5. Define the first kinematic chain by picking the end button in the Define Chain box. Select BODY12 from the list. While pressing the Alt key on the keyboard, select BODY08 from the list. Pressing Alt enables you to select the "Start" of the kinematic chain without actually clicking on the button. Define the second kinematic chain by selecting BODY11 from the list without pressing Alt. Press Alt again and select BODY07. Click on the Joint Precedence button at the lower center of the screen and set the precedence at End to Start.

6. Click on the Follow Object button at the top of the screen. IK now asks for a "follow object" for BODY11. Be sure that the "Solve for orientation" and "Follow object motion is relative" check boxes are enabled. Select R-DUMMY and click on OK. IK solves for joint positions. Select BODY12 from the list and make sure that the three bones in the first kinematic chain are highlighted. Click on the Follow Object button and select L-DUMMY as the follow object for BODY12. IK solves for joint positions.

7. Click on the Interactive button. Activate the Front view. Click on the double-right arrow button to preview the IK animation of the legs. The feet remain in place and the legs bend appropriately. Cancel out of the interactive window.

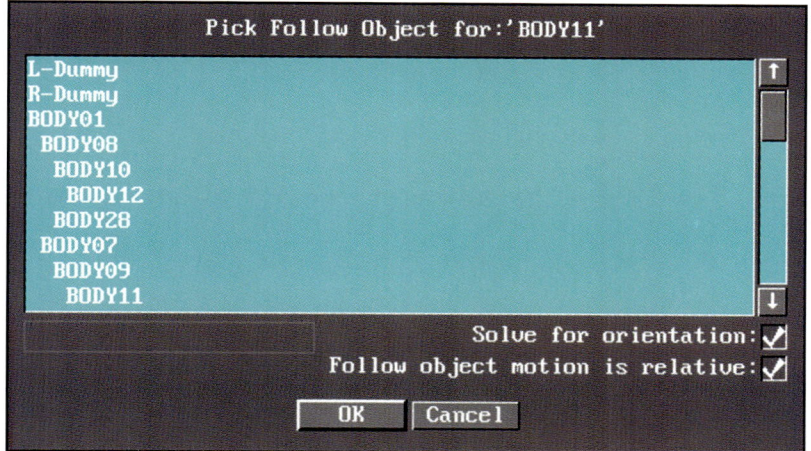

Figure 2.25
In the Pick Follow Object window, verify that the "Solve for orientation" and "Follow object motion is relative" boxes are checked.

8. Click on OK at the bottom of the Inverse Kinematics main screen. IK now places all the appropriate keys to animate the legs.

9. After you return to Keyframer, you can preview the animation again. The entire skeleton should now move smoothly. Save your IK work in another file, named something like **PUMPED2.PRJ**.

Setting the Bones Influence

The next step is to set the influence for the bones in your skeleton. If you aren't already in the Keyframer, press F4 to switch. Next, check to be sure that your primary mesh and all bones use the same naming convention, such as BODY, BODY01, BODY02, and so on. You can do this quickly by choosing **Info/Scene Info**. If you find any irregularities, you can easily change them choosing the **Object/Attributes** command in the cascading menu at the right.

1. Let's take a look at the Bones interface. Choose **Program/KXP Loader**. Select BONES from the list of available KXPs. Examine the Bones Pro interface (see fig. 2.26). You can use this dialog box to designate the main mesh object, determine each bone's area of influence, and preview the mesh deformation.

2. First, let's take a look at the button definitions.

★ **Main Mesh Object.** Click on the box in this area to select the main mesh object (in this case BODY).

★ **Selected Bones.** The buttons in this area enable you to choose the bones to be affected. These five buttons are described in the following sublist:

- **All.** Selects all bones for the main mesh object.

- **None.** Removes all selection designations.

- **Invert.** Reverses the selection state of all bones.

- **Choose.** Allows the selection of bones, by name, from a list.

- **Pick.** Enables you to click on the bones to select them.

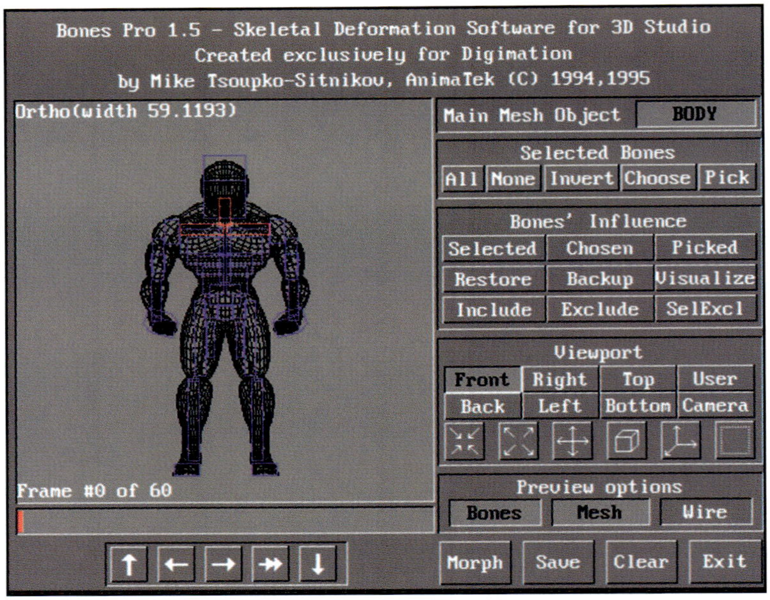

Figure 2.26
The Bones Pro interface. where you modify the influence your bones have over the vertices of the Main Mesh Object.

- **Bones' Influence.** The buttons in this area enable you to change the zone and scale of a bone's area of influence. It affects any vertices that fall within a bone's area of influence. For example, if you rotate a bone, all vertices falling into its area of influence rotate accordingly. The following sublist describes the nine buttons in this area:

    - **Selected.** Allows you to change the influence of all bones selected under the Selected Bones option, simultaneously.

    - **Chosen.** Allows the selection of the bones, whose influence you wish to modify, by name, from a list.

    - **Picked.** Allows you to pick the bone, whose influence you wish to modify, from the preview window using a mouse.

NOTE: When you choose Selected, Chosen, or Picked, a dialog box appears. The top of the box tells you the number of bones for which you will set the influence.

* **ZONE.** Describes the influence of a bone as a percentage of the bone's size.

* **MULTIPLIER.** Determines the rate of "falloff" of a bone's influence.

NOTE: Most bones will share their influence with other bones. An example would be, if you have an upper arm bone and a lower arm bone in a humanoid arm, the area of vertices that reside around the point where the bones meet is influenced by both bones. By modifying the Zone and/or Multiplier of one of the bones, you can give more or less influence over that area of vertices to that bone. You can have a different ZONE and MULTIPLIER for each bone. However, you cannot animate these settings. They remain the same throughout the animation.

* **Restore.** Allows you to load PRX files from disk.

* **Backup.** Allows you to save the current influence configuration to disk in a user-specified PRX file.

NOTE: These PRX files do not take the place of saving data directly to an object using the Save button. They allow you to try different bones settings and save these settings to disk for future use.

* **Visualize.** Provides a quick and easy way to determine which areas of your mesh are affected by a particular bone. Clicking on Visualize while pressing Ctrl displays a bone's maximum influence area. The maximum influence area defines where the influence of the given bone exceeds the influence of any other bone. Clicking on Visualize while pressing Alt enables you to select a bone, by name, from a list.

* **Include.** Enables you to restore a selected bone's or bones' influence over the chosen bone. The primary use of this button is to reverse the effects of Exclude.

- **Exclude.** Allows you to prevent, in whole, a selected bone or bones from influencing the chosen bone.

- **SelExcl.** Selects all bones (turns red), previously Excluded from a given bone. All other bones turn to a deselected (blue) state (see fig. 2.27).

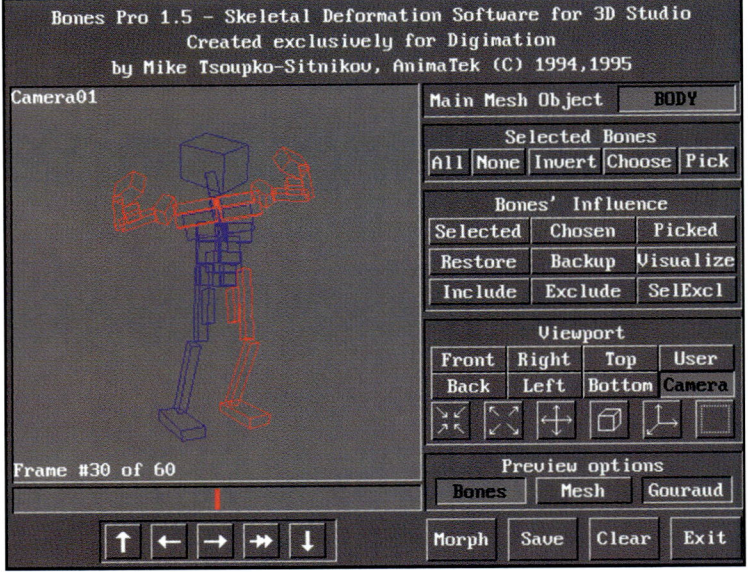

Figure 2.27
Bones that have been selected turn red, while deselected bones remain blue.

- **Viewport.** You use the eight buttons in this area to determine the view you want for your Bones Pro preview window. The Zoom, Pan, and Rotate icons here work the same as the icons in 3D Studio's main display.

- **Preview options.** Click on the Bones button to see the bones displayed in the preview window. Click on Mesh to see the main mesh object. When you activate the Mesh button, the main mesh object appears, regardless of whether or not you hide it in the Keyframer. The third button, acts as a toggle between Wire, Flat, and Gouraud, the three types of shading in the preview window.

- **Morph.** Enables you to create mesh objects from the deformed main mesh object, and places them in the 3D Editor and Keyframer. You can do this for a single frame or a range of frames. This can be very useful for creating morph targets.

★ **Save.** Obviously enough, saves your work. Click on the Save button to write the deformation data to 3D Studio, which stores the Bones data in the mesh object.

★ **Clear.** Removes all Bones Pro data from an object and exits the dialog box.

★ **Exit.** Returns you to the Keyframer.

> **Stop:** You can exit Bones Pro without saving the data. This doesn't write the appropriate data, however, and the mesh will not render with your bones setup.

3. If the main mesh object is not already selected, you must do so. Click in the box next to Main Mesh Object, and select BODY. You can now preview the animation you've created.

4. You can use the arrow keys or the slider under the preview window to move to any frame in your animated sequence. The double arrow plays the preview as fast as possible. The speed of the preview is in direct proportion to your computer system's performance level and inversely proportional to the complexity of the displayed mesh.

> **NOTE:** Sometimes after you create an animation, you discover that the bones influence a larger or smaller area of the mesh than you intended. You can change the area of influence of one or more bones, as necessary, to obtain the effect you want. Notice that the hands and thighs of the main mesh object are being stretched and distorted over the range of the animation (see fig. 2.28). Not to worry, you correct this shortly.

5. For most bones, the default Zone and Multiplier of **100** and **1**, respectively, work quite well. As described earlier, you have at your disposal essentially two ways to control a bone's influence, modify the Zone and Multiplier, and use the Exclude and Include commands. For purposes of this exercise, you use both.

6. The only bone you cannot easily control using only Exclude is BODY21. Set the Zone for BODY21 to: **40** and set the Multiplier to: **1.55**. This action gives BODY21 the influence neccessary to rotate the helmet in a rigid manner.

Figure 2.28
A preview of the test animation in the Bones Pro interface. Notice the vertex distortion. By changing the influence of individual bones, you can eliminate this undesirable effect.

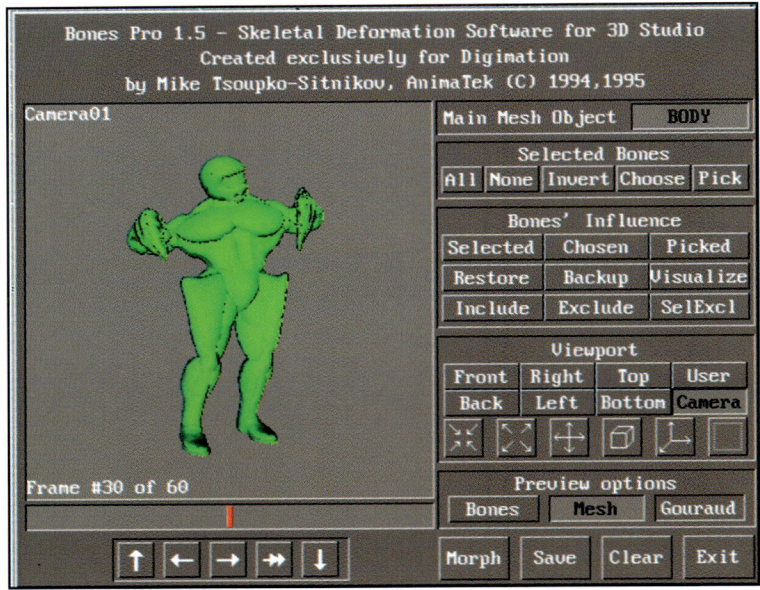

7. Next, you use Exclude to a greater extent to control which bones affect which areas of your mesh. Selectively, Exclude bones according to the following table:

Bone Name	Bones To Exclude
BODY01	BODY15-20,22,23
BODY02	NONE
BODY03	NONE
BODY04	NONE
BODY05	NONE
BODY06	NONE
BODY07	BODY05,06,08,10,12,13-20,22-25,28
BODY08	BODY05,06,07,09,11,13-20,22-25,27
BODY09	BODY05,06,08,10,12,13-20,22-25,28
BODY10	BODY05,06,07,09,11,13-20,22-25,27
BODY11	BODY05,06,08,10,12,13-20,22-25,28
BODY12	BODY05,06,07,09,11,13-20,22-25,27
BODY13	NONE
BODY14	NONE

Bone Name	Bones To Exclude
BODY15	BODY01-04,06-12,14,16,18,20,21,23,25-36
BODY16	BODY01-05,07-13,15,17,19,21,22,24,26-36
BODY17	BODY01-04,06-12,14,16,18,20,21,23,25-36
BODY18	BODY01-05,07-13,15,17,19,21,22,24,26-36
BODY19	BODY01-04,06-12,14,16,18,20,21,23,25-36
BODY20	BODY01-05,07-13,15,17,19,21,22,24,26-36
BODY21	BODY01-03,07-20,22-36
BODY22	BODY01-04,06-12,14,16,18,20,21,23,25-36
BODY23	BODY01-05,07-13,15,17,19,21,22,24,26-36
BODY24	BODY15-20,22,23
BODY25	BODY15-20,22,23
BODY26	NONE
BODY27	BODY05,06,08,10,12,13-20,22-25,28
BODY28	BODY05,06,07,09,11,13-20,22-25,27
BODY29	BODY15-20,22,23
BODY30	BODY15-20,22,23
BODY31	BODY13-20,22,23
BODY32	BODY13-20,22,23
BODY33	BODY13-20,22,23
BODY34	BODY13-20,22,23
BODY35	BODY13-20,22,23
BODY36	BODY13-20,22,23

8. Turn on the Mesh button and switch the Preview options button to your choice of Wire, Flat, or Gouraud. Preview the animation. The animation now no longer shows any erratic vertex movements (see fig. 2.29). Save your Bones Pro data. If the BONES.AXP has not yet been assigned, a dialog box prompts you for how you would like it to be. If you select Yes, it automatically is assigned. Select Exit to return to the Keyframer.

Figure 2.29
Preview of the test animation in the Bones Pro interface. Notice the vertex distortion. By changing the influence of individual bones, you can eliminate this undesirable effect.

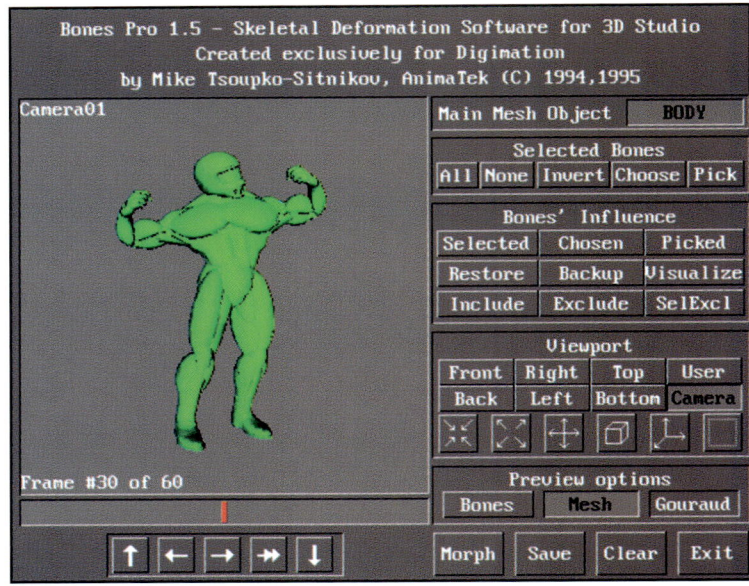

Render the Test Animation

First save your work in a new PRJ file. Then select the resolution and output, then render, to disk, the sample animation. This should go quickly, as this exercise is not cluttered with excess geometry, spotlights, texture maps, and reflections. The rendered animation should look something like MUSC-A.FLI, on the CD-ROM.

Conclusion

The Bones Pro IPAS routine opens up a whole new world of animation possibilities for 3D-Studio. Since its release, I have animated some two dozen organic meshes. I am sure that you have seen several organic, multi-object, animated sequences. The problem with multi-object characters is that there is continuous polygon intersection; and no stretching or contracting of fleshy/muscular areas. Bones Pro has conquered these problems.

Its uses are albeit, limitless. You can use it to animate everything from a broken hydraulic hose whipping back and forth and spewing fluid; to causing a tree's branches to wave gently in the wind. Currently, I'm having quite a bit of fun making monsters beat the (you know what) out of each other.

Remember, the two most effective pieces of motion capture equipment in the world reside in round sockets in your face. If you've seen it, you can re-create it. Experiment with MUSC-A.PRJ. Use IK to make the bones run. Animate the chest heaving. Make it do a jump flip. Animate your own organic meshes. Try to make a "Blob" (remember that movie?) ooze across a floor. Open up your imagination and let your creativity flow.

Gizmo Lightning

Effect 3

by Paul Taylor
San Anselmo, California

Equipment and Software Used

- 90 MHz Pentiums with 128 MB RAM and 17" monitor
- Macintosh 7100 Power PC with 80 MHz and 40 MB RAM
- PhotoShop 3.0
- Autodesk 3D Studio Release 4
- MetaREYES Metaballs
- Positron's Meshpaint 3D
- Yost Group's Disk 3, 6, and 7
- Bones Pro 1.5
- HP Scanner

Artist Biography

Paul Taylor started out as an illustrator after getting his degree at the Academy of Art College in San Francisco. He spent a period of time working as a storyboard artist for advertising agencies in San Francisco. After he got a PC with 3D Studio, he started freelancing for the multimedia community in the Bay area. He then was hired as lead artist at Amazing Media, and after six months was offered the Art Director position. Taylor then proceeded to art-direct *Frankenstein*, as well as two other CD-ROM titles in the works at Amazing Media.

Effect Overview

The Gizmo Lightning effect shows how to animate an image modeled and rendered in 3D Studio using the Layers feature in Adobe Photoshop 3.0. 3D Studio and Photoshop 3.0 are invaluable for doing animation effects for CD-ROM game titles. The GIZMO.FLI animation on the CD-ROM was done for the CD-ROM game "Frankenstein, Through the Eyes of the Monster" (an Interplay presentation, produced by Amazing Media). GIZMO.FLI is an example of the powerful results you can produce when you use a scene created in 3D Studio as a background for animating.

One inevitable challenge when you create an environment is the high face count you need to make a scene look realistic. Therefore, I want to emphasize the importance of good texture mapping and lighting, two things I find many 3D artists skimping on. If you start out with a high-quality image, any effect you add makes it look that much better. If you start with a weaker image, on the other hand, any effect you add might not help it as much, and might even make it confusing.

> **STOP:** You must have Photoshop 3.0 or Painter 3.0 before you can continue this effect, because you need the Layers feature or the Floater feature. I have found that Photoshop's Layers feature seems more intuitive and stable compared to Painter's floaters.

Procedure

To get started, load the GIZMO.3DS model from the CD-ROM provided with this book. The GIZMO.3DS objects consist mostly of primitives or very simple lofted objects. Combined with proper texture maps and lighting, however, they look complex. Play the GIZMO.FLI file located on the CD-ROM. Not many pixels actually move in the FLI file, because the animation had to be a certain size to play back as a quicktime movie off a double-speed CD-ROM drive. However, the FLI gives the illusion of full-screen motion. This kind of screen space conservation is one challenge you face when you design animations to stream off of a double-speed CD-ROM with a data rate of only 300 KB/sec.

Look at the mesh in the 3D Editor shown in figure 3.1.

Figure 3.1 shows two scientific-looking pieces of machinery on top of a lab table. A hidden cylinder (which should remain hidden until later) encloses them. The cylinder, combined with a good texture map, is all you need to establish the illusion of being in a tower in Dr. Frankenstein's castle. In the Camera viewport, you see a Jacob's ladder on the left and a Mickey

Mouse–looking device on the right, each connected by a bundle of wires. The picture frame on the wall was created using a program called Cybermesh, by Knoll Software, available as a plug-in for Photoshop. Cybermesh works like the Yost Group's Displace from their IPAS Disk #7, which uses the brightness values of a bitmap for displacement map modeling. One thing Cybermesh does that Displace doesn't, however, is drop out any black pixels, which enables you to cookie-cut a model—perfect for intricate molded frames (see fig. 3.2). To see the grayscale image used to make the molded picture frame, view FRAME.TGA on the CD-ROM—render it or view the GIZMO.TGA from the CD-ROM.

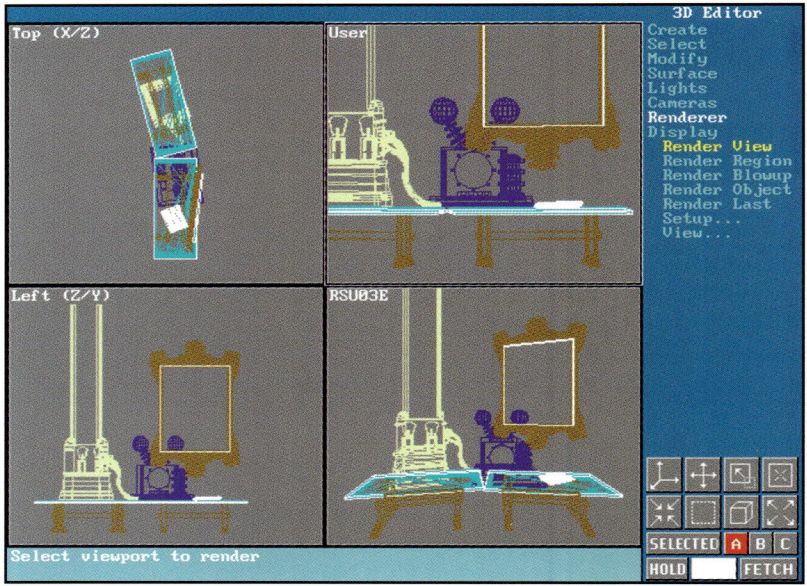

Figure 3.1
Notice that most of the models in this scene are either simple primitives or simple lofted objects.

NOTE: If you plan to have your own models enclosed in a cylinder, remember to flip the surface normals of your cylinder so that when it renders you can see the texture map.

Re-Creating the Lightning Effect

To re-create the Gizmo Lightning effect, do the following:

1. Make the Front viewport the active viewport and press W to make it fill the screen.

2. Press U and click the left mouse button (but DON'T move the mouse), to change the Front viewport to a User viewport with the Mickey Mouse

gizmo aligned in it. If it isn't perfectly aligned, use the left- and right-arrow keys on the keyboard to rotate the viewport until you can see a flat view of the gizmo (see fig. 3.2).

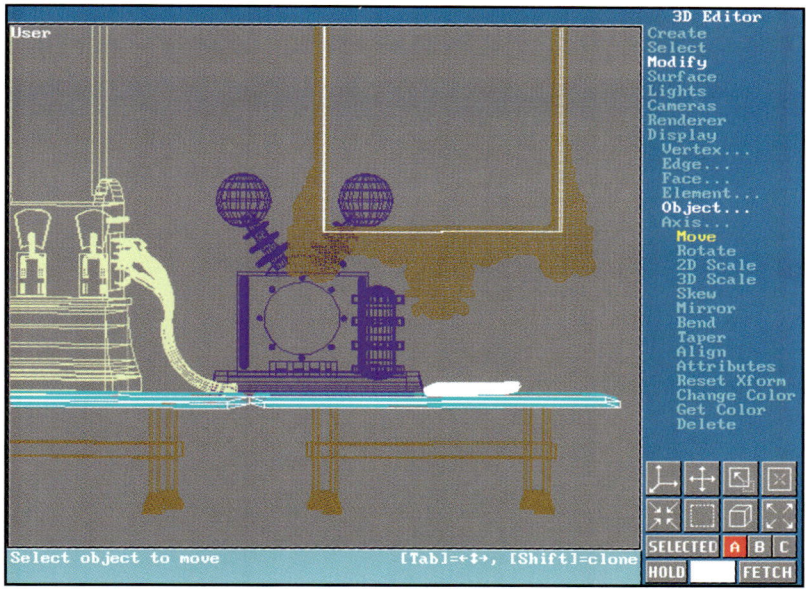

Figure 3.2
You need to use the User viewport in order to align the mesh so that it is flat and facing you.

TIP: When you rotate a mesh in a User viewport, you can hold down the Shift key to rotate in increments of 1 degree. The default is 10 degrees.

3. With the User viewport still active, switch to the 2D Shaper by pressing F1.

4. From the 2D Shaper, choose **Display/3D Display/On**. Then choose **Display/Choose**. After the dialog box appears, select All, then click on OK.

5. If you can't see your meshes from the 3D Editor, click on the Zoom Out icon in the lower right corner of the screen several times or until you can see your meshes. They appear as grayed versions of the meshes in the 3D Editor—as if you used **Display/Freeze**.

6. Now that you can see your meshes, use the Zoom icon to center the Mickey Mouse gizmo on-screen so that it looks like figure 3.3.

Figure 3.3
Use the Zoom icon to center the Mickey Mouse gizmo on-screen.

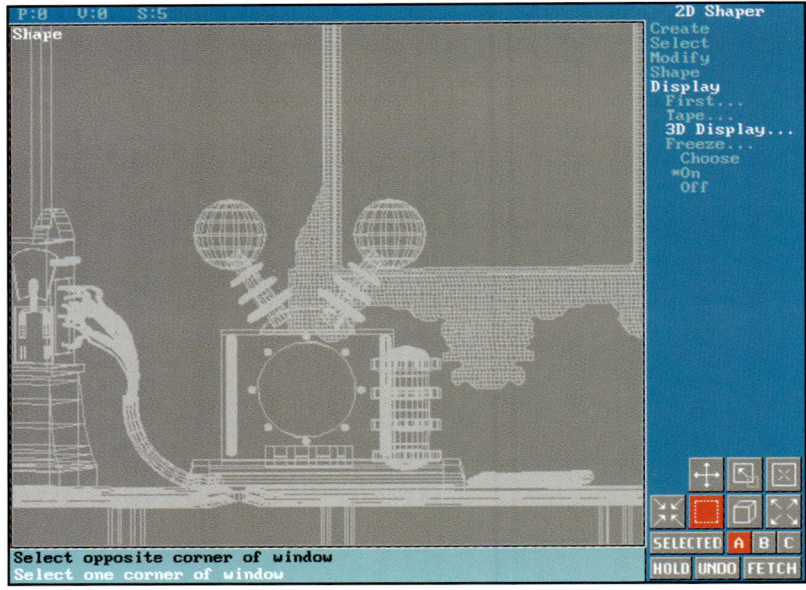

7. Use the **Create/Quad** command to make a Quad that encloses the Mickey Mouse gizmo. You use this to texture map the lightning animation on in the 3D Editor.

8. Press F3 to switch to the 3D Editor. From the 3D Editor, choose **Create/Object/Get Shape**. After the prompt appears, name the object **LITNING** and then click on OK to import the 2D Quad shape into the 3D Editor from the 2D Shaper.

9. Click on the Zoom Extents icon with the right mouse button. This makes every mesh in every viewport visible and enables you to find the 2D Quad you created, because it probably isn't exactly where you want it yet. Use the Top viewport and the User viewport to position the Quad on the Mickey Mouse machine. Make sure that the LITNING Quad is in the middle of the two spheres, as shown in the Top viewport of fig-ure 3.4.

10. Press F5 to switch to the Materials Editor. Assign a dark gray material to the LITNING Quad so that when you import it to Photoshop, your animated lightning stands out against it.

TIP: Choosing Modify/Object/Move and using the "hit" key (letter H) brings up a list of all the objects in your scene not frozen or hidden, for you to pick by name. This comes in very handy when you work on complex models.

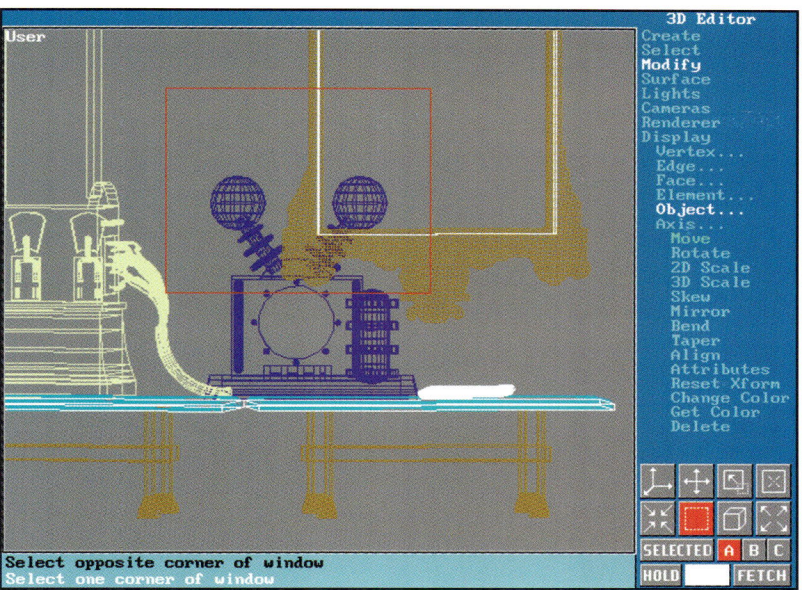

Figure 3.4
The LITNING Quad should be in the middle of the two spheres.

Photoshop 3.0

The next section will describe how to prepare the template for animating in Photoshop.

Animating the Lightning

We now have the model set up for the following steps, which will enable you to render the model from the User viewport and take it into Photoshop 3.0 as a background image so that you can animate the lightning effect using the background as a template.

1. Center the Mickey Mouse gizmo in the User viewport, render the User viewport to disk at 640 × 480, and call it **GIZ_USER.TGA**. Make sure that the Quad is in the middle of the two spheres of the gizmo. The Quad becomes your guide when you paint the lightning in Photoshop (see fig. 3.5).

2. Now save your model in its current state and call it **GIZMO.3DS**. Important: You need the User viewport you just rendered to remain stationary so that you can align the animated texture map properly after you create it in Photoshop.

3. Quit 3D Studio and launch Windows. From Windows, launch Photoshop. Choose **File/Open** and load the GIZ_USER.TGA image from your \3DS\IMAGES directory.

Figure 3.5
Make sure that from the Top viewport the Quad is in the middle of the two spheres, and from the User viewport it is centered around the two spheres.

4. Open the Layers palette under **Window/Palettes/Show Layers** and make six new layers by repeatedly pressing on the Layer icon at the bottom left of the Layer window or by going to the top right and clicking on the arrow and selecting New Layer. You can leave the default names that Photoshop gives each layer—you rename them later when you separate them.

5. Choose a light color that is very bright and saturated, like yellow, green, blue, or whatever. (I chose yellow for my lightning, but any color will do since Dr. Frankenstein has strange and near-magical machinery in his lab!) Paint your lightning on each layer, randomly changing where and how it moves. You can temporarily hide a layer by clicking on the Eye icon at the left of the Layers palette if it starts to get confusing.

NOTE: Be sure to paint on the appropriate layer, not the background. You might make some mistakes along the way and paint on the wrong layer if this is new to you and you don't use layers regularly. Just remember to periodically check which layer is highlighted before you begin to paint.

6. Paint lightning in each layer, and be sure not to go outside the polygon you use as a reference.

7. After you finish painting and are satisfied with your lightning, you need to separate each layer and make it a unique Targa file. Start by carefully using the Marquee tool (the upper left icon on the Tools palette) to select the reference polygon. Choose **Select/Save Selection** to save this selection. Saving the entire file at this point would be a good idea as well.

8. Turn off the eye in front of the Background layer. Important: If you leave the Background layer on, you can't separate the Lightning from the background.

9. Next, you need to systematically highlight each layer and define them as patterns and fill them into a new file using the **Edit/Define Pattern** and **Edit/Fill** commands. A submenu appears after you execute **Edit/Fill**. Select **Contents:/Use:Pattern.** The **File/New** command automatically sets the file size to match the Marquee selection for you, if you first make sure that the Background is selected and you use **Edit/Copy** while your Marquee selection is still active. Be sure to make the background of each new file black so you can use it as an alpha channel. Also, name these files **LIT0001.TGA** through **LIT0006.TGA**.

> **NOTE:** Step 9 might seem rather long—you might be asking yourself why you need to do all that when a simple copy-and-paste would do the trick. Well, you could copy and paste, but what the Define Pattern and Fill (with pattern) provide is registration. Without it, you cannot accurately place your animation.

Finishing the Effect

After you save each of these files, quit Photoshop and Windows, but do not launch 3D Studio yet. You first need to make an IFL (Image File List) file out of the LIT0001.TGA through LIT0006.TGA files. You can use IFL in the Materials Editor as an animated bitmap file, as an animated Opacity, Self Illumination, and Shininess map.

To create an IFL, do the following:

1. From within the 3DS directory, type **MAKEIFL**. This brings up on-screen the simple directions for making an IFL.

2. After you read the directions, type **MAKEIFL LIT LITN 1 6,** which creates a file named LIT.IFL. You will use this file in the mapping channels of the Materials Editor in 3D Studio.

Now that you have an IFL, launch 3D Studio and load the GIZMO.3DS file you saved earlier, and then follow these steps:

1. Press F5 to switch to the Materials Editor. From there, create a material that has all the default settings and add the LIT.IFL file to the Texture, Opacity, Self Illumination, and Shininess map channels (see fig. 3.6). Keep the sliders set to 100% for each of the mapping channels.

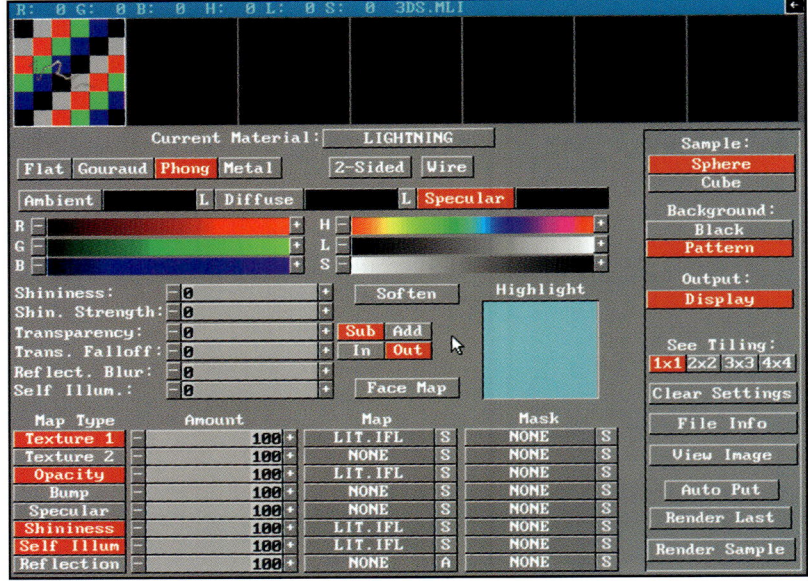

Figure 3.6
Create a material with the LIT.IFL in the following channels—Texture, Opacity, Self Illumination, and Shininess.

2. Press P to put this material in the current Materials Library. This brings up the current Materials Library and prompts you to name your material. Name it **GIZMO LIGHTNING**. Then save your Materials Library by pressing Ctrl+S. You can save it as a unique library or as the 3DS.LIB.

> **TIP:** Many users would prefer not to clutter up the default Studio Material Library with extraneous materials. A more efficient approach, rather than putting it to the library and resaving the library, would be to Put (the material) To Current.

3. Now, press F3 to switch back to the 3D Editor. In the User viewport that you aligned earlier, apply planar mapping coordinates to the LITNING Quad by choosing **Surface/Mapping/Adjust/Scale** while holding down the Alt key. This snaps the planar mapping coordinates to the LITNING Quad and should match perfectly the IFL file you created.

4. Choose **Modify/Object/Attributes** and select the LITNING Quad. When the Attributes dialog box appears, turn off both the Receive and Cast Shadows options, as shown in figure 3.7. Important: If you don't, the LITNING Quad casts a shadow and ruins the effect.

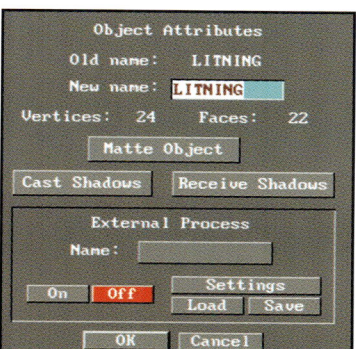

Figure 3.7
Be sure to turn off both the Receive and Cast Shadows options.

5. Choose **Surface/Materials/Choose** and **Surface/Materials/Assign**, respectively, to assign the material GIZMO LIGHTNING to the LITNING Quad. (If you chose to use Put To Current in step 2 instead of saving the material to the library, you only need to choose **Surface/Materials/Assign/Object** here.)

6. From the Top viewport, move the LITNING polygon to the front of the Mickey Mouse spheres to ensure that when you render the animation you don't embed it in the mesh.

Now you should repeat the steps for the Jacob's ladder. The only difference is that the lightning should be animated crawling up the Jacob's ladder instead of sparking about randomly. After you finish, remember to use **Display/Unhide/All** to unhide all objects in the scene, which reveals the cylinder used for the wall and floor. You can render the scene as an animation and you even can move the camera around as long as you don't go too far to the side of the flat polygons.

Conclusion

You can use this effect for many other things besides lightning, such as cracks animating in a stone wall, water gurgling out of those cracks, paint peeling away form a wall, torches rotoscoped in a castle, and many more. The possibilities are limitless. The effect might seem time-consuming—because it is! But don't let it get you down, because the results are worth the effort. If you stick to it and devote the hours, your images and animations will stand out and all the hard work will eventually pay off. Many people have a working knowledge of 3D Studio but few create artistic, "punchy" images. The market for people who both know how to use 3D Studio and have an artistic eye is growing fast, especially in the gaming industry. And think about this: A mega-hit game can make more money now than a mega-hit movie!

Time Machine

Effect 4

by Greg R. Phillips
Indianapolis, Indiana

Equipment and Software Used

- IBM PC–compatible, Pentium 90, 64 MB of RAM, and 1 gig drive
- Video output to DPS Personal Animation Recorder
- Iomega ZIP 100 MB drive
- 3D Studio Release 4.0
- Adobe Premiere 4.0
- Animator Studio
- Fractal Design Painter 3.0

Artist Biography

Greg Phillips is an award-winning 3D computer graphic artist and President of the Multimedia Group at Phillips Design Group, Inc. in Indianapolis, Indiana. He works with many types of software including 3D Studio, Animator Studio, Fractal Design Painter, Photoshop, CorelDRAW!, Premiere, Alias Power Animator, and many more. He is coauthor of the book *3D Studio Special Effects* and contributed to *Inside 3D Studio 3.0*. His 3D designs have appeared in New York, San Francisco, and all around the world in design publications, books, cover art, art galleries, animations, exhibits, and many published articles. He is currently working on design and development of interactive CD-ROMS, kiosks, and Internet WWW design for many national companies. He can be reached via CompuServe at 102363.373 or via Internet at greg@dgs.com.

Effect Overview

This chapter describes techniques for using 3D Studio to create exciting lighting effects and animated texture maps. The Time Machine effect simulates a time machine spinning up views of different years. The 3D models in this chapter were created in 3D Studio 4.0, and the texture maps are from 3D Studio and Autodesk Texture Universe. This effect uses files from different software packages, such as Adobe Premiere, in which you will use AVI video files to create animated texture maps for the Time Machine effect of people walking in a city. In addition, this chapter shows color strobe lighting effects created from the holes in geometry that you will animate.

Procedure

Start 3D Studio, choose **File/Load Project**, and select file TIME.PRJ from the \TIME\PROJECT directory of the CD-ROM included with this book. See figure 4.1.

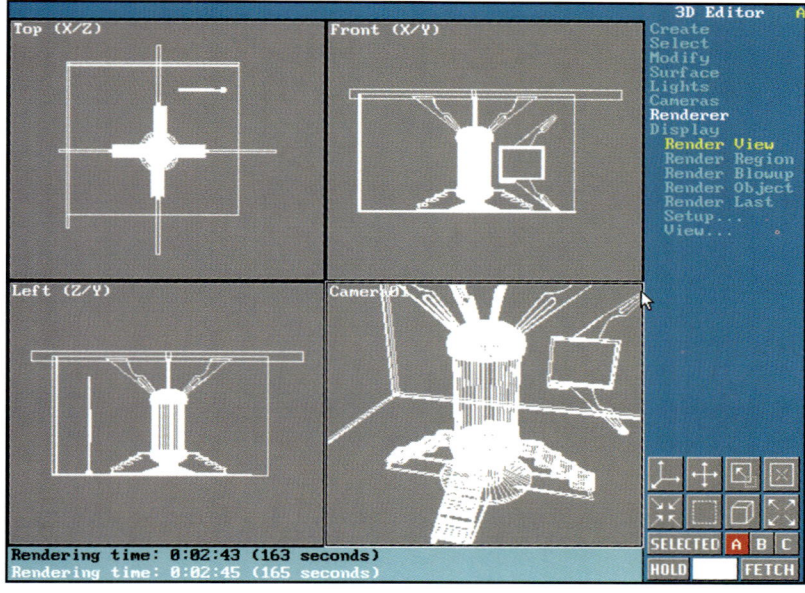

Figure 4.1
View of the project file for creating the Time Machine effect.

Then choose **Info/Configure**, click on Maps Paths in the Program Configuration menu, and add the CD-ROM directory \TIME\MAPS to access the images and maps necessary for this chapter.

See table 4.1, which lists the objects and assigned materials for this project.

Table 4.1 Objects and Assigned Materials for this Project

Objects	Material	Mapping
Step 1,2,3,4	Chrome Metalcool	Applied
Support T1, T2	Purple Metal	None
Base 1,2,3	Sky Metal	Applied
Floor	Bump Plate	Applied
Ring 1,2	Purple Metal	None
Spin 1,2	Sky Metal	Applied
Time ball 1,2	Chrome Metalcool	Applied
Time text	Green Neon	None
Time tube	Sky Glass	Applied
Top cap	Sky Metal	Applied
Top base	Chrome Metalcool	Applied
Top Steel 1,2	Gray Default	None
Wall 1,2	Bump Plate	Applied
TV mount	Purple Metal	None
TV screen 1	Chrome Metalcool	Applied
TV screen 2	TV Screen	Applied

NOTE: If you need to access these materials at any time, choose **Surface/Material/Get Library** from the 3D Editor, and select the file TIME.MLI from the \TIME\MATLIBS directory of the CD-ROM. You also can choose **Material/Get from Scene** in the Material Editor.

The file TIME.PRJ contains the 3D models for completing this effect.

I created most of these models in the 2D Shaper and used the 3D lofter to create bevel modifications to the geometry. To get started, use the following procedures:

1. Use Adobe Premiere to find two 240×180 AVI video files that contain plenty of motion, color, and length to match your animation, then export your AVI files to a FLC file and save to your maps directory. These files will be used for the creation of animated texture map effects in this chapter. If you don't have an AVI file editor, these files have been created for you as FLC files and materials that come with this chapter (in \TIME\MAPS on the CD-ROM).

> **NOTE:** You must have Adobe Premiere, Animator Studio, or other editing software to export and edit AVI files.

2. Go to 3D Studio's Materials Editor, choose **Material/Get Material**, and select SKY GLASS. This material uses texture maps and FLC files to create an animated texture map you can modify. Look at the material settings and the different texture maps and create your own.

   Figure 4.2 shows the materials combined for the animated texture map effect.

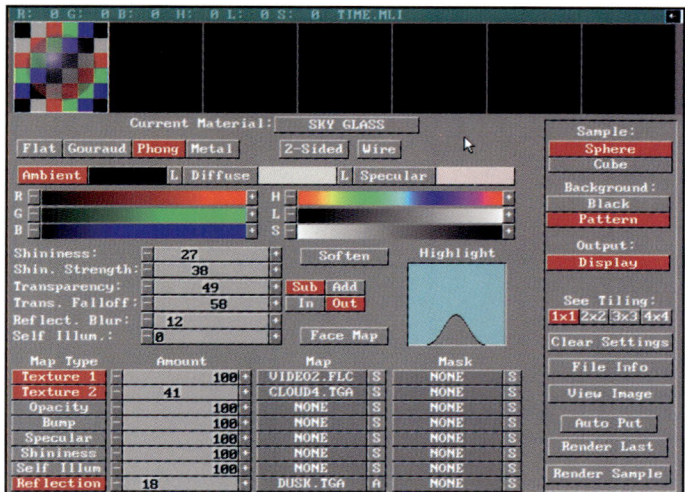

Figure 4.2
Materials Editor showing FLC files and texture maps from the material Sky Glass.

Next, go to the 3D Editor, choose **Surface/Mapping/Type**, and choose Cylindrical. Go to **Mapping/Adjust/Scale**, hold down the Alt key, and select the object (Time Tube). This will autoscale the Cylindrical mapping to the object Time Tube. Select **Mapping/Apply Obj.** and apply mapping to the object Time Tube. Next, choose **Surface/Material/Choose**, select the material Sky Glass, and **Assign/By Name** to the object (Time tube). Go to **Modify/Object/Attributes**, select the object (Time Tube), and turn off Cast Shadows and Receive Shadows.

> **TIP:** Try different texture maps and FLC files to create many dynamic multiple mapping effects of your own. Try changing texture maps and transparency, for example, to create different types of clouds and smoke effects.

The camera was created for you in this project. To change or modify, select **Cameras** and use **Adjust,Move,FOV..** to modify the camera for different perspectives or lens types.

3. Next, choose **Lights/Spot/Create**. Then create a spotlight in the Top viewport, name it **LIGHT**, and give it settings (RGB 235,235,235), Cast Shadows on, Show Cone on, Hotspot 119.25, and Falloff 119.75 (see figure 4.3 for location, direction, and angle of spotlight).

Figure 4.3
Spotlight location and creation for the Time Machine effect.

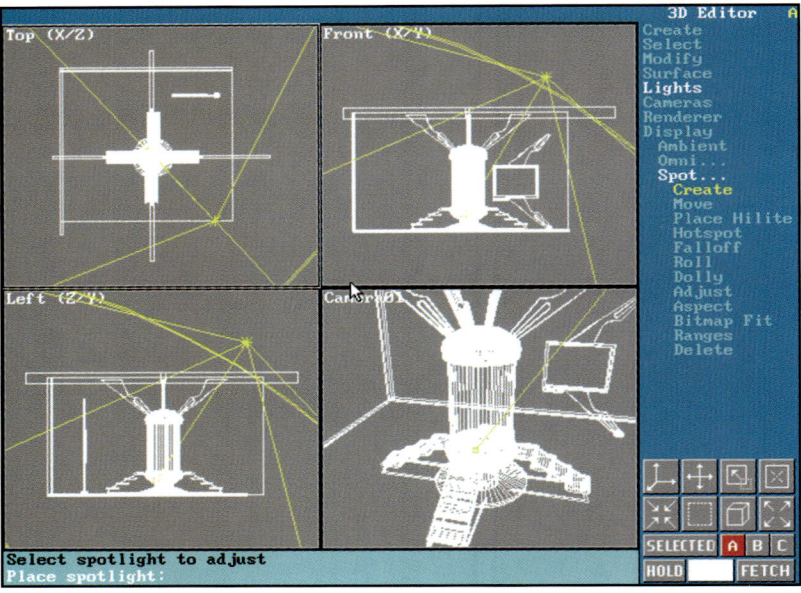

4. In the 3D Editor, choose **Display/Hide/By Name** and hide everything except (base 1, top base, spin 1, spin 2). See figure 4.4.

Figure 4.4
Hiding objects for strobe spotlight creation.

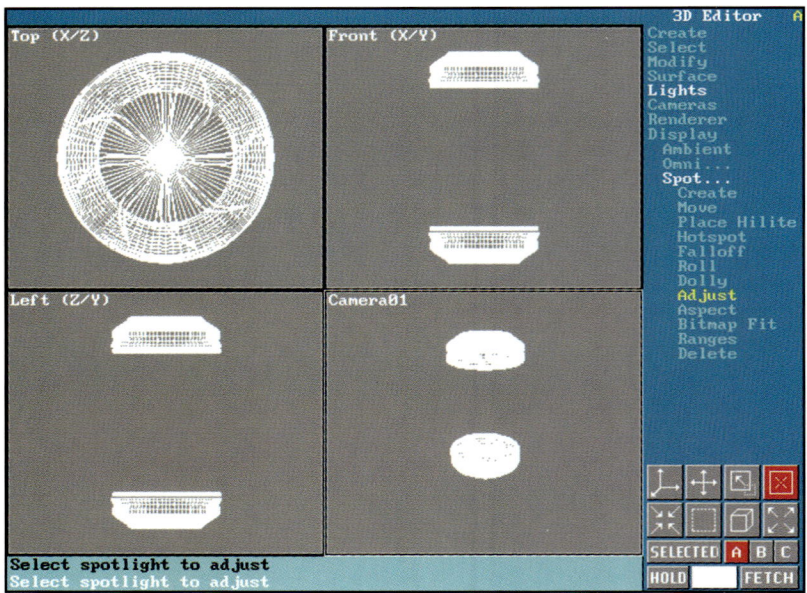

5. Choose **Light/Spot/Create** and create a spotlight inside the object base 1 and under the object spin 1, move it to the center of the object, and place the target in the center of the top base. Name the spotlight **YELLOW** and create a yellow light (RGB 218,218,0), Hotspot 174.0, Falloff 174.5, Cast Shadows on, and Show Cone on (see fig. 4.5).

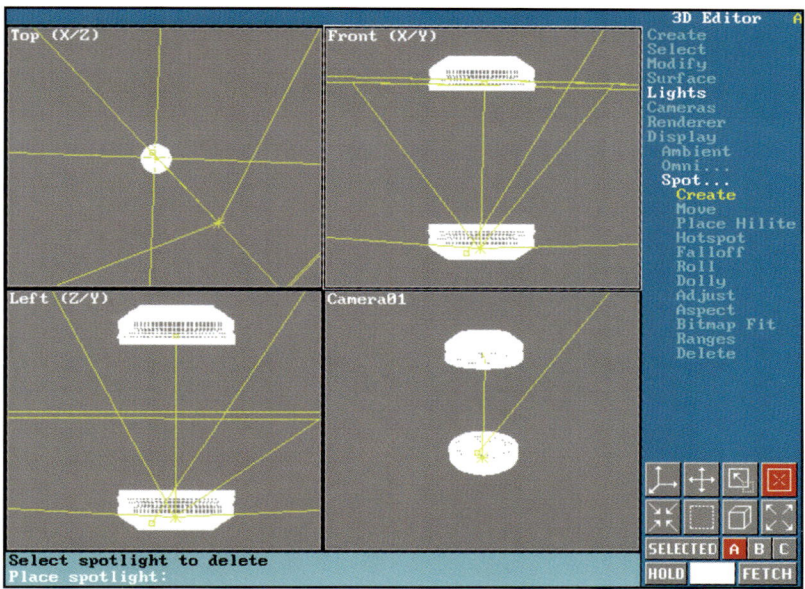

Figure 4.5
Showing the yellow spotlight creation and location for strobe effects.

6. Create the third spotlight. Choose **Light/Spot/Create** and create a spotlight inside the top base and the target facing object base 1.

   Name the spotlight **RED** and create a red light (RGB 255,0,0), Hotspot 64.25, Falloff 136.75, Cast Shadows on, and Show Cone on (see fig. 4.6).

7. Go to **Display/Unhide/By Name**, unhide wall 1, wall 2, and floor, and render the Camera viewport to 640×480 and view the image. To compare this image to your image, look at TIME\IMAGES\TEST.TGA on the CD-ROM.

8. Next, choose **Display/Unhide/All** and unhide all objects, render the Camera viewport to 640×480, and view the effects of lighting and materials. See figure 4.7 or view full-screen from the CD-ROM TIME\IMAGES\TIME.TGA.

Figure 4.6
Showing the red spotlight creation and location for strobe effects.

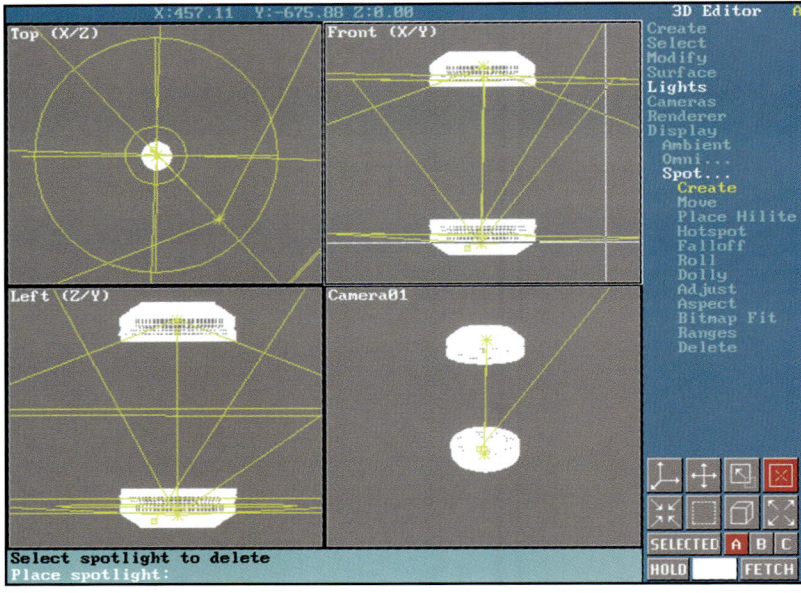

Figure 4.7
Rendering showing setup of color spotlight effects.

> **TIP:** Try different color lighting and animated lights for other effects. For example, when applying texture maps to the spotlight using Spotlight Definition/Projector, change color or try animated texture maps swirling from the lights.

9. Go to the Keyframer and set number of frames to 330+ frames. This setting is based on the time length of your animated texture maps that you created.

10. Move to your last Keyframe, zoom in around the center of the object Time Machine. Next, choose **Object/Rotate Abs.**, then select the object spin 1, and press A on the keyboard to turn on Angle Snap. Then press the Tab key to change the axis and rotate +430, which spins the disk with vents and creates the strobe effect from the yellow light below it (see fig. 4.8).

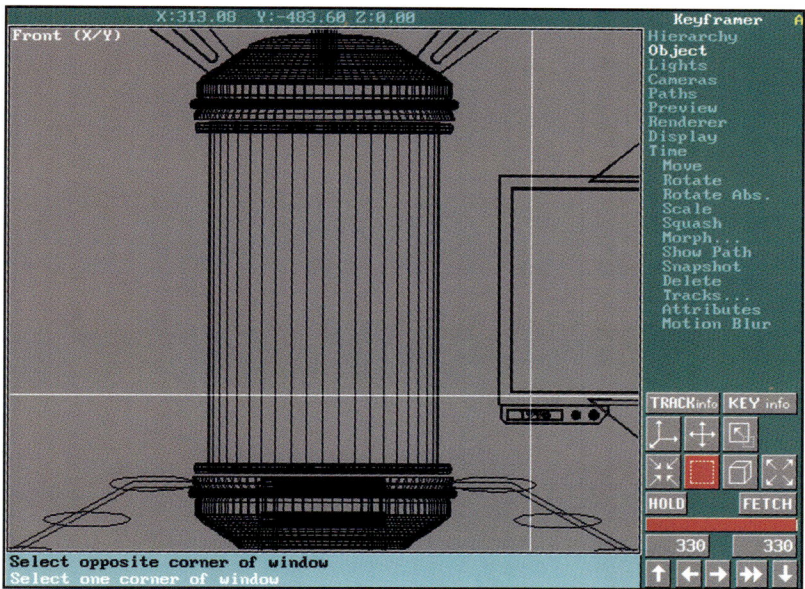

Figure 4.8
The creation of the spinning disk for strobe effects.

> **TIP:** Try different disk patterns like the one on object spin 1 to create new strobe effects. This creates new light patterns from the different holes and designs that you create in your models.

11. Move to your last Keyframe, zoom around the center of the object Time Machine, and choose Object/Rotate Abs. Then select the object spin 2, and press A on the keyboard to turn on Angle Snap. Next, press the Tab key to rotate −430. This spins the disk with vents in the other direction and creates the strobe effect from the red light above it.

> **NOTE:** Note the animated texture map assigned to the object TV Screen 2. This is an FLC file with reflection and transparency map types that you can modify or change.

12. Start rendering your animation. The length and time of your animation will vary according to your system performance, you could lower the resolution or change the frame rate to save time. If you want to view the completed Time Machine animation for this chapter, see TIME\FLICS\TIME.FLC on the CD-ROM.

Conclusion

When you play your next 3D game or see your next movie, look for the special effects and try to re-create them. 3D games and movie special effects are here to stay and can only get better.

Experiment with different variations of lighting colors, texture maps, and IPAS plug-ins in the animation effects you create. Never stop experimenting in 3D Studio. Try everything, use your imagination and creativity, and you will find some great effects of your own.

The Tail of the Comet

Effect 5

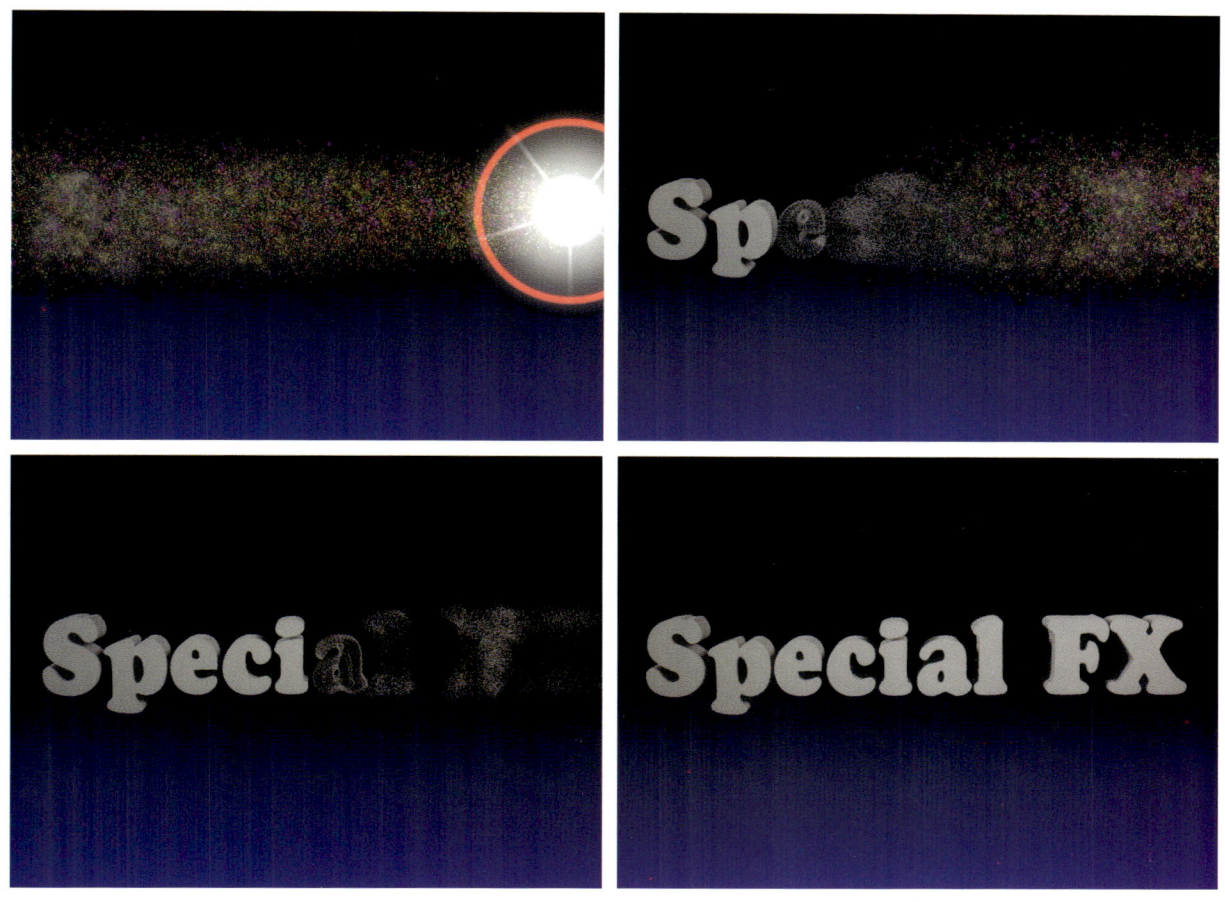

by Kirk O. Nash
Bolingbrook, IL

Equipment and Software Used

- IBM compatable 486/66 with 32 MB of RAM
- IBM compatable P120 with 64 MB of RAM
- Wacom 12×12 Tablet
- TARGA + 64 Framebuffer
- PJPS PAR with TBC IV
- Number 9 Imagine 128 SVGA Display Card
- 3D Studio Release 4
- Magic 4 from Digimation
- Disintegrate from the Yost Group particle systems disk
- Glow from the Yost Group image processing disk (optional)
- Lens Flare from the Yost Group image processing disk (optional)

Artist Biography

For the past 12 years, Kirk O. Nash has worked in various areas of the multimedia field. First, as a freelance photographer, he did projects ranging from slide-tape presentations to fine art B&W photography, and his work was shown in several exhibitions. In 1988, he started Creative Digital Images, which provided photographic as well as video production services.

Creative Digital Images now provides 3D animation, digital compositing, and special effects for both the corporate and broadcast video markets, as well as for CD-ROM titles and interactive kiosks. Animations produced by Creative Digital Images have been broadcast nationally and internationally.

Kirk also is very active in a Chicago 3D Studio users group, The Loop Group, where he puts on demonstrations of animation techniques and IPAS routines. Kirk also spent a year as the editor and writer for The Loop Group newsletter.

Effect Overview

There is nothing more boring than a character generator creating 2D titles that the audience is forced to read. 3D-generated titles are a step up, but again, audiences today are used to seeing letters fly on-screen. The Tail of the Comet effect starts off with an eye-catching particlization that draws the viewer into seeing what will be created. In this effect, you use particle animation and image processing to create the effect of a comet traveling from left to right across the screen with pieces of the tail joining to form the words, "Special FX." The particles from the comet will have a soft glow, and the head of the comet will be a lens flare.

This chapter steps you through creating the letter objects, then creating and assigning box objects to the type to control the particles that come together to form the words. You tessellate the faces of the letters to control the denseness of the particles when they come together, and you use the Hide function in the Track dialog box to make the solid letters appear. You then modify an AXP cube to form the comet, clone the cube, and use the Copy Tracks function to assign the same motion to all copies of the AXP cubes. You then apply custom self-illuminated materials to the AXP cubes to be used for keying image processing effects in Video Post. Next, you create a sphere to use as the flare object, and you adjust the flare settings to track the sphere as it travels across the screen at the head of the comet. Last, you create and modify a Video Post Queue to control the image processing.

Procedure

Start 3D Studio, choose **File/Load Project** and select COMET.PRJ from the \COMET directory on the CD-ROM supplied with this book. Now might be a good time to take a look at the COMET.FLC to get a feel for your target finished animation. I rendered this file at 640×480, the speed of your machine determines playback speed (it plays back in three seconds in real time). I didn't use 320×200 because the particles are so small that you lose much of the effect in the lower resolution.

Text

First, you create the text that the comet reveals.

1. Press F1 to switch to the 2D Shaper. You see the Polygons spelling out "Special FX" already created. Choose **Shape/Assign/None** to make sure no polygons are assigned.

2. Choose **Shape/Assign,** then click on the letter S to assign it.

3. Press F2 to switch to the 3D Lofter. The path in the lofter module isn't the default path. I've scaled and moved the path to work with this animation, so don't alter it.

4. Choose **Shapes/Get/Shaper** to load the assigned *S* shape into the 3D Lofter. Don't use align or center to change the orientation of the shape because after you loft each shape, the letters are in proper relationship to each other to form the words "Special FX" in the 3D Editor.

5. Choose **Objects/Make** to loft the letter *S*. Refer to figure 5.1 for proper settings of the object lofting controls. Name the lofted object **S**.

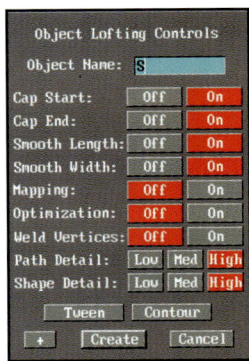

Figure 5.1
Lofter settings for creating text.

6. Repeat steps 1–5 for each appropriate letter, naming each respectively: "**p**," "**e**," "**c**," "**i**," "**a**," "**l**," "**F**," and "**X**."

7. Press F3 to switch to the 3D Editor. You should now see the text "Special FX" in proper order and placement. Click on the Camera viewport to activate it. Press Alt+E to show safe frame for the Camera viewport, then press W for a full frame view. The right and left edges of type should just touch the green boundary of the safe frame as in figure 5.2. The safe frame option gives you a visual cue (of the inner green box) of where in your work area objects can be in order to be in frame on all video monitors. The yellow enter box is the area and aspect ratio of your current display settings. Press W again to toggle the full screen view off.

Text AXP Objects

Now that you have the proper text, you can clone the letters to make the AXP "Stand-in" objects. The "stand-in" objects cause the particles to join to form the individual letters. By making nine individual objects for the letters rather than one object for all the letters, you can make the letters form sequentially as the comet tail passes. If you used just one object, everything would join all at once.

Now, you can clone objects in a variety of ways in the 3D Editor, but in a situation like this, you want the letters to lie exactly on top of the old letters. I have found the following to be the quickest and easiest way to clone each letter:

1. Press Alt+A to select all objects. Each of the letters should turn red to show that they are selected.

2. Make sure that the local Axis icon is turned off. Pressing X toggles the icon on and off. (Red means on.)

3. Make sure that Angle Snap is on. An "A" appears in the upper right hand corner when Angle Snap is on. Pressing A toggles Angle Snap on and off.

4. Choose **Modify/Object/Rotate**. Toggle the selected icon to on by pressing the spacebar. The selected icon turns red when on.

5. In the Front viewport, while holding down Shift, choose **Modify/Object/Rotate** again and rotate all selected objects –10°. When the "Copy objects to" box appears, click on Multiple. 3D Studio adds "01" to the old name of each object. Accept these new names. You should now have two sets of letter objects, one selected and in the proper position and one unselected and rotated –10° clockwise from the selected set (see fig. 5.3).

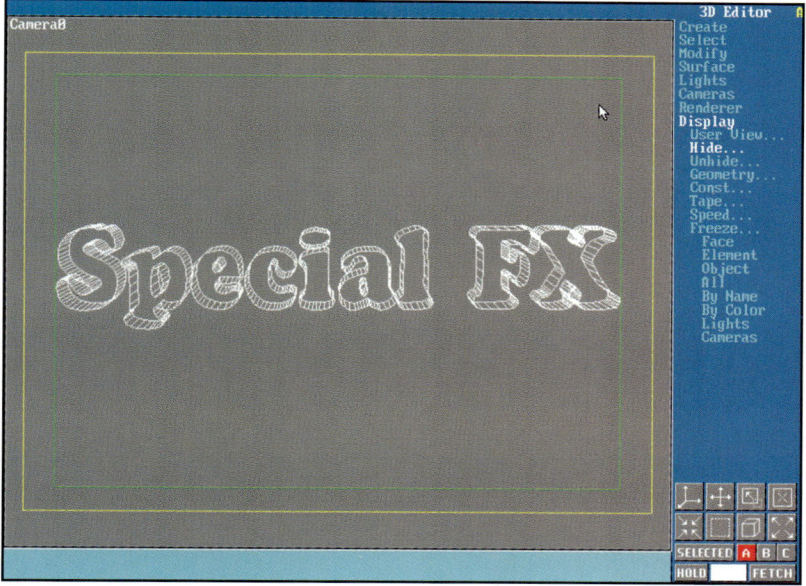

Figure 5.2
Full frame view in 3D Editor showing all lofted text in relationship to safe frame.

6. Choose **Select/Invert** to deselect the original objects and select the 01 versions.

7. Repeat step 4.

Figure 5.3
Original and copied letter objects.

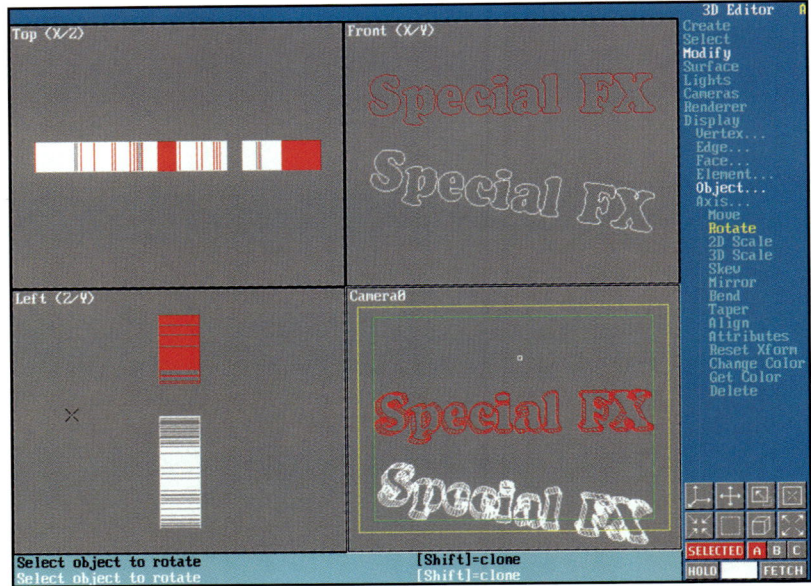

8. In the Front viewport, choose **Modify/Object/Rotate** and rotate the selected 01 version objects 10° so that they line up with the original objects. All views should now show one set of type.

9. You are done with the original set of objects for now, so choose **Select/Invert**, choose **Display/Hide/Object,** press the spacebar to turn on the Selected button, and then click in the Front viewport to hide the original set of objects. You need to redraw all viewports now, by pressing Alt+~.

10. Choose **Display/Unhide/Object/By Name** and select BOUND-BOX from the Unhide dialog box. Press Enter to accept. A box now surrounds all the type in each view (see fig. 5.4). Choose **Display/Hide/Object/By Name** to verify that only the new 01 versions of the letter objects are unhidden as well as the Bound-Box object.

11. Now you must assign the DISINTEGRATE IPAS to BOUND-BOX. Choose **Modify/Object/Attributes,** click on BOUND-BOX, and then click on the blank External Process name box. The AXP Selector dialog box appears. Select DISINT and press Enter.

STOP: You must have the Yost Group's Disintegrate IPAS to complete this section of the effect. You should already have read the manual that came with the IPAS so that you are familiar with using Disintegrate.

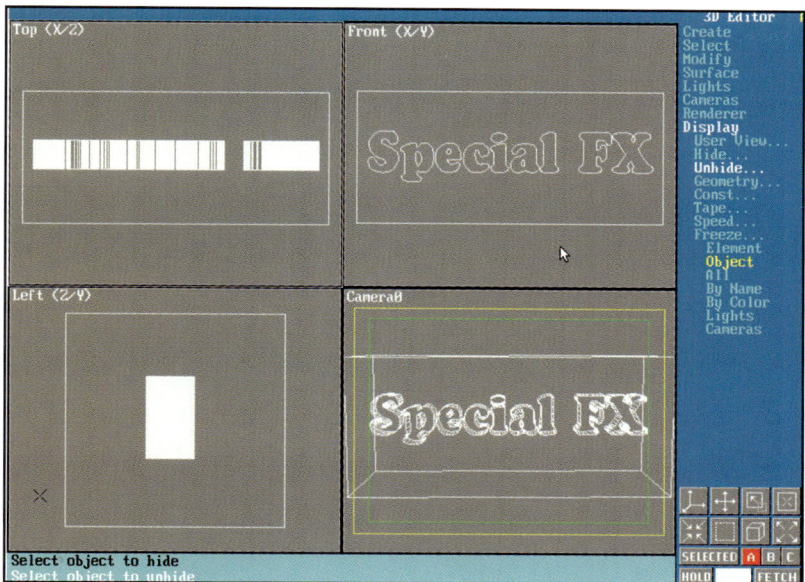

Figure 5.4
Relationship of bounding box to text.

12. The present settings for DISINT are the default values. Select Load to get the custom settings that you will use. You will now select COMET1.PRM from the \COMET directory on the supplied CD-ROM, press Enter to accept. Click on the Settings button to see the custom settings (see fig. 5.5). Press Enter after you finish.

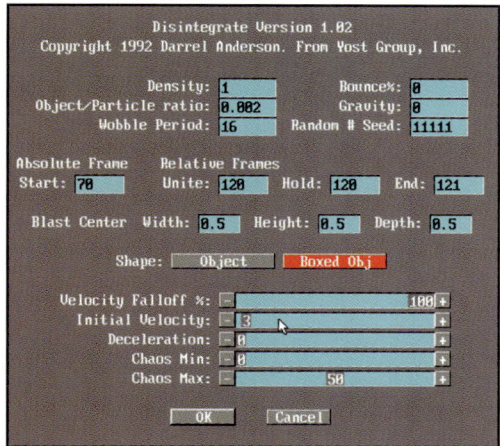

Figure 5.5
Custom Disintegrate IPAS settings.

I designed these settings for this particular animation. If you decide to create your own text, logo, or whatever, you probably will need to make adjustments. The original sets of IPAS processes provided no previews, so plenty of trial and error testing was necessary. I would suggest at least starting with the supplied settings to save yourself some of these test renders. The supplied settings might not be an exact match for what you need, but they should at least be a good starting point.

13. After you apply the AXP and settings to BOUND-BOX, you need to replicate the object for each letter. Just as for copying the letters, you use Rotate to clone the box. The Local Axis icon still should be off and Angle Snap on. Choose **Modify/Object/Rotate**. Next, while holding down Shift, click on BOUND-BOX in the Front viewport, rotate –10°. Name the new object **S_BOX** and press Enter to accept.

14. Repeat step 13 eight more times for all letters and name new objects **p_BOX**, **e_BOX**, and so on.

15. You now have nine new boxes rotated –10° from BOUND-BOX. Press Alt+N to deselect all objects, then choose **Select/Object/By Name**. Select the names of the nine new boxes and press Enter to accept and select the nine boxes.

16. Choose **Modify/Object/Rotate** and press the spacebar to turn on the Selected button. Click in the Front viewport and rotate selected objects 10° so that the new boxes line up with BOUND-BOX. You now are done with BOUND-BOX; you can delete or hide BOUND-BOX.

17. You now need to attach the stand-in objects to the bounding boxes. The order in which you attach the objects is crucial. Choose **Create/Object/Attach,** then click on S. You need to select the stand-in object first. Now, because all nine boxes are on top of each other, press H to open the Click on Object Name dialog box. Select S_BOX and press Enter. S and S_BOX are now the same object, S_BOX.

18. Repeat step 17 for the balance of the eight stand-in objects and bounding boxes.

19. Next, you need to change the Random # Seed for eight of the nine AXP settings, otherwise, the particles will have the same path for all nine objects. Choose **Modify/Object/Attributes** and press H to select p_BOX. Select settings from the dialog box and change the Random # Seed to 22222.

TIP: The exact number for the Random # Seed isn't important, it just needs to be different for all nine objects. Using five of the same number (i.e., 11111, 22222, 33333 ...) makes it easier to keep track of the numbers you use. Use whatever system you can, just be consistent.

20. While still in the settings dialog box, you need to change the Absolute Start Frame Number (see table 5.1).

Table 5.1 Absolute Start Frame values for the Disintegrate IPAS

Object Name	Absolute Start Frame
S_BOX	70
p_BOX	76
e_BOX	82
c_BOX	88
i_BOX	94
a_BOX	100
l_BOX	106
F_BOX	112
X_BOX	118

Adding six frames to each consecutive object causes the particles to converge sequentially in the same direction the comet travels. Press Enter to accept these settings.

21. Repeat steps 19 and 20 for the remaining seven objects: e_BOX, c_BOX, and so on.

22. Before you have sufficient particles to make the letters dense enough to be recognized when they come together, you need to tessellate the stand-in AXP objects. Disintegrate places particles based on the vertex count of the stand-in object. The more vertices, the more particles, up to 64,000 faces per object. Choose **Create/Element/Tessellate** and click on the letter S in the Front viewport. You need to tessellate each element letter twice, except for the X, which you tessellate only once. Also, be sure to tessellate both the upper and lower elements of the i—the riser and the dot. See figure 5.6 for a full screen front view of the final tessellated elements.

Figure 5.6
Tessellated elements.

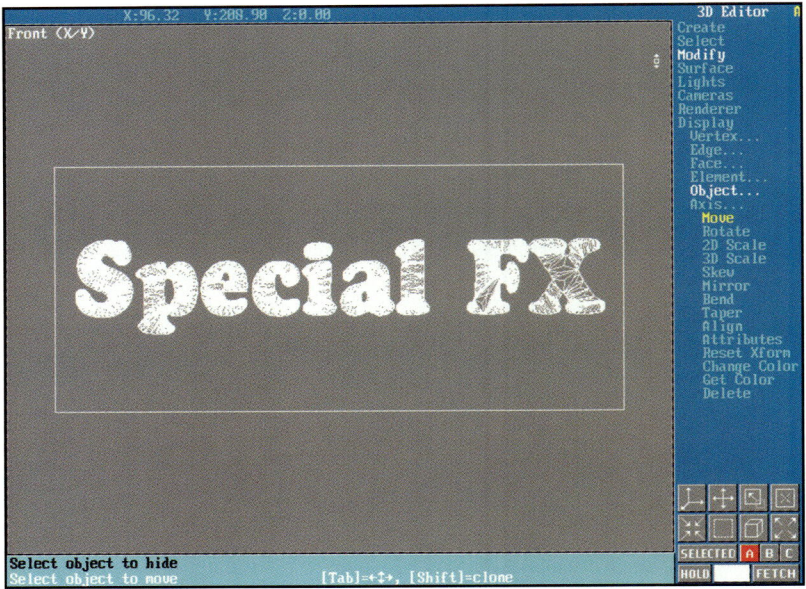

23. You can leave the material as Default for all the objects you've created so far.

24. Press F4 to switch to the Keyframer module. Before the particles can arrive on-screen at the appropriate time and the solid letters also appear at the correct time, you need to adjust the hide portion of the Track Info dialog box accordingly.

25. Click on the Front viewport, then press W to make the Front viewport full screen.

26. Click on the Track Info button. Press H to pick an object by name. After the dialog box opens, select S_BOX and press Enter.

27. At the bottom of the Track Info dialog box is the Hide line. Select the Add button and click on Frame 0 of the Hide line. Then, using the frame number scroll bar near the bottom of the dialog box, scroll until you can see Frames 150–200. With the Add button still selected, click on Frame 162, then on Frame 191 of the Hide line. The white section of the Hide line, Frames 162–190, represents when S_BOX is visible while rendering. The dark gray portion of the line represents when the S_BOX is hidden while rendering (see fig. 5.7). Press Enter to accept these settings.

28. Repeat steps 26 and 27 for the remaining _BOX objects and for the letter objects: S, p, c, e, and so on (see table 5.2 for the hide and unhide frame numbers for all the appropriate objects). Notice that when S_BOX hides at Frame 191, S unhides. This helps create the effect of particles coming together to form a solid object.

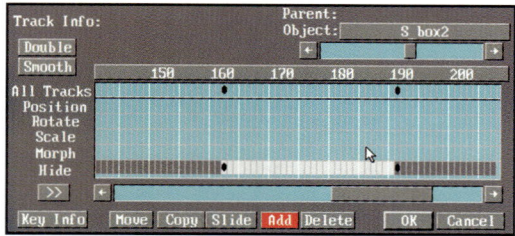

Figure 5.7
Hide information in the track info dialog box for S_BOX.

Table 5.2 Hide and unhide frame numbers for the Track Info dialog box

Object	Hide	Unhide	Hide
S_BOX	0	162	191
p_BOX	0	166	197
e_BOX	0	170	203
c_BOX	0	174	209
i_BOX	0	178	215
a_BOX	0	182	221
l_BOX	0	186	227
F_BOX	0	192	233
X_BOX	0	196	239
S	0	191	-
p	0	197	-
e	0	203	-
c	0	209	-
i	0	215	-
a	0	221	-
l	0	227	-
F	0	233	-
X	0	239	-

29. Press F3 to return to the 3D Editor and choose **Display/Hide/All**. You are finished with the letters and are ready to create the comet.

The Comet

Now for the comet. Like the _BOX objects, to create the particles for the tail of the comet, you use an AXP IPAS. This time you don't need a stand-in object to control the particles; a simple cube suffices. I have provided one in the COMET.PRJ file that already is the right size and has the proper orientation.

STOP: You will need Digimation's Magic 4 to complete this section of the effect. Be sure to read and complete the tutorials that come with Magic 4 so that you are familiar with how to use Magic 4.

1. From the 3D Editor, choose **Display/Unhide/Object/By Name**. Select box-YEL and press Enter.

2. To assign the AXP IPAS Magic, choose **Modify/Object/Attributes**, then click on box-YEL.

3. As you did for the _BOX objects, click on the blank External Process Name box. Select Magic 4 from the AXP Selector and press Enter.

4. Select Load to acquire the custom settings I used for this effect. The file is COMET2.PRM, located in the \COMET directory on the CD-ROM.

5. Select Settings to view the COMET2.PRM parameters (see fig. 5.8). Once again, these settings are designed for this effect with the supplied text. If you customize the text, you need to modify the parameters for your own needs. As with the Disintegrate IPAS, you don't have preview, and you have to do a good deal of trial and error to achieve the desired effect. These settings give you a good starting point. Press Enter to accept these settings.

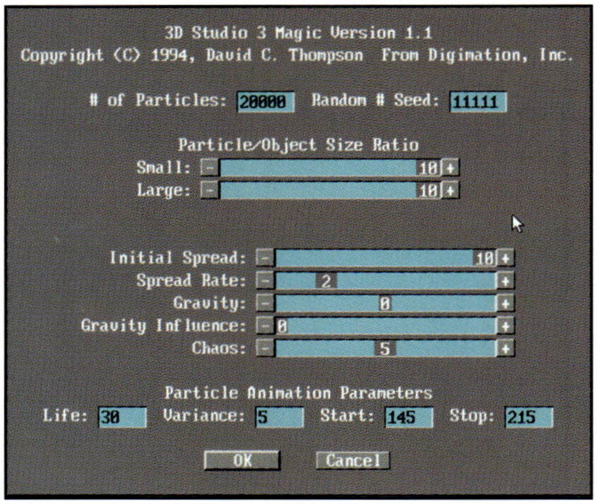

Figure 5.8
Custom Magic IPAS settings.

6. To get the quantity of particles necessary for a dense particle trail, you need to copy box-YEL four times so that you have five Magic AXP cubes. Use the same technique to clone the bounding box for the Text AXP objects; steps 13–16. Name the new cubes **box-GRN**, **box-ORN**, **box-VIO**, and **box-WHT**.

7. You now need to change the Random # Seed for the four new box-objects. Repeat step 19 from the Text AXP objects section of this chapter.

8. Next, you apply materials to the box- objects. Make sure that COMET.MLI is the current material library. To do this, choose **Surface/Material/Get Library**. COMET.MLI should be the current file name if it is the currrent library. If it is, press Esc to cancel. If COMET.MLI is not the current library, choose it. COMET.MLI is located in the \COMET directory on the supplied CD-ROM. Choose **Surface/Material/Choose**, select MAGIC YELLOW from the Material Selector dialog box, and press Enter. Now choose **Surface/Material/Assign/By Name**, select box-YEL, and press Enter to apply.

9. Repeat step 8 to apply MAGIC GREEN to box-GRN, MAGIC ORANGE to box-ORN, and so on. These are custom self-illuminated materials designed to key the optional Glow image processing IPAS in Video Post at rendering time.

10. The last part of the comet is the head. For this effect, the head is a lens flare. From the 3D Editor, choose **Unhide/Object/By Name** and select BALL, then press Enter to unhide. You should now see a small sphere aligned with the right side of the cubes in the Top and Front viewports. BALL is approximately centered in the Left viewport (see fig. 5.9).

11. You can now apply a material to BALL. Choose **Surface/Material/Choose** and select WHT PLSTC ILUM, then press Enter to accept. Choose **Surface/Apply/By Name** and select BALL, then press Enter to assign WHT PLSTC ILUM to BALL. You now have all the necessary objects to create the "Tail of the Comet" effect with the correct attributes and materials applied.

12. Press F4 to switch to the Keyframer. The object box-YEL already has position keyframes assigned. You need to make all of the box- objects move exactly the same. To accomplish this, choose **Object/Tracks/Copy**, press H, select box-YEL as the source object, and press Enter. Now, press H again, select box-GRN, and press Enter. Activate the Absolute button in the Copy Tracks dialog box and press Enter to accept.

> **NOTE:** When you create your own version of this effect, you can move the original box-YEL object in the Keyframer before you make the clones in the 3D Editor. Using the Absolute option causes the clones to line up exacly on top of each other, even if you moved box-YEL on frame 0.

Figure 5.9
Flare object. BALL in relationship to box- objects.

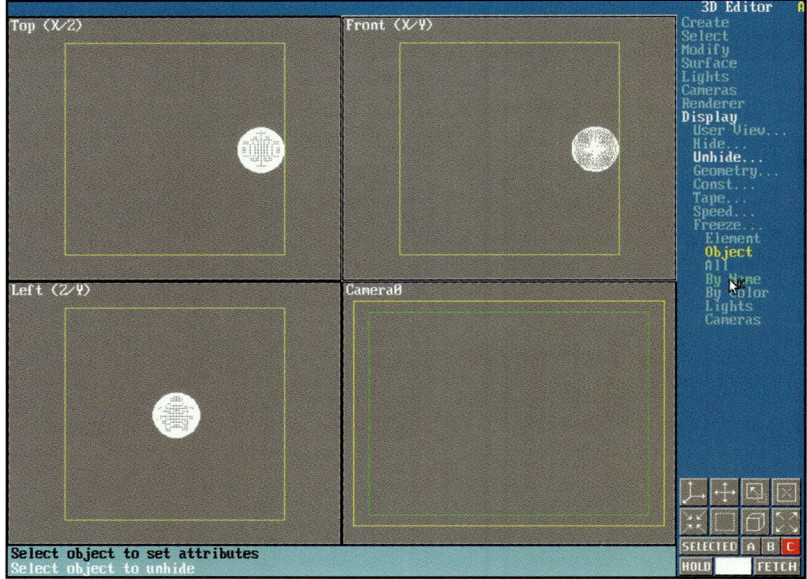

13. Repeat step 12 until all five box- objects have the same tracks.

14. You now need to make the BALL object move with the box- objects. Choose **Hierarchy/Link** and click on the BALL object to make it the child object. Now press H and select box-YEL as the parent object.

> **NOTE:** When using the Magic 4 IPAS, your Magic AXP object should not be at the end of your hierarchical chain. The IPAS might not behave predictably.

Now if you drag the frame slider at the bottom of the screen, you see the box- objects and the BALL object move across the Camera viewport from frames 145–190. This is the only physical object movement for this effect. The bounding boxes and the AXP settings control all the particle animation for the letters.

Video Post

Now that all of the objects are in place with movement and AXP processes assigned, you are ready for the last step: applying Video Post Image Processing effects and rendering.

1. Choose **Render/Video Post** and click anywhere in the Camera viewport, which opens the Video Post Queue dialog box.

2. Click on the Add button, to activate it. Now click on the first, then second, then third lines, just below the word "Queue" in the blue area, to add three [KF Scene]s to the Video Post Queue.

3. Activate the Edit button, then click on the first [KF Scene] line, which should open the Queue Entry dialog box. Activate the Gradient button. Now click on the far right rectangle next to the Gradient button, which opens the Define Gradient Colors dialog box. Set the B slider to 26, then press Enter to accept. Press Enter again to accept the Queue Entry dialog box.

4. With the Edit button still active, click on the third entry in the Queue. The Queue Entry dialog box appears again. Next click on the blank box next to the Process button. Select Glow for the IXP Selector and press Enter. Click on the Setup button next to the button that now says Glow_I.IXP. The Glow Filter dialog box should now be open. Before Glow can process the appropriate pixels, you should set Key off to Hue. Adjust the Hue slider to 43, which is the hue value for Magic Yellow material (see table 5.3 for the attributes of all the materials used in this project). Set Var to 0, this will cause only the pixels with an exact Hue value of 43 to be affected by the Glow IPAS. And since the Magic Yellow material is self-illuminated, most of the particles will have a Hue value of 43 since they will not be affected by light sources or shadows. Set Brightness attenuation to 70 and effect size in pixels to 13 (see fig. 5.10). Press Enter to accept these settings.

Table 5.3 Materials Attributes for Comet.MLI

Material Name	R	G	B	H	L	S	Self Ilum
Magic Green	0	200	0	85	100	255	80
Magic Orange	200	52	0	11	100	255	80
Magic Violet	200	0	200	213	100	255	80
Magic White	198	205	205	128	201	17	80
Magic Yellow	200	200	0	43	100	255	80
WHT PLSTC ILUM	247	255	254	122	251	255	100

Figure 5.10
Glow Filter IPAS dialog box.

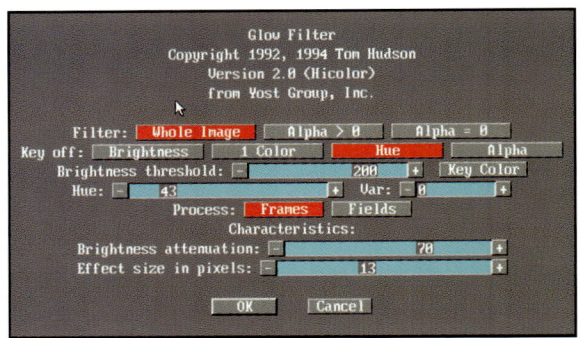

5. Back at the Video Post dialog box, you need to copy the Glow_I.IXP entry so that you have five Glow entries. Activate the Copy button, click on the Glow_I.IXP entry, and then drag it down to the next available position in the Queue. Repeat the copy step until you have five Glow_I.IXP entries.

6. You now need to adjust the Hue Keying settings for the four new Glow_I.IXP entries to match the appropriate materials. Again, refer to table 5.3 for the Hue values for each of the five MAGIC materials. Click on Setup and adjust the Hue settings. All the other settings are okay, because you copied the first Glow_I.IXP values.

7. Repeat step 6 until all five Glow_I.IXP entries have the proper settings.

8. The last entry you have to make is to add the Flare IPAS to the Video Post Queue. As in step 2, add a new entry to the next available line in the Queue. Edit the new entry, and add Flare to the Process line as you did for Glow in step 4. You Key the flare from the object position. Object to Flare should be BALL. The name you enter for Object to Flare *must* be exactly the same as the object you want to Key off of (see fig. 5.11 for the balance of settings for the Lens Flare). After all the settings are correct, press Enter to accept. Press Enter again at the Queue Entry dialog box.

> **NOTE:** In order for the Flare IPAS to work, Render/Output/Coords must be set to On in your 3DS.SET file. On is the default value.

9. After you make all the entries to the Video Post Queue, it should look like fig. 5.12. Press Enter now to save all the entries you made. If you click on Cancel now, you save nothing from the Queue. Save your work now if you haven't been doing so already.

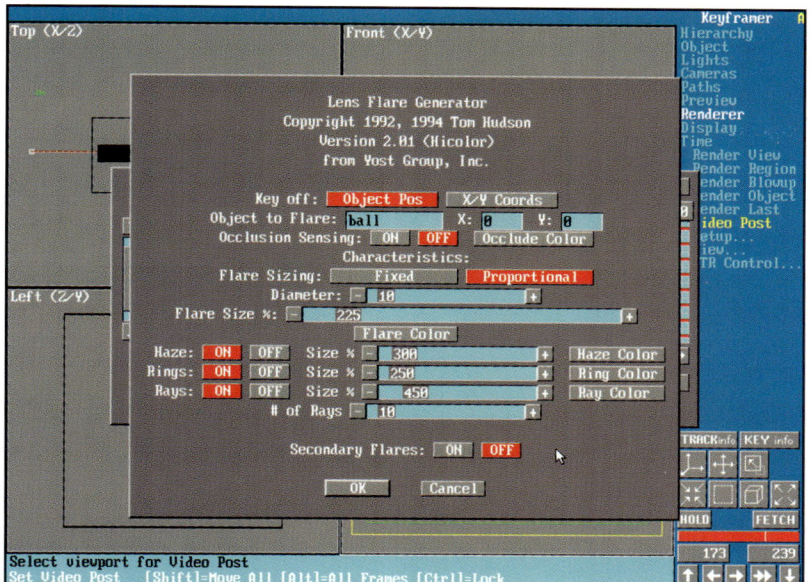

Figure 5.11
Lens Flare IPAS dialog box.

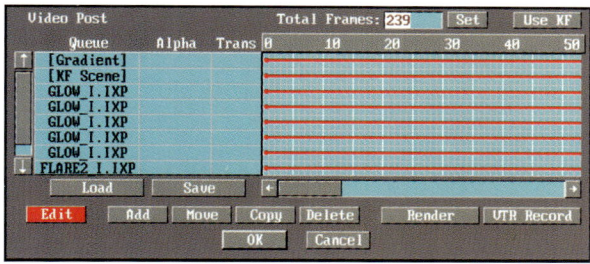

Figure 5.12
Video post queue with all entries.

STOP: If you render a FLIC, be sure to wait to render when you have plenty of uninterrupted CPU time available. On a P120 with 64 MB of RAM, the COMET.FLC on the CD-ROM took several hours to complete. Some frames took 4 minutes to render and used over 56 MB of RAM. Particle Animation and Image Processing are extremely memory- and CPU-intensive.

10. Choose **Render/Video Post** and click on the Camera viewport to get back to the Video Post dialog box.

11. Select Render and configure the output for the best of your system's capabilities, TGA frames for video recording or a FLIC with the Vibrant driver using the default resolution. Again, because the the particles are so small, a 320×200 FLIC really loses a lot of the nuances of the finished effect.

12. Set the frames to Range and render Frames 149–239 to disk.

Conclusion

All of the IPAS processes used to create Tail of the Comet can produce some very powerful effects. By experimenting with settings you can change the spread of the comet's tail or the size and density of the letter's particles, to name just two variations. Experiment with materials, try different colors for different letters, or perhaps even make all the comet's particles one color. Try adding Starbursts (using the Highlight IPAS) to the comet's particles in Video Post. Perhaps the camera could follow the comet and then swing around to reveal the particles coming together for your logo. You don't have to use a flare for the head of the comet either, the head can be a product, logo, or even text.

Because each of the IPASs used for this effect have no preview, you might need to generate a number of test frames and animations to get the "right" effect, but the final results can definitely be worth the time and effort.

Tornado!

Effect 6

by George Maestri
Los Angeles, California

Equipment and Software Used

- IBM-Compatible Pentium 90 with 32 MB RAM
- 3D Studio Release 4.0
- Adobe Photoshop 3.01 for Windows
- Autodesk Animator Studio

Artist Biography

George Maestri is a writer and animator who lives in Los Angeles. His computer experience dates back to the age of 12, when he taught himself programming on a Honeywell mainframe. This talent blossomed into an early career in computers, and by the age of 16, George was programming for a living on the Altair 8800, the original microcomputer. He soon graduated to Unix, where he spent many years as a Systems Engineer. After more than a decade in the computer business, George abandoned his trade to learn traditional animation at DeAnza College in Cupertino, CA. From there, he worked in animation and eventually wound up developing stories and animating on the pilot for "Rocko's Modern Life." He later wrote for the series, gaining a Cable Ace nomination. George has returned to computers as a tool for animation, directing both traditional and computer animation for a number of studios. He currently develops new projects for Film Roman.

Effect Overview

The Tornado effect is one way to create a realistic spinning, animatable tornado. The effect relies on animated texture and opacity maps to achieve a particle-like effect. Although 3D Studio does have a tornado IPAS particle system, you can't control the shape of the particles, nor can you reshape the system. Also, creating large numbers of particles using motion blur can tax even the fastest renderers. This method works well and renders much faster.

Procedure

The tornado consists of three nested sets of 24 stacked toruses. To make the tornado look more natural, you need to create several toruses of different sizes and thicknesses, then mix them up a bit to make a stack.

Building the Funnel Stacks

1. From the 3D Editor, choose **Create/Torus/Values**. Select a rather low number, such as the default of 8 sides and 16 segments.

2. To make things easier when you animate the tornado, you need to be sure to precisely center the toruses so they all spin around the same axis. Choose **Modify/Axis/Place**. Center the axis in the Top viewport.

3. Choose **Create/Torus/Smoothed**. In the Top viewport, create a torus centered on the axis with an inner radius of 20 and an outer radius of 25. (These numbers are just suggestions, if you need to work bigger, just keep approximately the same proportions.) Name the torus **Outer-01**.

4. You need to assign mapping coordinates to the torus. Because you copy it, assigning the mapping first is best so the mapping copies with the object. Choose **Surface/Mapping/Type** and select cylindrical mapping. Choose **Surface/Mapping/Adjust** to size and adjust the cylinder so it fits roughly around the perimeter of the torus. Choose **Surface/Mapping/Assign/Object** and click on Outer-01.

5. Repeat this procedure two more times to create a slightly fatter and a slightly thinner torus. Be absolutely sure to center these on the axis as well. For the fat torus, I chose values of 18 and 26, and for the thin torus, I chose 21 and 23. Name these **Outer-02** and **Outer-03**.

6. Assign mapping coordinates to these toruses, as in step 4.

Now that you have a few different types of toruses, you can start building your outer funnel cloud. You should start from the bottom and work your way up (see fig 6.1). First, you need to stack the three toruses you've already created to make the bottom of the funnel.

Figure 6.1
Begin building the outer funnel cloud by stacking the three toruses to make the bottom of the funnel.

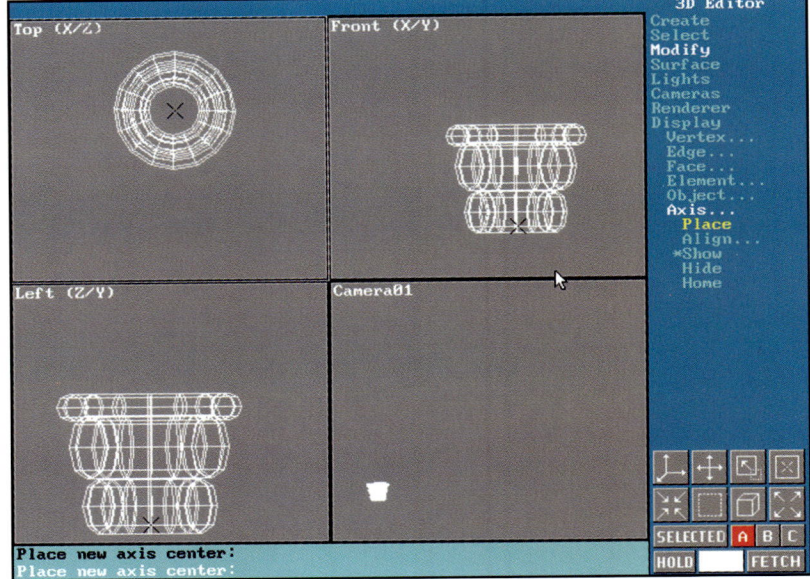

7. Choose **Modify/Object/Move**. Select the Front or the Left viewport. Press the Tab key so that you move only the toruses along the Y axis. Move the toruses so that they are stacked and overlap a bit.

Now you need to copy these three and resize the copies to make the funnel.

8. Choose **Create/Object/Copy**. Press the Tab key so that the cursor arrow points along the Y axis only. Select a torus and copy it.

9. Choose **Modify/Object/3D Scale**. Resize the new torus so that it is slightly larger than the one on top. Choose **Modify/Object/Move** and position the torus on top of the stack. Select a different torus and repeat this procedure to make an ascending stack. My stack was 24 toruses high. Figure 6.2 shows a completed outer funnel cloud.

> **TIP:** How you build the funnel is really an aesthetic decision. You might want to make the tornado tall and thin or more squat. The important thing is to mix up the three different sized toruses as you enlarge them to keep the patterns random, to make the tornado look more natural. One thing I did was scale the copied toruses along the Y axis using **Modify/Object/2D Scale**, which gave me an even greater variety of shapes.

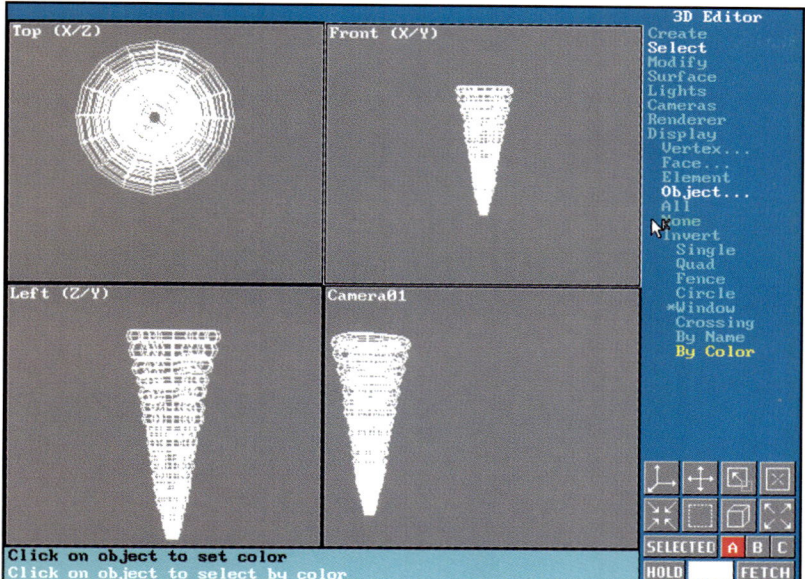

Figure 6.2
The first funnel cloud is now complete.

After you build the outer funnel, you can create the two inner funnels simply by copying the toruses.

10. Choose **Select/Object/Quad** to select all the toruses.

11. In the Front viewport, copy all of the toruses at once. From within the Front or Left viewport, choose **Create/Object/Copy**. Press the spacebar to toggle the selected indicator on. Press the Tab key to make sure the cursor arrow points horizontally. You want to keep these at the same level. Copy the stack of toruses to multiple objects named **Inner01** through **Inner24**.

12. Repeat this to create a third stack, named **Core01** through **Core24**.

    You now have three stacks, all the same size. You need to scale them down so that they nest properly.

13. Choose **Select/None**. Now choose **Select/Object/Quad** and select stacks Inner01 through Inner24. Draw a box around the objects.

14. Choose **Modify/Object/2D Scale**. From within the Top viewport, scale the stack down somewhere around 75 percent. The stack should now appear taller and thinner in the Front and Left viewports.

    Repeat this procedure for the Core stack, making it about 60 percent smaller that it originally was.

Effect 6: Tornado! 103

15. Now that you have three stacks, you should assign them different colors to help when you switch among them for animation, because you can display or hide by color in the Keyframer. Choose **Modify/Object/Change Color** and assign each stack it's own unique color (see fig. 6.3).

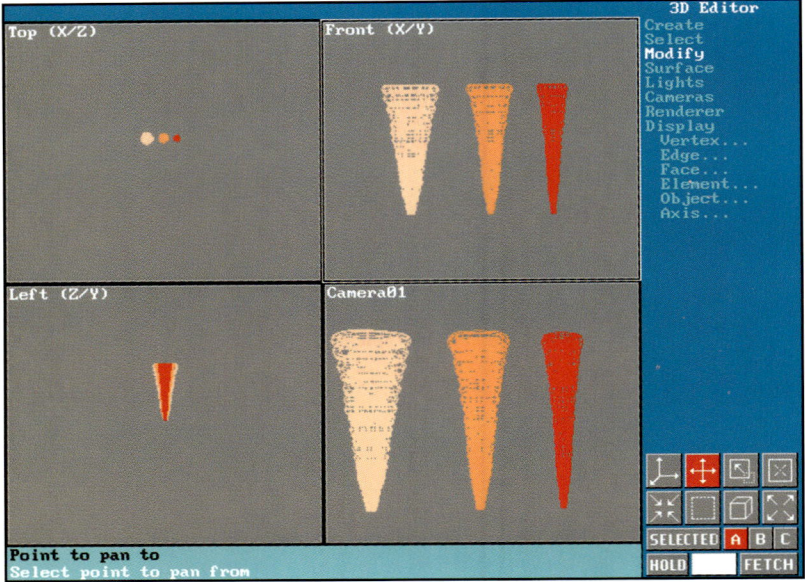

Figure 6.3
The finished funnel stacks.

Textures

Now that you have the three main elements of the funnel, you can assign your textures. You can use three predefined textures for the three funnels; they are named Animated-Wisps, Animated-Smoke1, and Animated-Smoke2. The library TORNADO.MLI contains all of the textures used in the exercise.

Let me digress a bit to explain a little about these textures and how they were created. Each of these maps has simple animated textures and opacity maps. Animated-Smoke2 is intended for the inner ring, while Animated-Smoke1 is intended for the core of the tornado. Both use a simple FLIC named Smoke001.FLC as their texture map. The only difference is the transparency.

To make these textures:

1. From the Materials Editor, load SMOKE001.FLC as the texture.

2. Set Transparency to **40** and Transparency falloff to **60**.

3. Save the material as **Animated-Smoke1**.

Repeat the same procedure, but lower the Transparency to **20** and the Transparency Falloff to **25**. Name this material **Animated-Smoke2**.

The outer ring uses a wispy texture to simulate the particles and wisps of vapor that surround the tornado. They also nicely obscure the edges of the inner toruses so that they look less geometric.

To make the basic map, I created a black frame in Photoshop and painted some thin white wisps on the surface. I was careful to keep the majority of the frames black, so that when it's made into an opacity map, only the white wisps show. The black pixels are opaque. Liberal amounts of blur keep the edges soft.

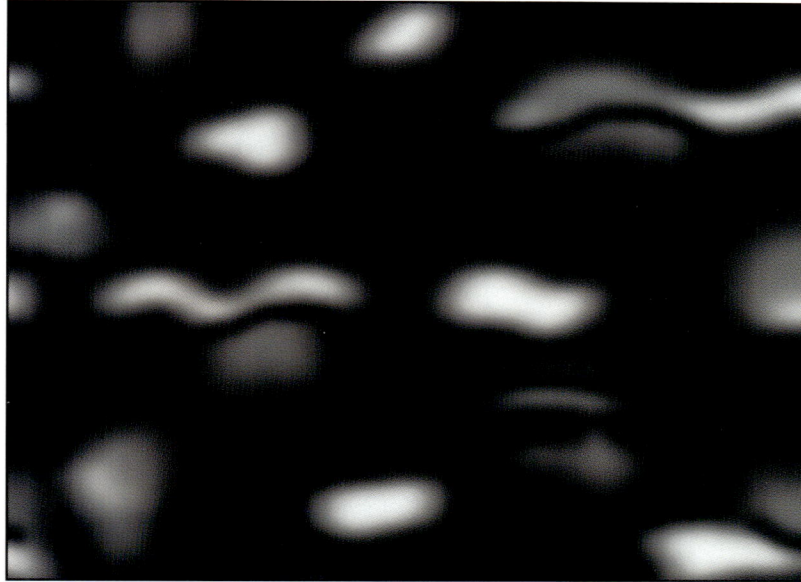

Figure 6.4
A frame from WISPS.FLC.

To make these textures:

1. From the Materials Editor, load WISPS.FLC as the opacity map (see fig. 6.4). Set the opacity to **100** percent.

2. Load SMOKE01.TGA as the texture map, and set the value to **85** percent.

3. Save this material as **ANIMATED-WISPS**.

After you set the textures, you can assign them to the three stacks.

1. From the 3D Editor, select each stack by color (choose **Select/Object/By Color**) and assign the following textures:

Animated-Smoke1—Core00 through Core24

Animated-Smoke2—Inner00 through Inner24

Animated-Wisps—Outer00 through Outer24

Finishing the Funnel Cloud

To finish building the tornado, you have to build a hierarchy and nest the outer stacks around the core.

1. Before you leave the 3D Editor, you should set up each of the stacks so assigning the hierarchies and keeping the elements centered will be easy. Move each stack so that their centers all fall along the same line (see fig. 6.5).

Figure 6.5
Align the stacks so they lie along the same axis.

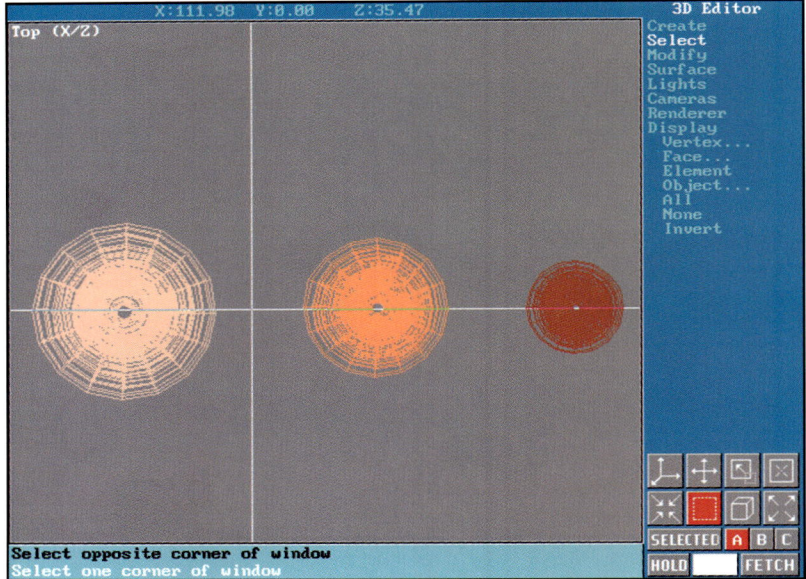

Now enter the Keyframer. You need to assign the hierarchies. The toruses in the outer rings are children to the inner rings. The inner rings are children to the core.

TIP: For this to work properly, you should be positioned at Frame 0 in the Keyframer. When you animate with hierarchies, all child positions are determined relative to Frame 0. Also, it's easier to work if you place the funnel stacks next to each other. You nest them later.

1. Set the current frame to 0.

2. From the Keyframer, choose **Hierarchy/Link**. Click on Outer00 as the child. Click on Inner00 as the parent.

3. As long as you're still in link mode, assign the next link.

   Click on Inner00 as the child. Make Core00 its parent.

4. Work your way up the funnel stack, assigning the hierarchies to each of the 24 levels of toruses.

   TIP: To test a link, simply choose **Object/Move** and move the parent. If the link is correct, the child moves with the parent. Left click to cancel the move command.

5. Create a dummy object for the core to be linked to. Choose **Hierarchy/Create Dummy**. Name the object **Dummy00**. Center the dummy beneath the bottom torus of the core.

6. Link each of the toruses in Core00 through Core24 to the dummy. Choose **Hierarchy/Link**. Click on Core00 and link it to Dummy00 as the parent. Work your way up the Core stack, using the following hierarchy:

Dummy	**00**
Core	00
Inner	00
Outer	00
Core	01
Inner	01
Outer	01
And so on	

7. Finally, you need to nest each of the funnel stacks around the core stack (see fig. 6.6). To do this, choose **Object/Move**. Highlight the front view. Press the Tab key so that the objects only move horizontally. Now click and drag each of the 48 Outer and Inner toruses so that you center both over the core.

Effect 6: Tornado!

TIP: If you placed the funnel stacks along the same horizontal line as directed, you don't need to worry about them being centered along the Z axis. Simply drag them horizontally in the front view and center them there. The rest will take care of itself.

Figure 6.6
The nested stacks.

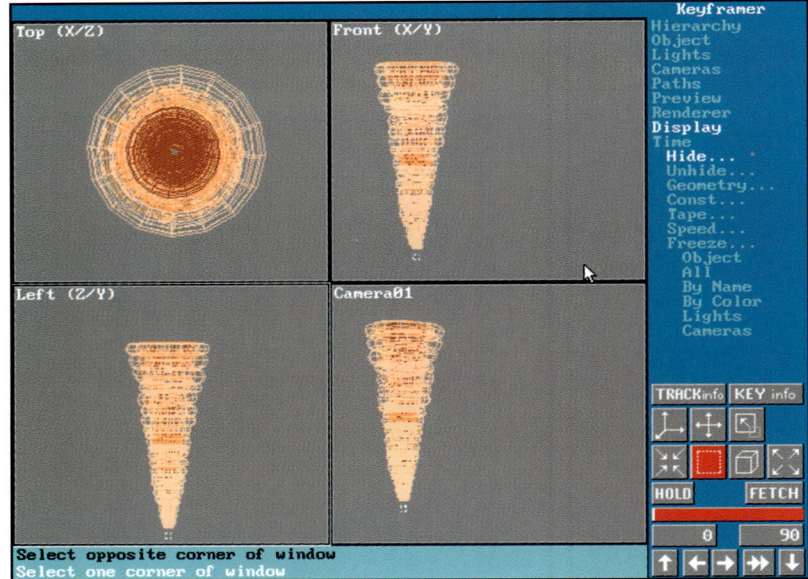

Animating the Tornado

Now you're ready to animate the tornado. First, you need to make the tornado spin, and then you move it and finally distort it. The rate of spin really depends on your specific scene. Generally, a tornado spins fairly fast. The only caveat is that you don't want to spin it so fast that it approaches the frame rate of the animation and starts strobing. For example, if you were to spin it 360 degrees per frame, the object would appear to be stationary. For this tornado, I suggest you go somewhere between 30 and 45 degrees per frame.

1. Make your active segment 90 frames long. Set the current frame to Frame 90.

2. Hide the outer rings. First, you need to spin only the core. Because it's linked to the outer rings, they spin along with it. Unfortunately, the outer rings now obscure the Core funnel. But because you assigned them different colors, hiding them is easy. Choose **Display/Hide/By Color**, then click on the outer funnel to hide all the toruses. Do the same for the inner funnel.

3. Spin each torus in the core stack. Choosing 45 degrees per frame gives you 45×90 = 4050 degrees of rotation through the entire scene. Choose **Object/Rotate**. Click on the bottom torus and drag. Tap the Tab key until the torus rotates around the vertical axis. Rotate it approximately 4050 degrees.

4. Repeat this for each torus in the stack. When you rotate the toruses, don't give them exactly the same value. If they rotate at slightly different rates, the tornado looks more natural. Also, the top of the funnel should move less quickly than the bottom. I varied the rates from about 3700 to 4100 degrees over the course of 90 frames.

5. Choose **Display/Hide/By Color** and click on the Core Funnel. It disappears.

6. Choose **Display/Unhide/By Color**. Click on the Inner Funnel's color. It appears.

7. Since the outer edges of the tornado need to move slower than the core, you need to rotate these back a bit. Choose **Object/Rotate** and rotate each torus in this stack back by approximately 10 to 20 percent, or –400 to –800 degrees.

8. Repeat this procedure for the Outer Funnel. Again, between –400 and –800 degrees is about right.

9. You now have the three funnels spinning properly, so you can move the funnel cloud across the landscape. Set the current frame to Frame 0.

10. Choose **Object/Move**. Move Dummy00 to the start of your tornado's path.

    The funnel should follow the Dummy to the start point.

11. Set the current frame to Frame 90.

12. Move the funnel to the final destination, again by moving Dummy00. Remember, big things move slowly. If you want to make your tornado look huge, you need to move it slowly.

Distorting the Funnel

Now that you have the basic motion, you can distort the funnel. A real tornado very rarely is straight up and down. Wind currents and other atmospheric effects distort the cloud so it snakes down to the ground. Constructing the cloud out of segments enables you to move these horizontally and still maintain the proper rotation.

1. Set the current frame to Frame 30.

2. Choose **Object/Hide/By Color**. Hide the outer two funnels, leaving the core.

3. Choose **Object/Move**. Move the individual toruses horizontally to distort the cloud. Be sure not to overextend the toruses and create break in the funnel. The funnel should form a continuous S shape from bottom to top.

4. Set the current frame to Frame 60.

5. Choose **Object/Move**. Slide the toruses horizontally to make another shape. Again, keep it continuous.

6. Repeat this for Frame 90. Figure 6.7 shows the distorted stack.

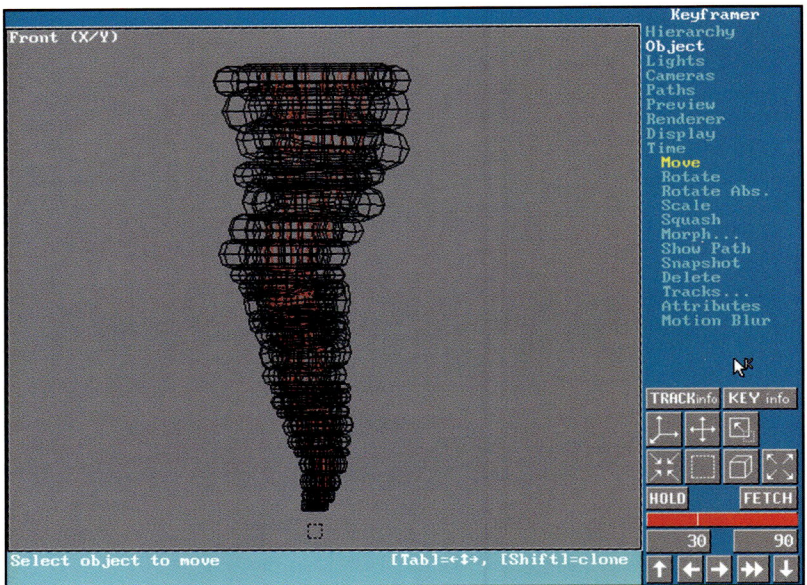

Figure 6.7
The distorted stack.

Rendering

The tornado should be ready to render. In the provided example, you have an object for the ground plane (Ground) and two objects for the clouds (Cloud0 and Cloud1). The clouds are just two variations of the same shape made using the Waves IPAS routine. Cloud00 morphs to Cloud01 over the course of the animation. I also turned on fog and lit the scene flat so that it looks even more murky and overcast.

1. Choose **Render/Render View** and click in the Camera viewport. In the Configure box, select the appropriate resolution.

2. Give the animation a name and render it. The final render is shown in figure 6.8.

3. On my Pentium 90 with 32 MB of RAM, the render times were about 2 minutes per frame at 752×480 (PAR) resolution.

Figure 6.8
The final render.

Conclusion

There's so much more you can do with this scene to make it look even more realistic. You can experiment with various particle system IPAS routines to make a dust cloud at the base of the tornado. You can experiment with color or add more layers, or with motion blur on the outer funnel. Finally, you can also make your tornado run into things such as buildings and make them explode. Explosions are always fun in 3D animation.

Interaction between Human and Computer Characters

Effect 7

by Kirk O. Nash
Bolingbrook, IL

Equipment and Software Used

- IBM Compatible 486/66 with 32 MB of RAM
- IBM Compatible P120 with 64 MB of RAM
- Wacom 12×12 Tablet
- TARGA - 64 Framebuffer
- DPS PAR with TBC IV
- Number 9 Imagine 128 SVGA Display Card
- Fractal Design Painter 3
- Bones Pro 1.5 from Digimation
- 3D Studio version 4.0

Artist Biography

For the past 12 years, Kirk O. Nash has worked in various areas of the multimedia field. First, as a freelance photographer, he did projects ranging from slide-tape presentations to fine art B&W photography, and his work was shown in several exhibitions. In 1988, he started Creative Digital Images, which provided photographic as well as video production services.

Creative Digital Images now provides 3D animation, digital compositing, and special effects for both the corporate and broadcast video markets, as well as for CD-ROM titles and interactive kiosks. Animations produced by Creative Digital Images have been broadcast nationally and internationally.

Kirk also is very active in a Chicago 3D Studio users group, The Loop Group, where he puts on demonstrations of animation techniques and IPAS routines. Kirk also spent a year as the editor and writer for The Loop Group newsletter.

Effect Overview

One of the hottest effects now in commercials and movies is computer-generated characters who interact with real world people and environments. This can be a very costly process that involves multiple video passes, blue screen shots, creating traveling mattes, and a great deal of post-production time. This chapter shows you how to make a 3D computer-generated character revolve around and interact with a human actor. You probably can create this effect using equipment and software you already have or can obtain without having to spend too much. When you finish this effect, you will have a final animation with a fully composited, computer-generated object and video background/foreground.

The basic story underlying this animation is as follows: A man hammering clobbers his hand, then becomes enraged and hurls the hammer, which in turn enrages the hammer's daddy, who reacts by deciding to avenge the man's offending behavior by squashing him. If you haven't viewed the animation yet, now would be a good time to do so, so you can get a feel for the effect. Choose **Render/View/Flic**. You can find the animation HAMMER.FLI in the\HAMMER directory on the CD-ROM for this book.

> **NOTE:** Before starting this effect, it would be a good idea to complete Effect 2, "Muscle Bot," first and become familiar with the concepts covered there.

This chapter first steps you through creating a 3D hammer using the lofter's SurfRev option and the Object Attach function to join the pieces of the hammer to form a single object. You then create a skeletal structure and specify a hierarchy and pivot points for the skeleton. Using Fast Preview in the Keyframer, you create a rough motion path for the hammer as it travels through the video environment. The Plug-In Bones Pro from Digimation is then used to give "life" to the hammer. (If you don't have Bones, you still can create this effect using morphing targets to bend and twist the hammer for its personality, or you can simply move the hammer without deforming it.) After you have the motion you want, you use Fractal Design Painter 3 to make the appropriate parts of the hammer disappear behind the actor. You might notice that the actor in the supplied video clip looks suprisingly like the author. He might not win any Academy Awards, but he works cheap and is always available. You might be fortunate enough to know someone like this if you decide to create your own test video clip.

Creating an interaction between a computer-generated character and real world video is a fairly advanced effect. You should have a good working knowledge of 3D Studio, because this chapter doesn't explain every keystoke for basic commands in great detail.

Procedure

Before you load 3D Studio, you need to create an image file list, IFL extension. The image file list controls the sequential series of TGA files used for the roto-scoped video background. The image file list tells 3D Studio to load the correct video frame for the background when you render. To create the image file list, switch to your directory that contains 3D Studio. Then type **MAKEIFL HAMR HAM1 0 0189** and press Enter, which creates an image file list named HAMR.IFL that has images named HAM1, frames 0 to 0189.

Start 3D Studio, choose **File/Load/Project** and select HAMMER.PRJ from the \HAMMER directory on the supplied CD-ROM. You need to add the directory that contains the TGA files for the video background to your map paths. Press * to open the Program Configuration dialog box. Click on the Map Paths button and add the \HAMMER\IMAGES directory to your list. You also can find the TIF files used for the supplied materials in the \HAMMER\IMAGES directory. You should be sure to include your 3D Studio root directory in the map paths. Any IFL you create will be located in the 3D Studio root directory.

Creating the Hammer

The HAMMER.PRJ file has all the objects already built with textures applied and with animation keyed using Bones Pro. If you are interested only in creating the effect of the hammer interacting with the actor, you can just render the animation as is and then skip ahead to the section "Image Manipulation."

1. Switch to the 2D Shaper module by pressing F4. Here, you see the polygons you use to create the head and handle of the hammer (see fig. 7.1).

Figure 7.1
2D Shaper hammer head and handle polygons.

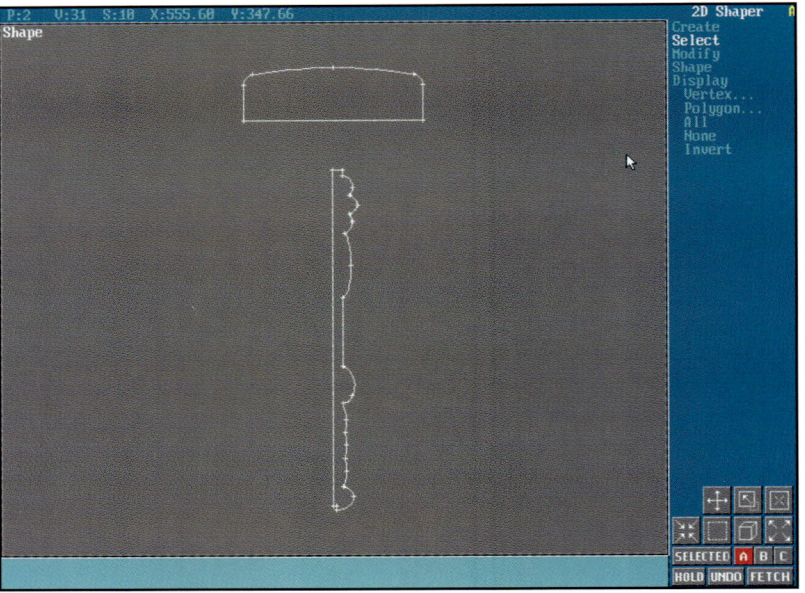

2. Choose **Shape/Assign** and click on the handle polygon.

3. Switch to the 3D Lofter module by pressing F2, and choose **Shapes/Get/Shaper**.

4. Choose **Path/SurfRev**. The Surface of Revolution dialog box appears. Set Diameter to 0.0001, Degrees to 360, and Vertices to 65, then press Enter. Press Enter again to replace the path.

5. Choose **Shapes/Align/Left**, which causes the handle shape to rotate around the straight edge and gives you the correct 3D shape. Choose **Objects/Preview** and activate the Contour button. Press Enter to generate the preview shape. Your screen should resemble figure 7.2.

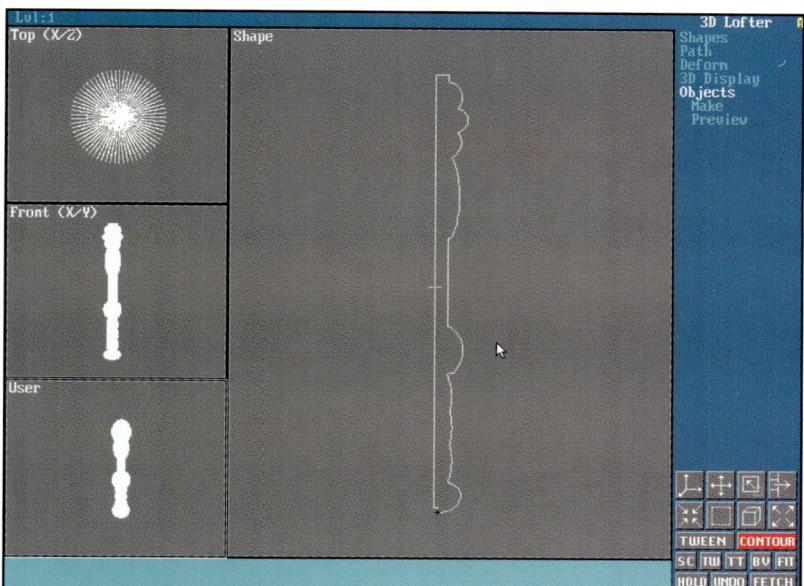

Figure 7.2
3D Lofter preview of the handle.

6. If your screen looks like fig. 7.2, then choose **Objects/Make** and see figure 7.3 for the Object Lofting Controls settings. Name this object **HANDLE**, and press Enter to create the 3D mesh. If your preview shape doesn't look like figure 7.2, make sure you aligned left, not right.

Figure 7.3
Object Lofting Controls dialog box settings.

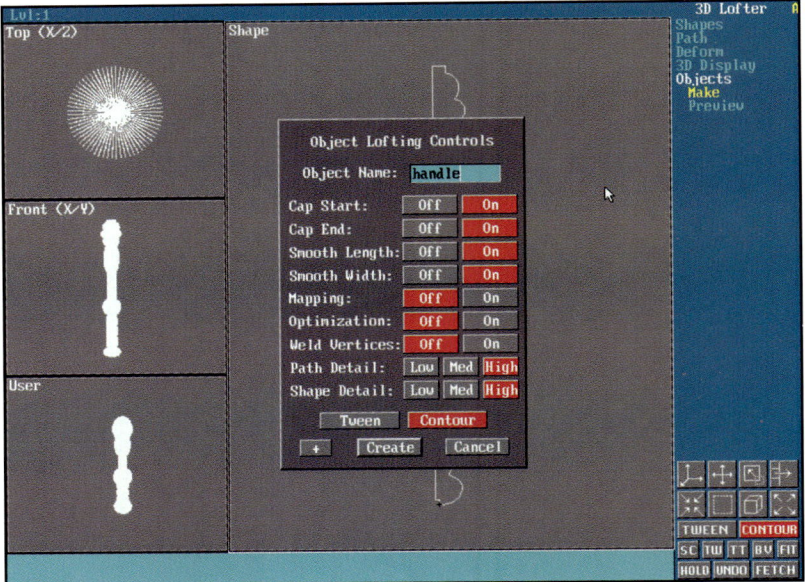

7. Switch back to the 2D Shaper. Choose **Shape/Assign/None**, then choose **Shape/Assign** and click on the top polygon, which is the head for the hammer.

8. Switch back to the 3D Lofter and choose **Shapes/Get/Shaper**, which loads the hammer head into the lofter. Choose Yes to replace the shape.

9. Now if you try to create the hammer head, it rotates around the wrong axis. You must rotate the polygon 90° in the Shape viewport. First, choose **Shapes/Center**.

10. Choose **Shapes/Rotate** and then make sure that Angle Snap is on. The letter A should appear in the upper right corner when Angle Snap is on. Pressing A toggles Angle Snap on and off.

11. Click on the hammer head shape in the Shape viewport and rotate 90°.

12. Choose **Shapes/Align/Right**. The hammer head shape now is ready to be lofted.

13. Choose **Objects/Make** and change the name for the lofted shape to **HEAD**. You can retain all the other lofting control settings from the last lofted object, HANDLE.

14. Switch to the 3D Editor by pressing F3. Make sure you can see all four views. You now have the hammer handle and head, but not in the proper position (see fig. 7.4). You have to move the object HEAD.

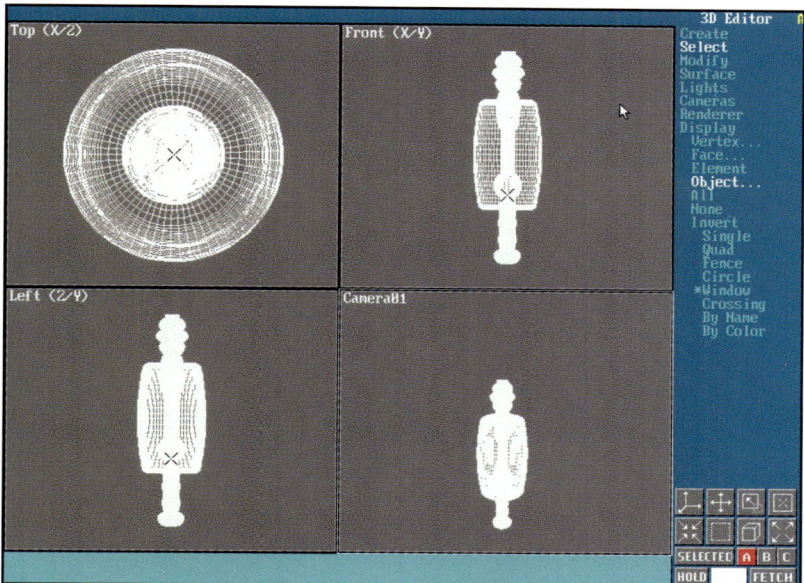

Figure 7.4
HANDLE and HEAD objects before HEAD has been rotated and moved.

15. Choose **Select/Object/By Name** and select HEAD. Press Enter.

16. Now click on the Front viewport and press W to toggle full screen to on.

17. Be sure to select the Local Axis icon. Choose **Modify/Object/Rotate**, press the spacebar to activate the Selected button, and rotate the object HEAD 90°.

18. Choose **Modify/Object/Move**. Toggle the Move directional cursor to vertical by repeatedly pressing the Tab key until it points straight up and down. Press the spacebar to activate the Selected button again and move HEAD up to the top of HANDLE approximately +418 units. Press the spacebar to deactivate the Selected button. Your Front viewport should now look like figure 7.5.

Figure 7.5
HEAD and HANDLE objects with HEAD properly oriented.

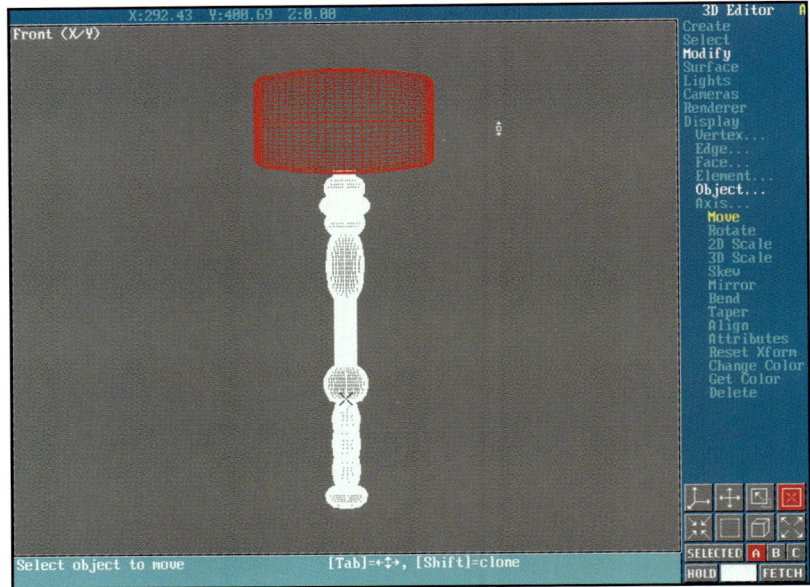

19. Press W to toggle the full screen view option to off. You now need to assign materials and mapping coordinates to each object. Choose **Display/Hide/Object/By Name,** select HEAD, and press Enter.

20. Choose **Surface/Mapping/Type/Cylindrical**. A mapping coordinates cylinder now should surround the object HANDLE as in figure 7.6. If not, you need to unhide the HAMMER object and choose **Surface/Mapping/Adjust/Acquire,** click on HAMMER, and then hide HAMMER.

Figure 7.6
Cylindrical mapping scale and position.

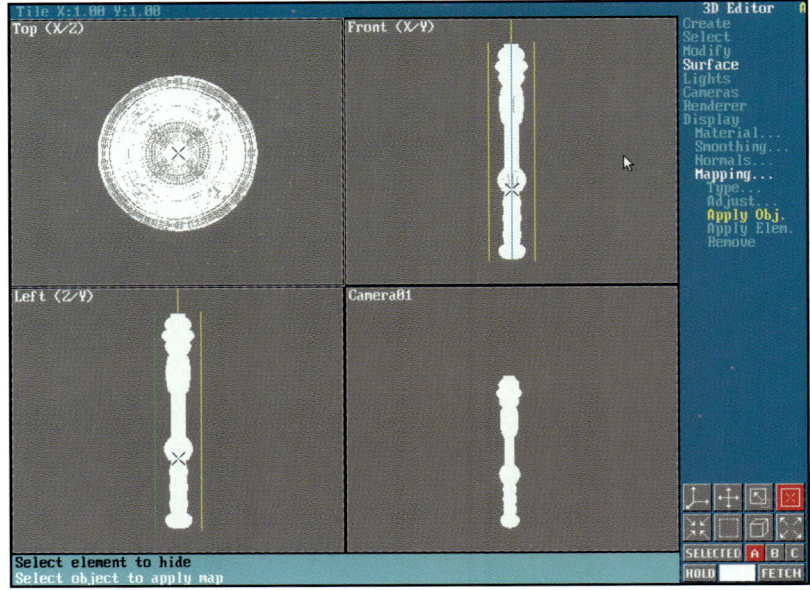

120 3D Studio Hollywood and Gaming Effects

21. Choose **Surface/Mapping/Apply Obj** and click on HANDLE.

22. Choose **Display/Unhide/Object/By Name** and select HEAD. Press Alt+N to deselect all objects.

23. Assign the same mapping coordinates to HEAD as you did to HANDLE. The texture in the material for HEAD is a flat color created in a paint program, so the coordinate type and alignment doesn't really matter. You just need mapping coordinates for HEAD.

24. You now can get the materials used for HANDLE and HEAD. Make sure HAMMER.MLI is the current material library. Choose **Surface/Material/Get Library**, HAMMER.MLI should be the current filename. If HAMMER.MLI is the current file listed, press Esc to cancel. If HAMMER.MLI is not the current file, choose it from the CD-ROM \ HAMMER directory. Choose **Surface/Material/Choose** and select HAMMER HANDLE (see fig. 7.7 for bitmap used in HAMMER HANDLE material), and press Enter. Choose **Surface/Material/Assign/Object** and click on HANDLE.

Figure 7.7
LEGMAP4.TIF bitmap used in HAMMER HANDLE material.

25. Choose **Surface/Material/Choose,** select HAMMER HEAD, and press Enter. Choose **Surface/Material/Assign/Object** and click on HEAD.

26. You can now join HEAD to HANDLE to make a single HAMMER2 object. Choose **Create/Object/Attach** and click on HEAD, then click on HANDLE.

27. Choose **Modify/Object/Attributes** to change name of HANDLE to **HAMMER2**. Use HAMMER2 because a HAMMER object already is hidden. If you haven't done so already, now might be a good time to render a test of HAMMER2. Choose **Render/Render View** and click on the Camera viewport (see fig. 7.8).

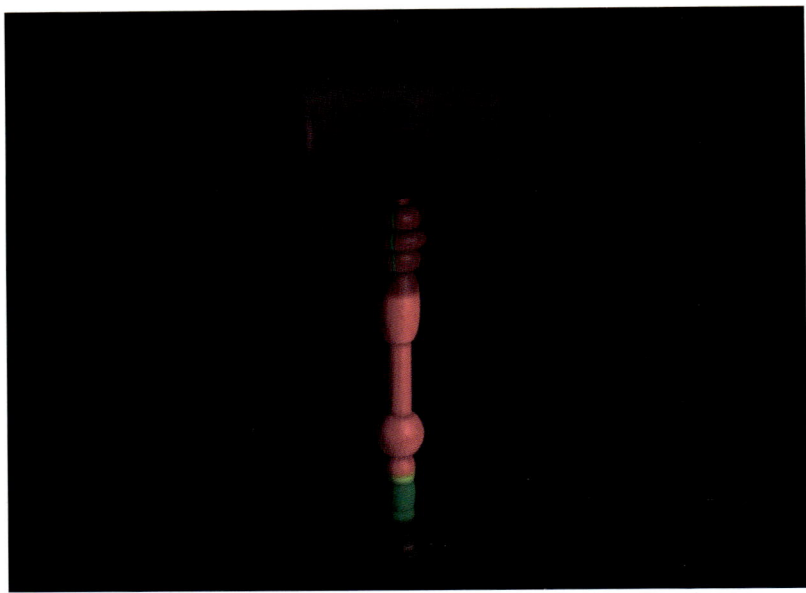

Figure 7.8
HAMMER2 object fully rendered with all materials applied.

Creating the Skeleton for the Hammer

In the supplied HAMMER.FLI, the hammer not only travels around the actor, but bends, wags its tail, and shakes its head up and down as if it's getting excited before it swoops down and eventually splats on the camera lens. All these additional actions help give the hammer life and a personality. Now you can copy the HAMMER2 object over and over, making dozens of morphing targets bending, twisting, scaling, and pulling faces, or, you can use Bones Pro. If you've ever used morphing targets to do character animation, you know how quickly the vertex count climbs, reducing available RAM. You also know how time-consuming making all those morphing targets is. Bones Pro, on the other hand, lets you work with your original object and create a skeleton that you alter, and which in turn deforms your original object at rendering time. If you're a die-hard mighty morphing power animator, that's great, but I'm a convert. Using Bones Pro saves me an incredible amount of time on projects and allows me to do effects you simply cannot do effectively using morphing targets.

1. The skeletal structure of HAMMER2 contains a total of 12 bones. The handle has 9 bones, and the head has 3 bones. Figure 7.9 shows the skeleton used for the object HAMMER. Figure 7.10 shows the same skeletal structure

with HAMMER also visible so that you can get a feeling for where the bones are located within the HAMMER object. Fastdraw was turned on for the HAMMER object so that you can see the bones inside easier.

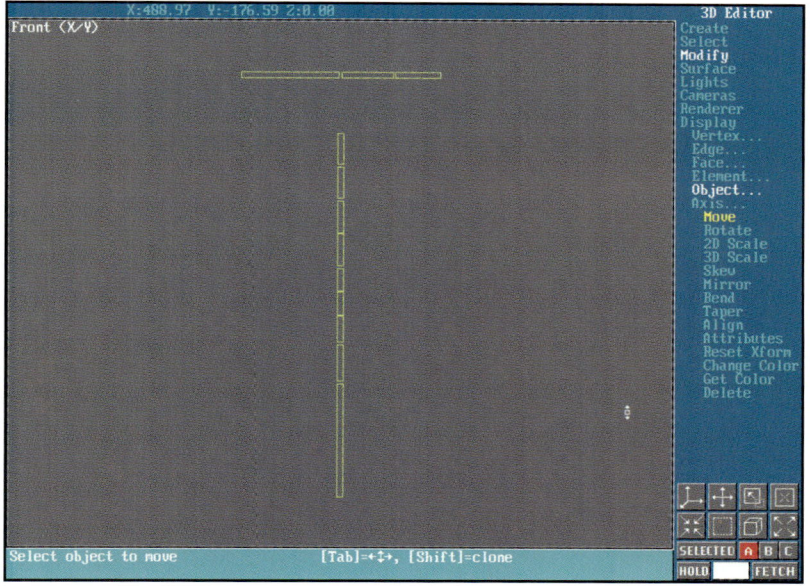

Figure 7.9
Skeletal structure for HAMMER object.

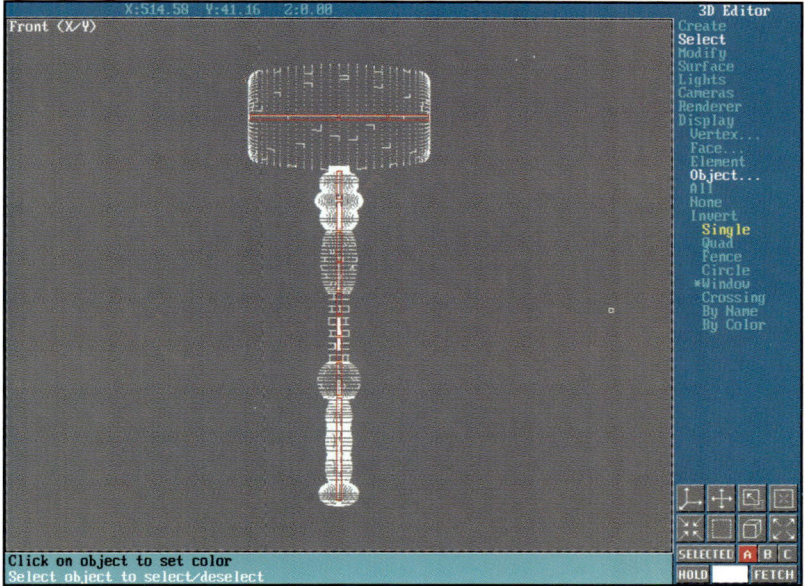

Figure 7.10
Skeletal structure for HAMMER with HAMMER unhidden and in Fastview mode.

2. Click on the Top viewport to make it active. Press W to toggle full screen on.

3. Choose **Display/Speed/By Name** and select HAMMER2. Press Enter to accept, then Choose **Display/Speed/Set Fast** and move the slider to 100. Press Enter. You should now see the HAMMER2 object in the fastest Fastdraw mode.

4. Choose **Create/Box**. While holding down the Ctrl key, create a box 10 units across in the center of the handle on HAMMER2. Name this object **HAMMER2_01**. Naming the bones is very important—the first part must be the same as the main mesh object HAMMER2. After the main mesh object name, the name must have an underscore (_), followed by 01 for the first bone, 02 for the second, and so on.

5. Press W, the new object HAMMER2_01 should appear approximately in the middle of the handle in the Front and Left viewports. You need to move, scale, and copy HAMMER2_01 to make the balance of the bones for the HAMMER2 skeletal structure. To simplify this task, choose **Display/Unhide/By Name** and select All. Then deselect HAMMER and press Enter.

6. Choose **Display/Freeze/By Name** and select All, then deselect HAMMER2 and HAMMER2_01. This will freeze the original skeletal structure used for the animation.

7. Choose **Display/Hide/Object** and click on HAMMER2. You now can use the original skeletal structure from HAMMER as a template as you scale, move, copy, and rotate HAMMER2_01 to create the skeleton for HAMMER2. The bones you create should line up with the original bones appropriately. Go ahead and create the skeleton for HAMMER2; there will be a total of 12 bones. From the Front viewport, HAMMER2_01 is the bottom bone in the handle, and HAMMER2_12 is the horizontal far right bone in the head.

8. You now assign the Bones Pro plug-in to HAMMER2. Choose **Display/Unhide/By Name**, select HAMMER2, and press Enter. Choose **Modify/Object/Attributes** and click on HAMMER2. Click on the blank External Process Name button. Select Bones and press Enter. Press Enter again at the Object Attributes dialog box—you don't adjust the settings for Bones Pro in the 3D Editor.

Animation

After you create all the objects, you need to set up the animation. You first create a rough motion path that makes HARMMER2 appear to travel around the actor.

1. Before you move any objects, set up the hierarchy. Press F4 to switch to the Keyframer. Choose **Display/Freeze/Object** and click on HAMMER2. Click on the Front viewport and press W to make it full screen.

2. Choose **Hierarchy/Link** and click on HAMMER2_12 to make it the child, then click on HAMMER2_11 to make it the parent of HAMMER2_12.

3. With Hierarchy/Link still the active option, click on HAMMER2_11, then on HAMMER2_10. Click on HAMMER2_10, then on HAMMER2_09. Keep going until you link HAMMER2_02 to HAMMER_01.

4. The last link is HAMMER2_01 to HAMMER2. You need to thaw HAMMER2 before you can link it. To ensure the correct hierarchical structure, choose **Hierarchy/Show Tree**. After the Object Attachment Tree dialog box appears, drag the view slider down until you can see the HAMMER2 tree. The tree should look like figure 7.11, except with the names HAMMER2 not HAMMER.

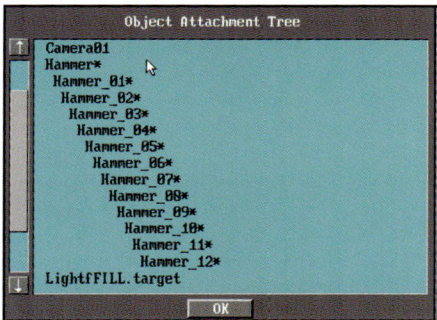

Figure 7.11
Hierarchical tree for HAMMER and its bones.

5. Now that you've placed the hierarchy, you have to place the object pivot points for each of the 13 bones. Start with HAMMER2. Choose **Hierarchy/Center Pivot** and click on HAMMER2. Now choose **Display/Hide/Object** and click on HAMMER2. Press ~ to redraw the screen.

6. Now for object pivot points for the bones. Choose **Hierarchy/Object Pivot** and click on HAMMER2_01. You want to make HAMMER2_01 pivot at the base. Refer to figure 7.12 for the proper placement of the object pivot. Adjust the pivot point in the Top, Front, and Left viewports until it looks like figure 7.12. After you set the object pivot properly, click on the yellow highlighted Object Pivot on the right side of the screen to set the pivot and return to normal mode.

Figure 7.12
Object pivot point for HAMMER2__01.

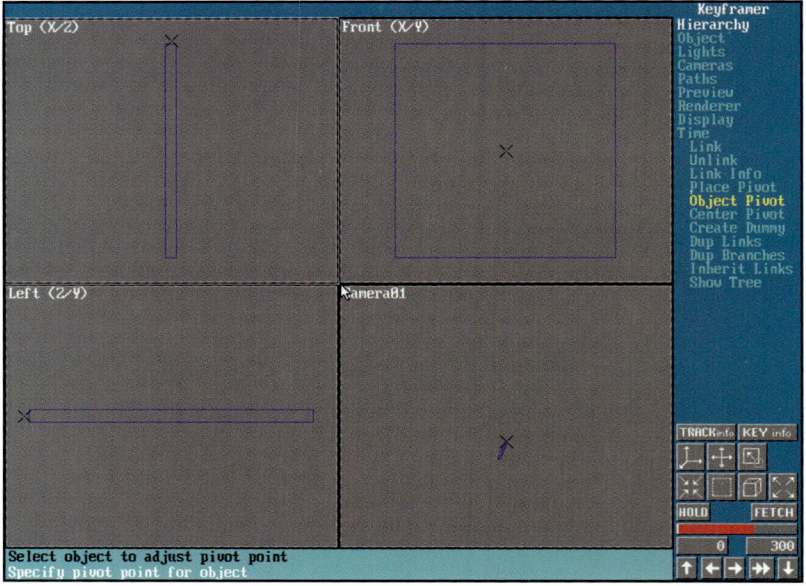

7. You repeat step 6 for the remainder of the bones. For HAMMER2_02, 03, 04, 05, 06, 07, 08 09, 11, and 12, the pivot point should fall between the selected bone and its parent object. See figure 7.13 for the placement of the object pivot for HAMMER2_02 as it falls between HAMMER2_02 and its parent object HAMMER2_01.

Figure 7.13
Object pivot point for HAMMER2__02.

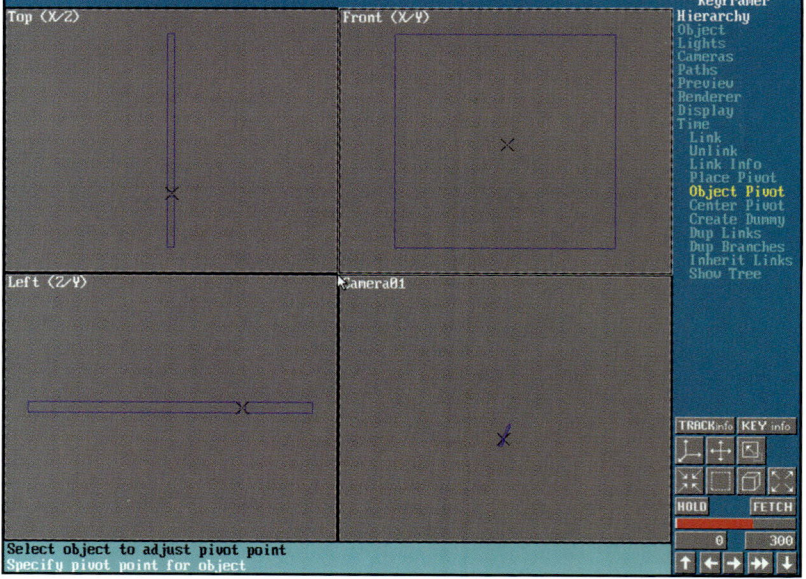

8. The object pivot for HAMMER2_10 is different because HAMMER2_10 and HAMMER2_09 are perpendicular to each other. See figure 7.14 for the placement of HAMMER2_10's pivot point.

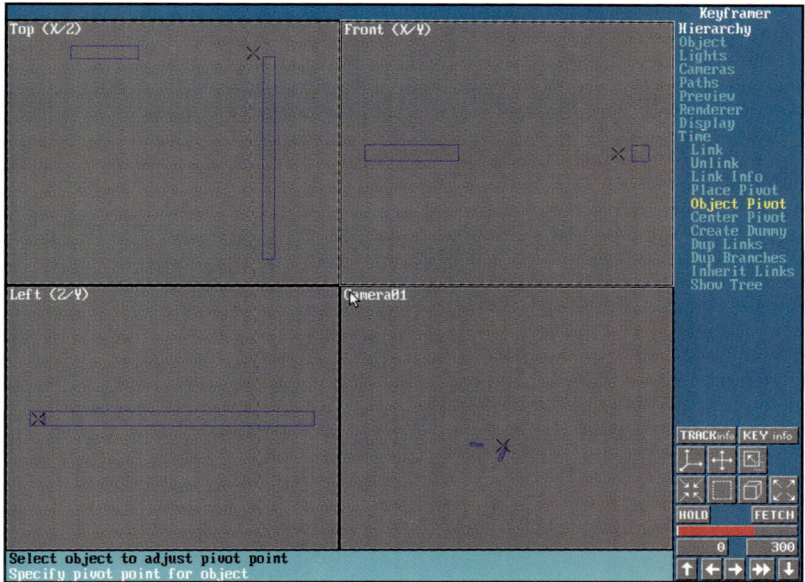

Figure 7.14
Object pivot point for HAMMER2__10.

9. After you place the object pivots, you should be able to rotate the HAMMER2 objects to make a shape similar to that shown in figure 7.15. Go to frame 10 so you don't change the values for frame 0.

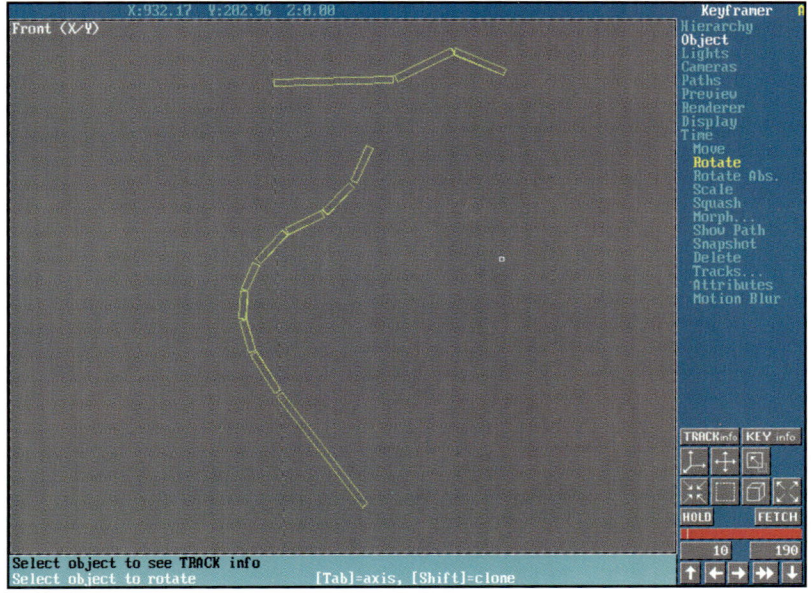

Figure 7.15
Rotated HAMMER__ object with the hierarchy and pivot points in place.

Effect 7: Interaction between Human and Computer Characters   127

10. When you're satisfied that the pivot points are in the proper location for each object, delete all the rotation keys for frame 10. Click on the Track Info button, then click on HAMMER2_01. Select Subtree for the Scope. Activate the Delete button and click on all tracks for frame 10. Press Enter. The HAMMER2 skeleton should now be back to the default settings.

11. You need to scale the objects you've created so far down to 40 percent in all three dimensions. Because HAMMER2 is the first object in the hierarchy tree, you only need to modify HAMMER2. Go to frame 1 and choose **Display/Unhide/By Name** and select HAMMER2. Press Enter.

12. Click on the Key Info button, then click on the HAMMER2 object. When the Key Info dialog box is displayed, activate the Scale button and click on Create Key.

13. To scale HAMMER2 to 40 percent, change the X, Y, and Z values from 1.0 to .4. Press Enter. HAMMER2 and all the child objects now are scaled to 40 percent.

You're now ready to create the rough motion path for HAMMER2. You might want to unhide HAMMER with all the child objects to see the Keyframes used for the HAMMER.FLI on the CD-ROM.

If you decide you want to create your own animation with custom video, before you ever record the first frame to tape, you should plan out the entire effect. If you have an actor who's going to interact with an object that doesn't exist, you need to be able to explain at all times where the object is and what it's doing. You want your actor to be able to physically and emotionally react to an object he can't see. You can create the best character in the history of animation, but if you don't have believable interaction between your character and the actor, the audience won't buy it. For this effect, I storyboarded out the whole effect first. When I went to shoot the video I knew, based on the boards, exactly what the hammer would be doing when it attacked. I knew to change my facial expression when the hammer was coming at me, even while it was still out of the audience's view. I knew which way to turn, where to move my arms, where to be looking when the hammer was getting ready to attack the second time, and when and where to turn and jump to avoid being hit by the computer generated menace.

The next step in creating the effect is to view the video and note the key movement frames so you can use them to adjust the position of the mesh object. Refer to figures 7.16 through 7.27 to view the key video frames for gauging the initial rough motion. See table 7.1 for production notes on key video frames.

Figure 7.16
Frame 65. "Reel" hammer leaves frame.

Figure 7.17
Frame 74. Actor's expression changes as he sees HAMMER, which is still out of frame.

Figure 7.18
Frame 84. Arms begin to go up and start to turn away from HAMMER.

Figure 7.19
Frame 93. Start to lean back.

Figure 7.20
Frame 105. Fully leaned back and turned 180°.

Figure 7.21
Frame 120. Standing upright and looking away from camera at HAMMER.

Figure 7.22
Frame 130. Backing up toward camera still looking at HAMMER.

Figure 7.23
Frame 137. Start to spin away from HAMMER toward camera.

Figure 7.24
Frame 143. Head is facing camera.

Figure 7.25
Frame 153. Left foot leaves ground as actor begins dive at camera.

Figure 7.26
Frame 161. Halfway into dive toward camera.

Figure 7.27
Frame 171. Actor goes out of frame.

> **NOTE:** You probably have noticed that the video frames in figures 7.16 through 7.27 have black bars on the left and right edges. This video was shot with a consumer VHS camcorder that doesn't fill the entire frame. Using BETACAM, S-VHS, and HI-8 greatly reduces or totally eliminates those black bars. The black bars are out of the video safe frame, so they won't appear if you render to tape. If you grab video from a source that doesn't fill the screen and render a FLIC, you can create a border to cover the area if the bars do cause a problem.

Table 7.1 Key Video Frames

Frame	Description of action
65	"Reel" hammer leaves frame
74	Actor's expression changes as he sees HAMMER, which is still out of frame
84	Arms begin to go up and start to turn away from HAMMER
93	Start to lean back
105	Fully leaned back and turned 180°
120	Standing upright and looking away from camera at HAMMER
130	Backing up toward camera still looking at HAMMER
137	Start to spin away from HAMMER toward camera
143	Head is facing camera
153	Left foot leaves ground as actor begins dive at camera
161	Halfway into dive toward camera
171	Actor goes out of frame

14. You don't use Bones Pro to make the rough initial motion, so choose **Object/Attributes** and click on HAMMER2. Click on the Off button to turn off Bones Pro. Press Enter.

15. Choose **Display/Hide/By Name**. Make sure that the Subtree button is active and select HAMMER2_01. Press Enter. HAMMER2 should now be the only object displayed.

16. Press W to toggle Full view off.

17. Choose **Renderer/Setup/Backgound** and click on the box to the right of the Bitmap button. Select HAMR.IFL from your 3D Studio root directory. Again, you should already have added the paths for HAMR.IFL and all the TGA files for the background located on the CD-ROM to your Map Paths. Accept the settings.

18. Go to frame 65. Here, the "reel" hammer has just left frame. Move HAMMER2 just out of frame to where the actor is looking.

19. Activate the Camera viewport and press F7 to start Fast Preview. The Camera viewport is black—you have to reassign the backgound for Fast Preview.

20. Click on the Backgrnd button. You now select the video background frame that matches the frame number you're on in the Keyframer. You're on frame 65, so select HAM10065.TGA from the /HAMMER/IMAGES directory on the supplied CD-ROM. Press Enter. Video frame 65 appears in the Camera viewport.

21. Make sure you can't see HAMMER2 in the Camera viewport. Press Esc to exit Fast Preview. Press Enter.

22. Go to frame 84, where HAMMER2 should be about halfway into the frame and the actor starting to physically react. Move HAMMER2 as appropriate.

23. Press F7 to enter Fast Preview mode again. Change the background to video frame 84, that is, select HAM10084.TGA. See how the changes you made to HAMMER2 look. Press Esc to exit Fast Preview, then press Enter.

24. At this point, you might or might not need to adjust HAMMER2. If you change HAMMER2, go back to Fast Preview to check your adjustments. Depending on the complexity of the change in the various frames, you might need to go back and forth between the normal Keyframer viewports and the Fast Preview several times.

25. When everything looks all right for frame 84, go to frame 93. Repeat steps 22 and 23 for the balance of frames listed in table 7.1, loading the proper background frame into Fast Preview accordingly. See figures 7.28 through 7.38 for examples. Feel free to adjust additional frames to make the rough motion test less rough.

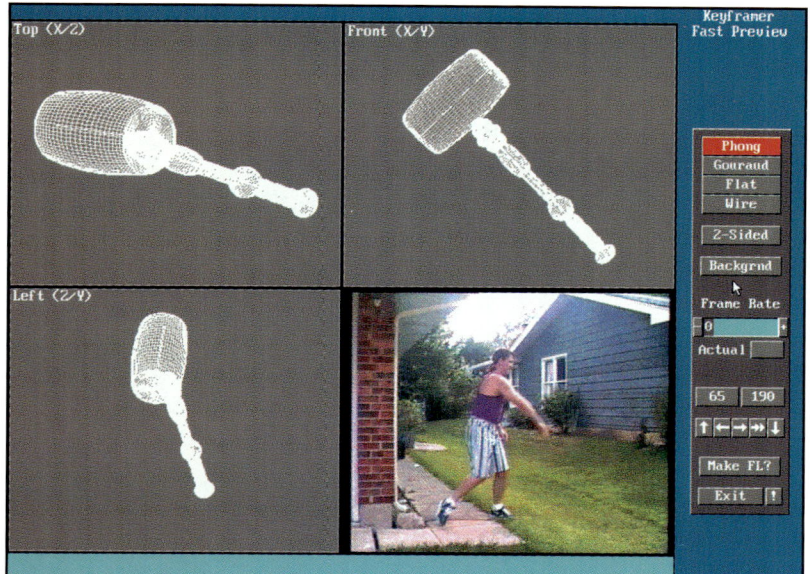

Figure 7.28
Frame 65.

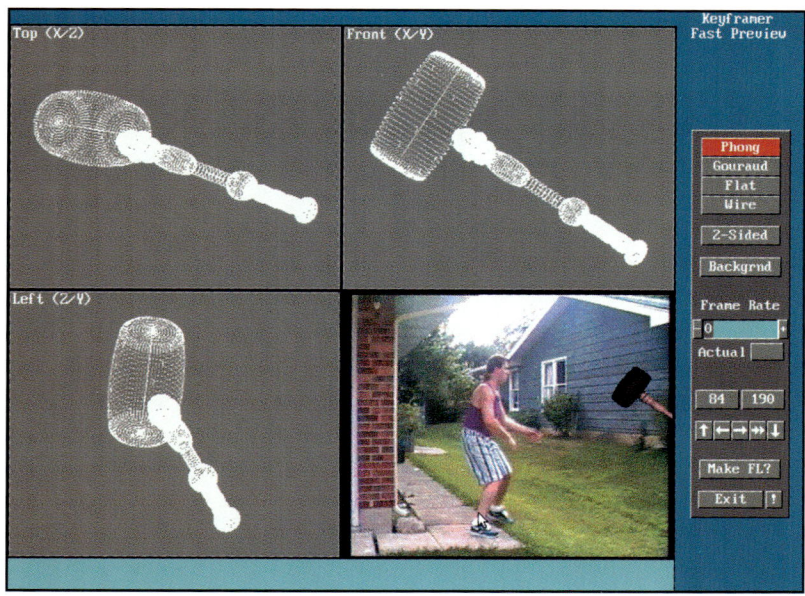

Figure 7.29
Frame 84.

Figure 7.30
Frame 93.

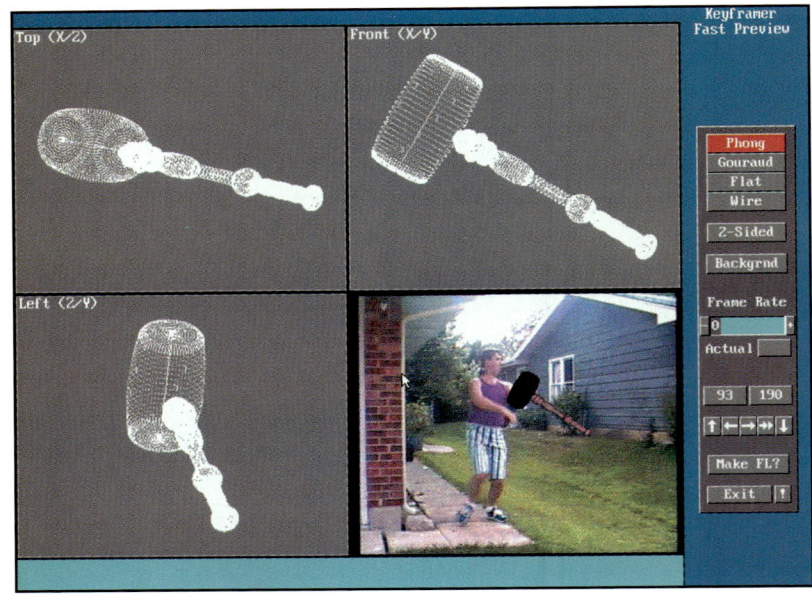

Figure 7.31
Frame 105.

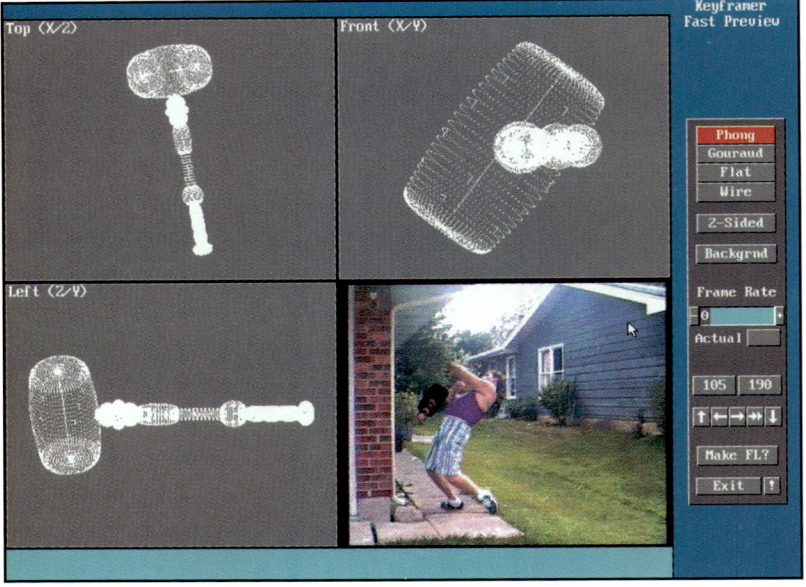

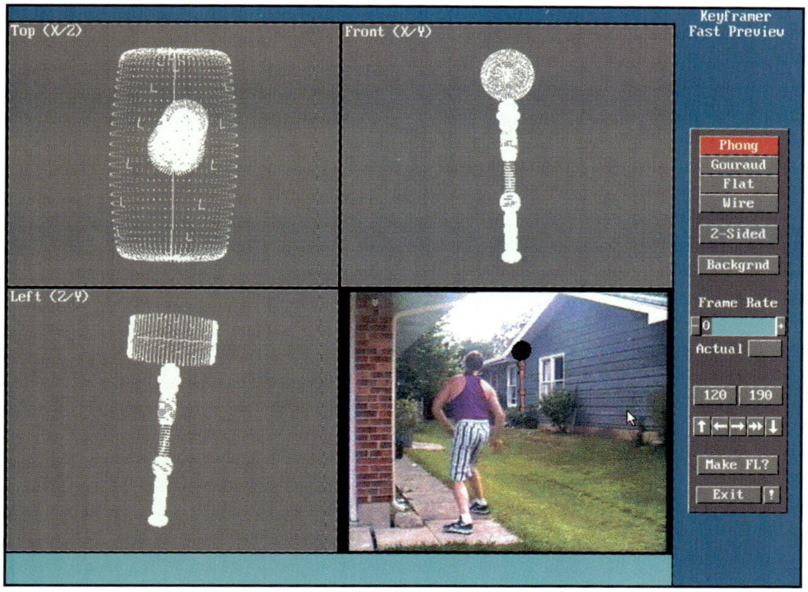

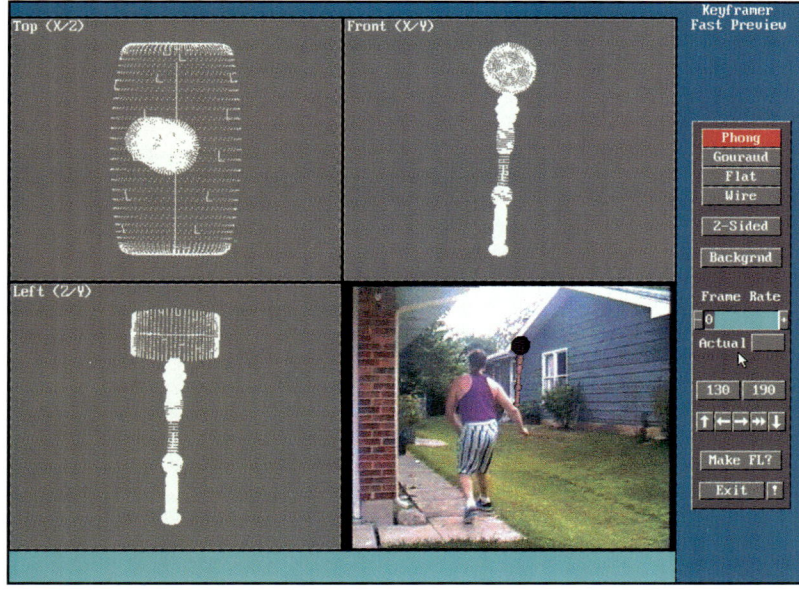

Figure 7.32
Frame 120.

Figure 7.33
Frame 130.

Figure 7.34
Frame 137.

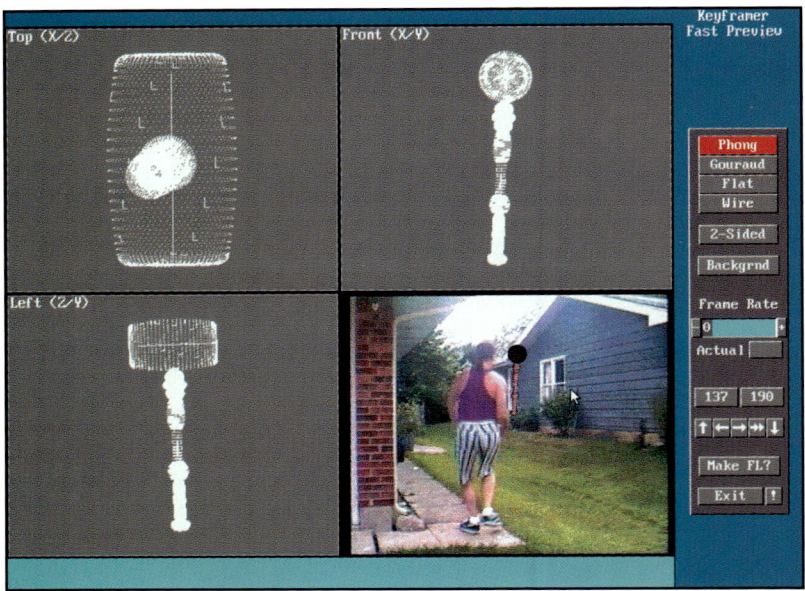

Figure 7.35
Frame 143.

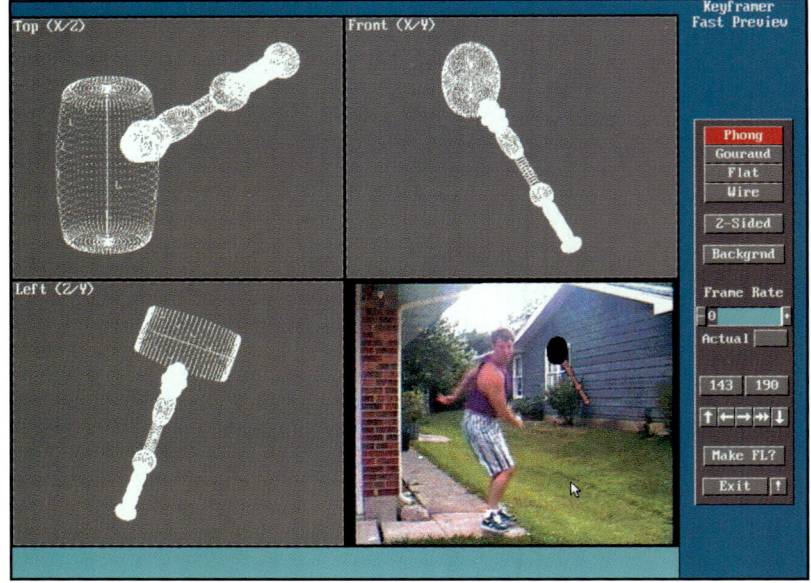

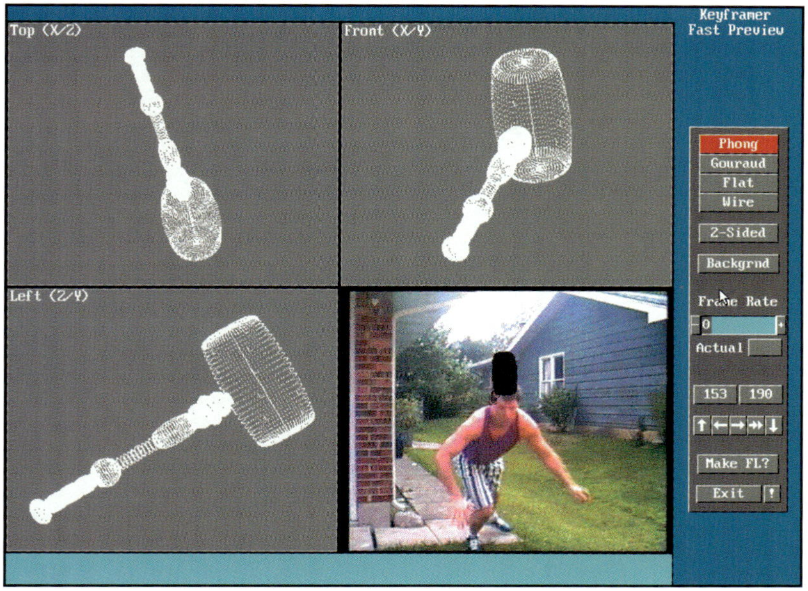

Figure 7.36
Frame 153.

Figure 7.37
Frame 161.

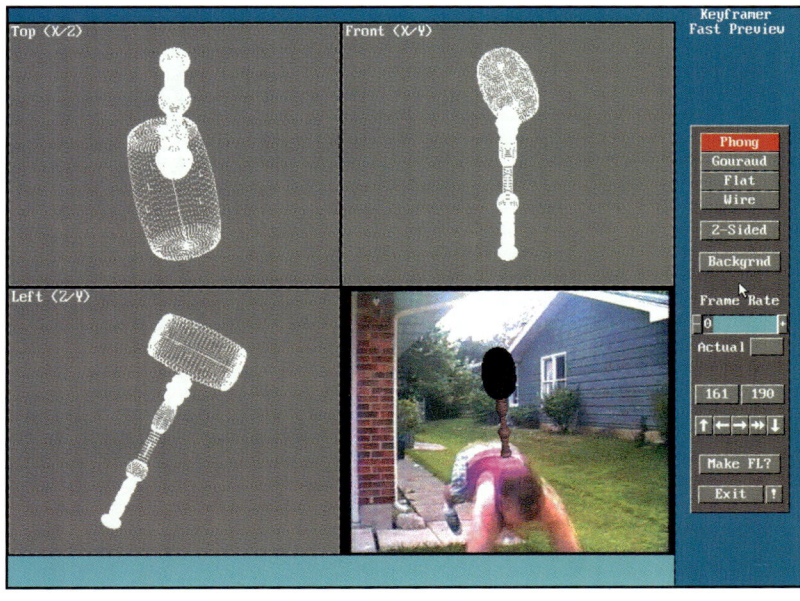

Effect 7: Interaction between Human and Computer Characters

Figure 7.38
Frame 171.

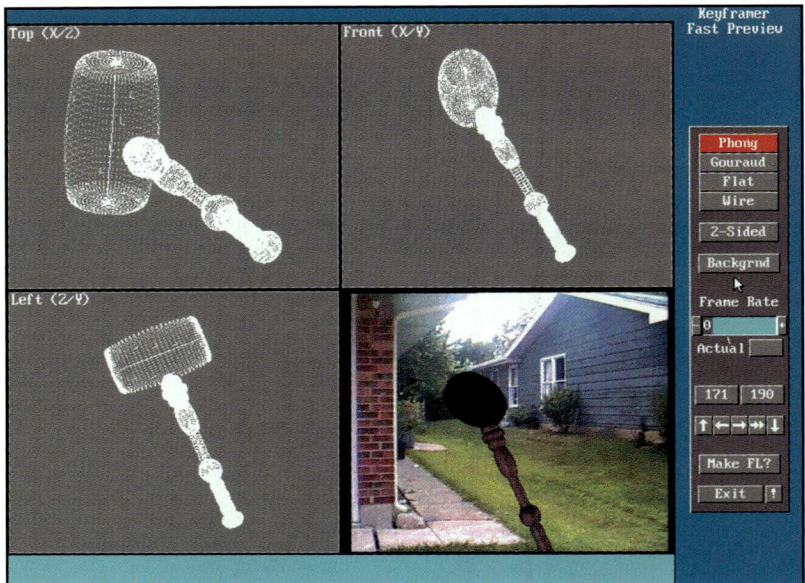

NOTE: For the first rough motion test, don't spend time adjusting the skeletal structure. You might spend a lot of time tweaking the bones, only to find you want to change the main motion of your object and you need to change all that fine-tuning you did.

After you finish making the rough motion, you should make the first motion test. Depending on your system configuration, make a FLIC or render TGAs to lay off to video. The Hammer flic on the CD-ROM was rendered at 320×200×1.0. The PAR files I used were 752×480×0.86. You can leave all the HAMMER2 objects hidden because you haven't made any Bones Pro deformations yet. Go ahead and render the first motion test, frames 0–189.

NOTE: Be sure to set Background to Rescale in the Render Animation dialog box. The furnished frames are 752×480×0.86.

View the first motion test. If you need to make changes, make them and render a second motion test. After you're satisfied with the main motion, you can go ahead and use the skeletal structure to tweak HAMMER2. Tweaking is where you really give your object life and personality; where you go from being an animator to being a character animator. This effect doesn't intend to teach character animation—volumes and volumes of books do that. If you aren't familiar with character animation, unhide the HAMMER object and its skeletal structure, the HAMMER_ objects. Study the supplied HAMMER.FLI

FLIC and see what types of modifications to the HAMMER_ objects achieved the various effects.

26. Choose **Display/Unhide/By Name**. Activate the Subtree button, select HAMMER2_01, and press Enter. All the HAMMER2_ objects should now be visible.

27. Choose **Object/Attributes** and click on HAMMER2. Click on the On button to turn on External Process, then press Enter.

28. Modify the HAMMER2_ objects.

29. Before you can see the effects of the modifications to the HAMMER_ objects on HAMMER, you need to press F12 for the KXP Loader. Select Bones and press Enter. You're now in the Bones Pro dialog box (see fig. 7.39). Click on Save, then press Esc to exit.

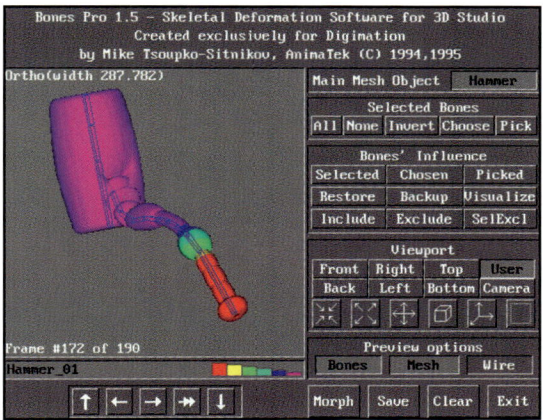

Figure 7.39
The Bones Pro dialog box.

NOTE: Whenever you make *any* changes to HAMMER2 or any of the HAMMER_ objects, you must go into the Bones Pro dialog box and click on Save. If you don't, no changes you make after the most recent save have any effect.

To see how the Bones Pro deformed HAMMER looks with the video background, you must do a full render of the frame. The good news is that you don't have to change the background bitmap to match the frame you're on; the image file list takes care of loading the proper TGA file. The bad news is that it takes longer to get visual feedback than when you use Fast Preview.

30. After you manipulate HAMMER2's skeleton, render another motion test.

31. View the motion test. Again, if you need to make changes, make them and render another motion test.

32. After you finish, you must render all the frames, 0–189, to TGA files. Use the prefix HAMZ for the final render. The TGA files are what you modify in Fractal Design Painter. If you have been rendering TGA files for your motion test, then you don't need to perform this step.

33. Write down the frame numbers of each frame that the HAMMER2 object passes behind the actor. Having a list of frames that you need to retouch saves time in Painter.

34. Be sure to save all work in progress as a project file, then press Q to exit 3D Studio.

Image Manipulation

Configure your system to run Windows.

1. Launch Windows and load Fractal Design Painter.

> **NOTE:** This chapter assumes that you already know how to use Fractal Design Painter's brushes and other tools.

2. Choose **File/Open**, then select the original video TGA file of the first frame that you need to retouch from the \HAMMER\IMAGES directory on the supplied CD-ROM. For the HAMMER object in the HAMMER.FLI on the CD-ROM, the first frame was 109, file HAM10109.TGA

3. Next, choose **File/Open** and select the corresponding TGA file of the animation you just rendered. I used the prefix HAMZ for the rendered TGA files, so for frame 0109, the file used was HAMZ0109.TGA. You should now see a frame from your animation with the HAMMER2 object in front of the actor. Depending on your animation, you need to make part of HAMMER2 go behind the actor. Most likely, you need to hide part of the HAMMER2's head.

4. With the animation frame as the current file being viewed, choose **File/Clone**. You now have a new image, named Clone of (your animation file name).

5. Now choose **File/Clone Source** and select the original video file name, which should be the first of three file names.

6. Make Cloners your current brush type, and you're now ready to retouch the first animation frame. See figure 7.40 for brush settings.

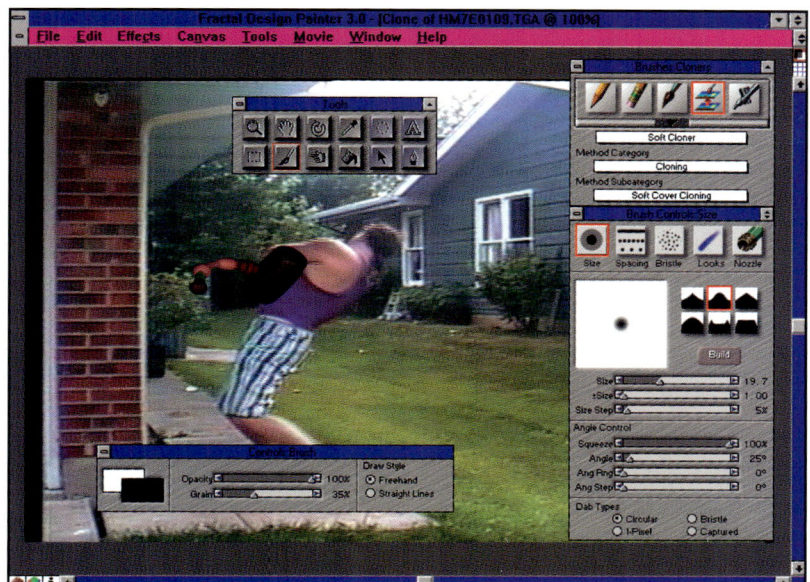

Figure 7.40
Clone brush settings in Fractal Design Painter.

TIP: When you clone, use a brush opacity setting of 100 percent to mask out large areas. When you mask out the edges where the actor and HAMMER2 meet, try a brush opacity setting of 24 percent.

Use the Tracing Paper function to help find the edges where HAMMER2 and the actor meet, Ctrl+T to toggle on and off. Use the Zoom In function (Ctrl++) to enlarge the area that you're working on if necessary. Adjust the brush attributes and size to help retouch.

7. After you finish retouching, save the cloned, manipulated image as the exact same name as the unretouched animation file in a different directory from the unretouched animation file so you don't copy over the original file.

8. Press Ctrl+W for each of the three image files you've been working with.

9. Repeat steps 2 through 8 for the remaining frames you need to retouch. See figures 7.41 and 7.42 to view an example of before-and-after retouching.

Figure 7.41
Frame 168 of animation before retouching.

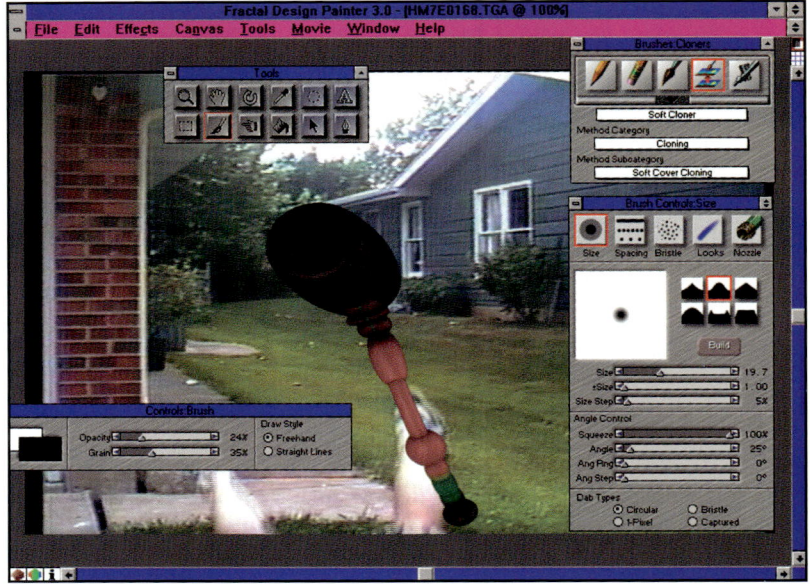

Figure 7.42
Frame 168 of animation after retouching.

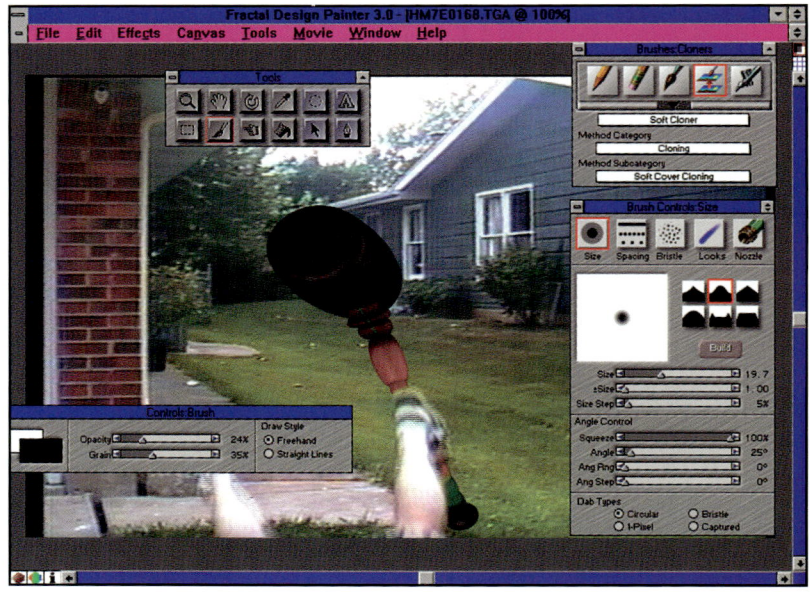

One of the nice features of using the Soft Cloner with a low opacity setting is with video frames that contain a great deal of motion. There are two fields in every frame of video. These two fields are every other scan line on a monitor. When you rendered this animation, the two fields were combined to make one frame. The areas of the frame where there is motion—the actor moving—will have a sort of blurry edge. This is the difference in motion between the two fields. Using the low opacity setting enables you to blend the computer generated object into the video subject with varying levels of opacity to match the "blurriness."

10. You now have all the frames you need to be able to create the final animation sequence. Exit Fractal Design Painter.

11. From the File Manager in Windows, move the original animation frame files that you retouched into a separate temporary directory.

12. Next, move the retouched files from the directory in which you saved them into the main directory in which you have the balance of animation files.

13. Exit Windows.

If you're going to lay the animation frames off to tape, you do that, then you're finished with this effect. If you can't go to tape, you have one last phase to complete.

Creating a FLIC from the Sequential TGA Files

1. Use the MAKEIFL command as you did at the beginning of this chapter to create a new Image File List (IFL) for the final animation TGA files. (**MAKEIFL HAMF HAM2 0 0189**)

2. Load 3D Studio.

3. Make sure that the new IFL's directory, the 3D Studio root directory, is in the image map path.

4. Choose **Render/Setup/Backgound** and add the new IFL as the Bitmap backgound. Press Enter.

5. Press F4 to switch to the Keyframer.

6. Set the total number of frames to 189. You should have 190 TGA files.

7. Choose **Render/Render View** and click on any viewport.

8. Configure the output for the type of FLIC you want.

9. Make sure Backgound is set to Rescale and Render Fields to No.

10. Render to disk.

You should now have a finished animation, in either video or FLIC format, in which a computer-generated hammer flies in front of, around, and behind the "reel" actor.

Conclusion

This was a basic sample of an economical interaction between the computer and "reel" world. The video was shot with consumer grade VHS equipment, something most of us already have at home. If you're creating an effect for a professional application, you will likely be using a higher quality video source than VHS.

The video was digitized using the PAR with a TBC IV. The video for this project was captured at a high compression setting to reduce the file size for the CD-ROM. When the video is grabbed at best quality on the PAR, the images can be of very high quality. If you don't have a PAR and TBC IV or other means of digitizing your video, find and go to a 3D Studio users group meeting. Odds are pretty good that you will meet someone who will be able to help you out cost effectively.

Compositing the computer graphics and video was done in 3D Studio. The image manipulation was handled in Fractal Design Painter, an inexpensive yet powerful paint program running on the same PC as 3D Studio.

The possibilities of effects that you can create when you combine computer generated characters with real characters are endless. Whether you have created a cute and fuzzy bunny or a three-headed dragon with chronic flaming halitosis, you now can have them romp with or eat your favorite actor or actress. Experiment with creating shadows or processing the computer graphics with grain to make them match the video better.

Warp Tube

Effect 8

by Ken Allen Robertson
San Francisco, California

Equipment and Software Used

- Pentium 90 with 32 MB RAM
- 3D Studio Release 4
- Scatter IPAS from Yost Group's Disk 6
- Stars IPAS in the Video Post Module
- Animator Studio (for the texture maps)

Artist Biography

Ken Robertson began his career as an actor/director for theater and film. He holds an MFA from the National Theatre Conservatory and appeared in many professional shows around the country. While studying future production methods, he discovered 3D Studio and became enthralled with it.

> "Orson Welles once said that a Hollywood Soundstage was the best toy train set a boy could ever have—Obviously, poor Uncle Orson never got to see this!"

Ken lives and works in San Francisco, where he is developing next-generation 3D games for computer, set-top systems, and possible Internet use. He also teaches classes in 3D Studio effects at the Computer Arts Institute in San Francisco.

Effect Overview

Computer animation is taking a more and more prominent role in the special effects world. For evidence, you need only look at the recent explosion of science-fiction films and television shows. Computer animation makes special effects cheaper and often quicker to produce, and pushes visual effects to a new high.

This effect is a staple of science-fiction entertainment. A light bursts from empty space, stretching out to engulf the cosmic traveler in a dance of plasma, and propel him/her through the cosmos at greater-than-light speeds. Although it has been called many different names, the warp tube is omnipresent in current space-inspired entertainment.

Procedure

It is always important to visualize the entire effect you wish to create before beginning construction. In this case, I wanted a tube of coherent purple light and energy moving towards the camera that dissipated into space at its mouth. Having the energy move towards the camera (instead of away) will enhance the illusion of speed.

Construction

1. Go into the 2D Shaper and click on **Create/n-gon/# of Sides.** Move the slider to select 32 sides and click OK. Now click on Circular and draw a circle approximately 100 units in radius.

2. Assign the shape as Current and go into the Lofter by pressing F2.

3. Scale the default path (**Path/2D Scale**) up to 400%. Scale the path up 400% again, and then scale it a third time, but only 200%. Click **Shapes/Get/Shaper** to pull your circle into the Lofter. Center the shape.

4. Now add two vertices to your path by clicking on **Path/Refine**—the first one about 2/3 to the top of the path, and the second halfway between the new vertex and the end of the path.

5. Press Page Up to move the active level to the first new vertex. Reimport your shape and center it. Click on **Shapes/Scale**, and scale the shape to about 130%. Go to the next level on the path and repeat the procedure scaling this shape up to about 175%. Go to the last vertex on the path and repeat the procedure again, scaling this shape to 215%.

Figure 8.1
Scaling shapes on the path.

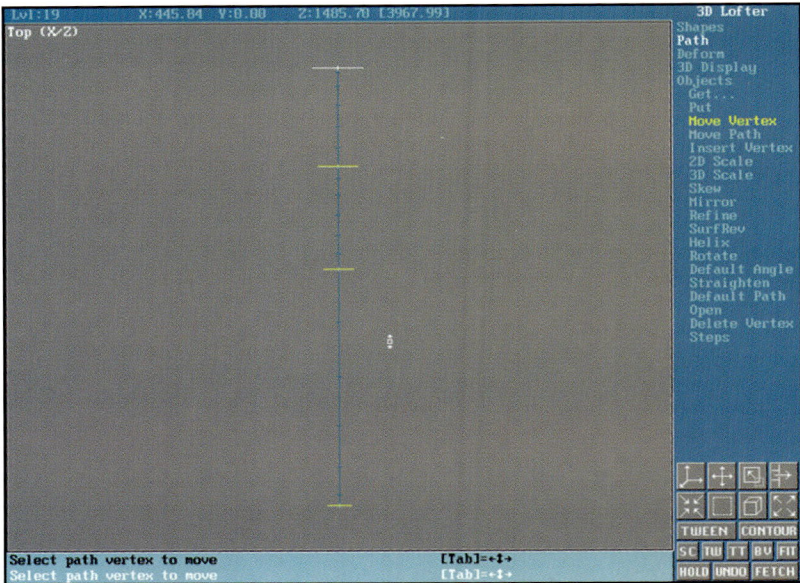

> **NOTE:** You can accomplish the scaling by using the deform-scale grids, but often it is more helpful to have a complete visual skeleton of what you can expect.

6. Now click on **Path/Move Vertex**. Click on the Top viewport to make it active, then hit the Tab key to toggle the cursor until its arrows only point vertically. Click and hold on the third vertex, and move it just below the second. Do the same with the top vertex, moving it just below the one you just moved.

7. Click on **Object/Preview**, and make sure the High Path and Shape Detail buttons are on.

   You should see the shape travel up the path widening into a funnel, then doubling back on itself and expanding even wider.

8. Make the object with the settings shown in the Object Lofting Controls dialog box (see fig. 8.2).

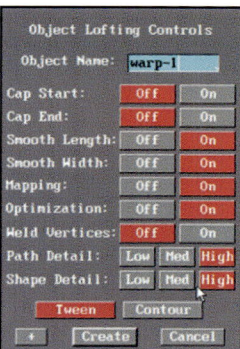

Figure 8.2
The Object Lofting Controls dialog box.

9. Name the object **Warp-1** and click OK.

Now go into the 3D Editor by pressing F3. You should have a tube that expands to the top, then doubles back on itself in an umbrella-like way. Because it was lofted with mapping coordinates on it, an animated map will travel from the base of the object to the top, and then back down the umbrella edge.

10. Rotate the object 90 degrees (with the local axis button inactive) so it lies along the positive X axis with its base at the global origin (see fig. 8.3). Click on **Display/Construction/Show** to see this.

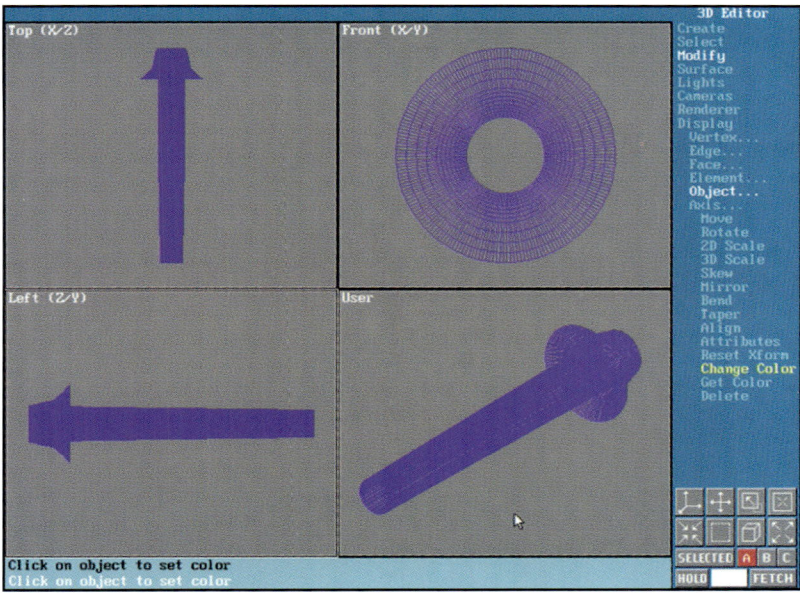

Figure 8.3
Rotating the object 90 degrees.

> **TIP:** Leaving the small end of the warp tube at the global origin (0,0,0) will make the object easier to animate later on.

Now go into the Materials Editor by pressing F5. It's time to create the real power of the warp tube.

Materials

1. In the top menu, click on **Info/Configure**, and then on the Map-paths button when the Configuration dialog box appears. Add **D:\warp** to your map-paths and click OK. (Substitute whichever letter designation is assigned to your CD-ROM drive if it is not D:.)

2. Click on the 2-Sided button in the top center of the Materials Editor, to make this a material that will render on the inside of the mesh.

3. Leave all the top controls in their current position, except the Opacity fall-off slider. Set this to 35.

4. Click on the None button next to the Texture 1 box on the bottom, and select PLASMA.FLC from the D:\warp directory. You can drag the name onto the view image button and watch the flic. It is a digitized fire animation that has been stretched to fill the entire frame (see fig. 8.4).

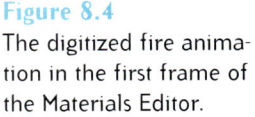

Figure 8.4
The digitized fire animation in the first frame of the Materials Editor.

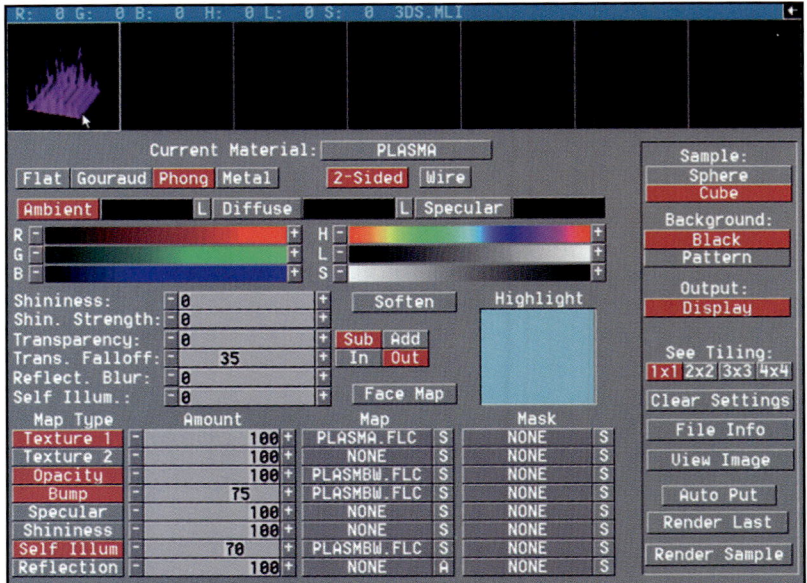

A plasma field should be much more unusual than a standard fire, however, so we will customize the material to make it look like something more celestial.

5. Click on the setup (S) button next to the material's name. The Material Setup dialog box will appear. Drag the blur slider to the right until it is set at about 30. Now click on the RGB tint button at the bottom of the dialog box.

6. Click on the None button next to the Bump box, and select PLASMBW.FLC. If you view the flic, you will see that it is a black and white version of the plasma flic. Press the Settings (S) button next to this material and move the Blur slider to about 20, and click OK. Move the Bump percentage slider to about 75.

7. Drag the PLASMBW.FLC name into the Opacity entry, and then again into the Self Illum (illumination) entry.

8. Leave the Opacity slider at 100, but move the Self Illum slider to about 70.

9. Render a sample of this material. You should have a smoothly bumped semitransparent purple flame.

10. Put this material into your library and name it **Plasma**. Press C and hit Return to make this the current material.

11. Press F3 and go back into the 3D Editor.

12. Assign the Plasma material to the Warp1 object by clicking **Surface/Material/Assign**. You will see Select object to make plasma shown in the bottom left of the screen. Click on the Warp1 object, and then click OK in the resulting dialog box.

Animation

To set up the animation, you will need to clone the warp tube into two morph target objects: the first a broad line of light extending across the horizon, and the second, a small star point of light.

> **NOTE:** Make sure the Local Axis button is off for the following animation. Otherwise, it will be difficult to line up the morph objects for proper animation.

1. To create the line, click on **Modify/Object/2D Scale**. Then go into the Left viewport and press the Tab key to toggle the cursor arrows to a horizontal-only position. Hold down the Shift key and click on the warp tube object. You should see a copy of your tube's bounding box scaling back towards the global axis, while your original object stays in place. If you don't see this, right-click your mouse to cancel the operation, and start the procedure again making sure the Shift key is held down before you click on the object.

2. Scale the object all the way back to 1%.

3. When the Object Name dialog box comes up, name this object **Warp-lat**.

4. Scale the object down to 1% again, and then make the Left viewport active.

5. Toggle the cursor so the arrows are now vertical only.

6. Press H to call up the object Hit-List, and select the Warp-lat object. Scale the object down to 1% again so it begins to resemble a flat line. When it is good and flat, toggle the cursor to the horizontal arrows position, and scale the Warp-lat object out 400%. Repeat this a few times so that the Warp-lat object stretches across the horizon.

7. Go back into the Left viewport, and toggle the cursor back to the four point position.

8. Click on **Modify/Object/3D Scale**, hold down the Shift key, and click on the original warp tube.

9. Scale this down to 1%, and name it **Warp-org**. Scale it down a few more times so it becomes a tiny speck (see fig. 8.5).

10. Go into the Keyframer, and set the total number of frames to **240**.

11. Create a dummy object at the far left end of the warp tube by clicking on **Hierarchy/Create Dummy** and name it **Marker**. This will serve as an origin marker later in the animation.

12. The first is to hide all but the Warp-org objects, so they won't be displayed in the final rendered animation. The Warp1 and Warp-lay objects will serve as the templates that the Warp-org object will morph into.

13. Click on the Track Info button in the lower right icon panel, and then click on the Warp1 object. The Track Info dialog box is shown in figure 8.6.

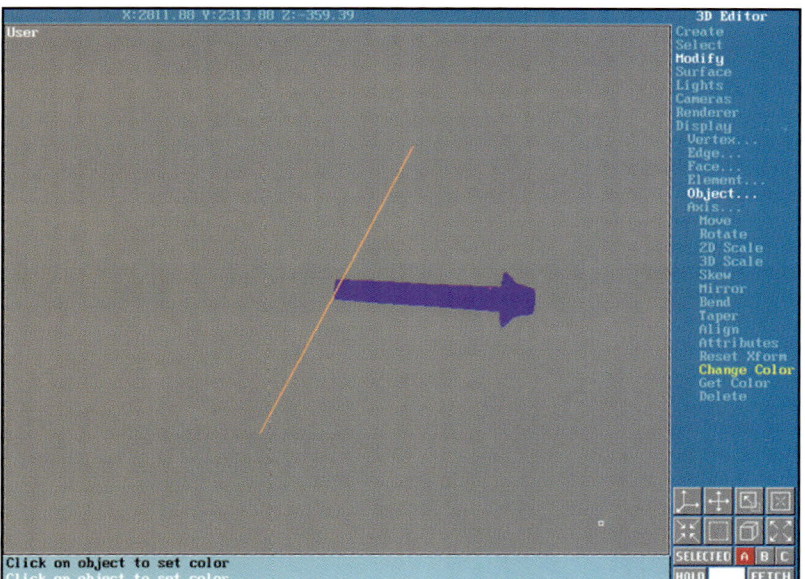

Figure 8.5
The scaled-down warp tube.

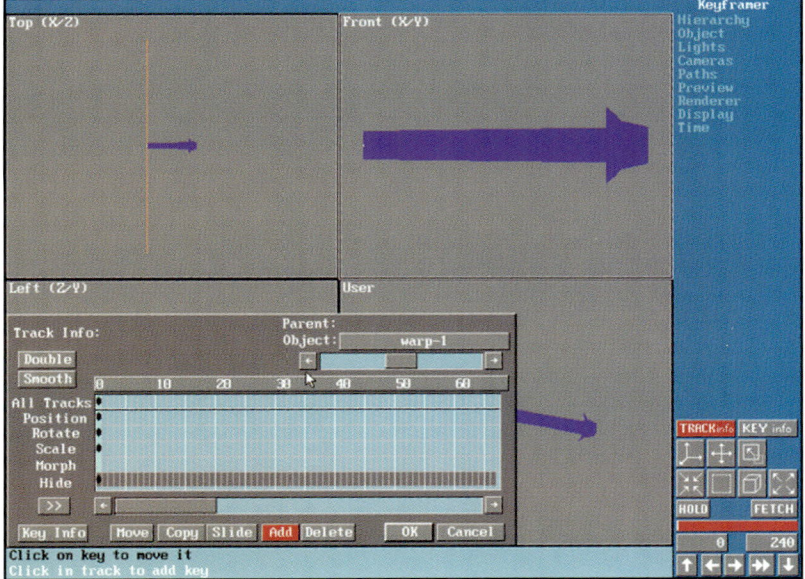

Figure 8.6
The Track Info dialog box.

14. When the Track Info dialog box pops up, click on the Add button to make it active. Now click on the Hide column at frame 0. A black dot will appear and the entire column will turn gray, hiding this object when you render the animation. Advance the object slider in the upper right of the Track Info box until the Warp-lat is displayed, and repeat the hide procedure.

Effect 8: Warp Tube   157

15. Now advance the object slider until Wrap-org appears. With the Add key still active, click on the Morph column at Frame 0. Add three more morph keys, one at Frame 30, the next at Frame 90, and the next at Frame 105 (see fig. 8.7). These will be used to create the slow-expansion-across-the-infinite-horizon animation, and the explosion of the tube itself.

Figure 8.7
Adding keys in the Morph column.

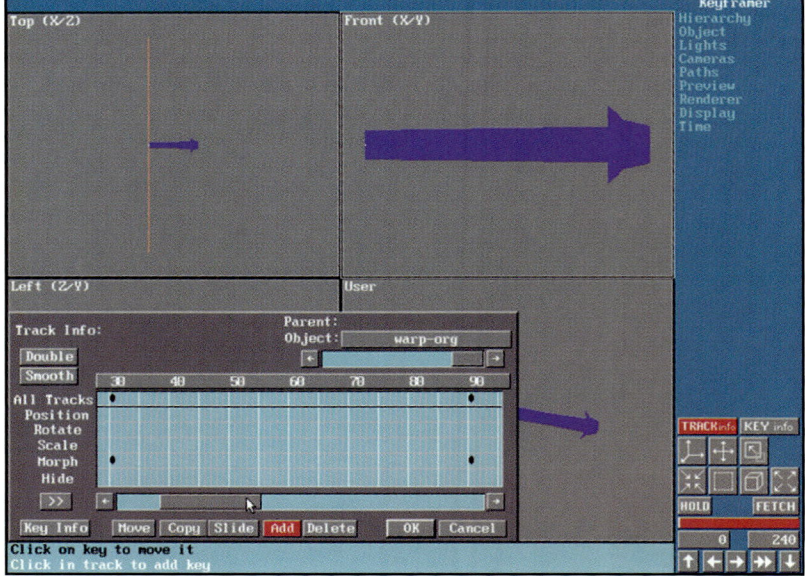

16. Click on the Key Info button in the lower left corner, and then click on the morph-key dot at Frame 90. When the Key Info dialog box pops up, make sure the Morph button is active (red).

If it isn't, click on it to make it active. The number box just below that button should have the number 3 displayed. Below that you should see a box with Warp-org displayed. Click anywhere in that box to call up the Morph Assign dialog box. In the Object list, click on Warp-lat and then click OK.

17. Now drag the EaseTo slider in the lower right all the way up to 50. This will slow the expansion as it nears completion, expressing strain and tension.

> **NOTE:** Do not adjust the morph assignments or any key info for the first two morph keys (Frame 0 and Frame 30). These have been added to tell 3D Studio that no morphing will occur for the Warp-org object until Frame 30.

18. Click on the advance arrow to the right of the key number box. When the number 4 is displayed, repeat the morph assign procedure, this time assigning the morph object as Warp-1.

19. Move the Ease From slider up to about 25. This will create a greater feel of explosion, and a smoother transition from the Warp-lat morph.

20. Click OK, and go back to the Keyframer's normal display, click on the Left display box to make it active. All your mesh objects should still be visible.

21. Click on **Cameras/Create** then go into the Left display. Make a new camera a short distance from the wide end of the Warp1 object. Pull the target a short distance towards the mouth of the tube, but not inside it (see fig. 8.8).

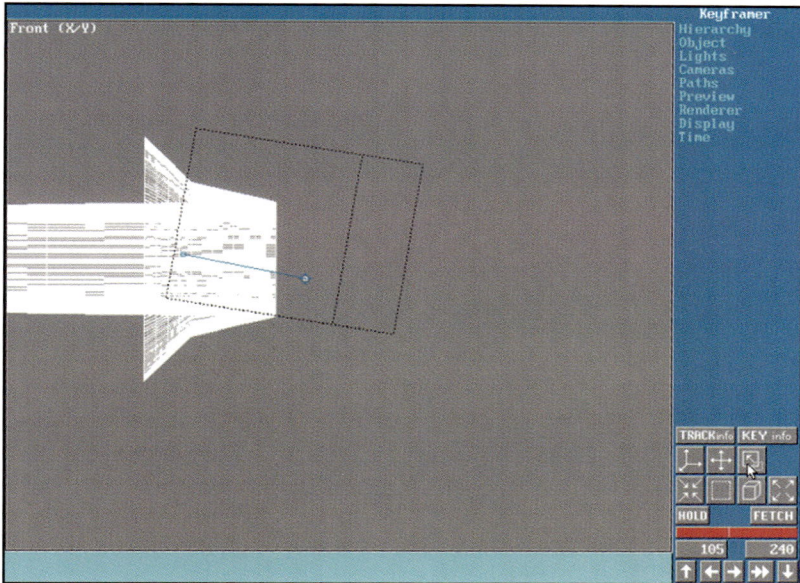

Figure 8.8
Pulling the target towards the mouth of the tube.

22. Now click on the lower Right viewport to make it active. Press the **C** key to make this a Camera viewport.

At this point, you might want to preview the animation by clicking **Preview/Make** and then clicking in the Camera viewport. If you want to do so, first click on **Display/Hide** and then on the Warp1 and Warp-lat objects, so they won't show up in the preview animation.

You will see the object expanding as it should, but scaling outward from the Warp-lat object, instead of moving forward toward your camera. Go to

Frame 105. Your warp tube should be at its full expansion. Modify its position by clicking on **Object/Move** and moving the warp tube so the far left end lines up with the Marker dummy object. If you preview the animation, it will now expand towards the camera.

If you feel confident with the animation as it stands, it's time to add the set dressing for a more convincing effect.

Video Post

1. Click on **Render/Video Post** to call the Video Post Editor. At the top right you will see a small (rather familiar) box that says Frames and displays the number 30. Next to that, you will see the Use KF button. Click on that button. When the dialog box pops up and asks if you want to set the total number of frames to those of the Keyframer, click Yes.

2. You will also see a large box with horizontal columns on the left side. Click three times in this box (the Queue entry box).

3. You should have three entries, each that say [KF Scene] followed by a long red stripe in the Track Info box next to it (see fig. 8.9).

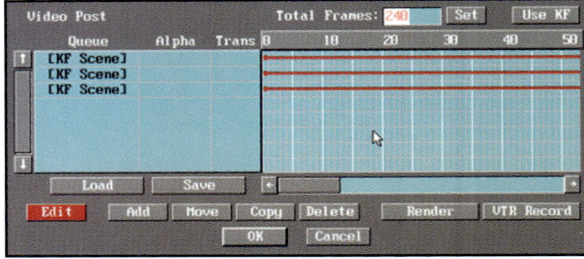

Figure 8.9
Long red stripes in the Track Info box.

4. Click on the Edit button at the bottom of the dialog box, then on the first [KF scene] in the Queue entry display. The Queue Entry dialog box appears (see fig. 8.10).

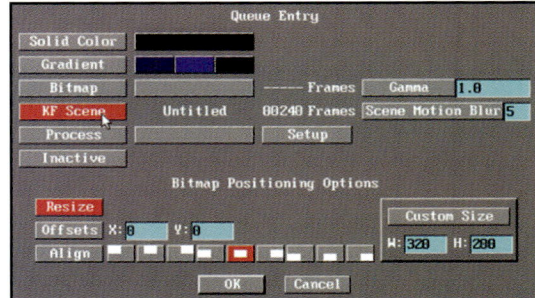

Figure 8.10
The Queue Entry dialog box.

160   3D Studio Hollywood and Gaming Effects

5. In the Queue Entry dialog box, click on the Gradient key. Click on the top color box in the Define Gradient Colors dialog box (see fig. 8.11), and make it a medium navy (Blue 85). Make the second box a dark navy (blue 30), and the last one the same as the first. Click OK in the Define Gradient Colors dialog box, and OK in the Video Post dialog box.

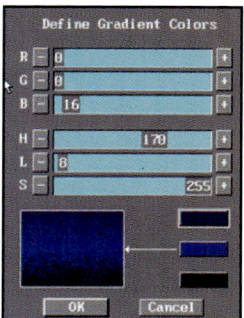

Figure 8.11
The Define Gradient Colors dialog box.

Now click on the second Queue entry to edit it. The Queue Entry dialog box reappears.

6. Click on the Process button this time, then click on the empty box next. When the list of available processes pops up, select Stars, and then click OK. Now click on the Setup button next to the process name. Leave everything with its current settings, but change the Brightness scale option to Logarithmic instead of Linear (see fig. 8.12).

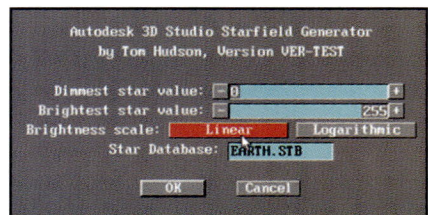

Figure 8.12
Changing the Brightness scale option.

7. Click OK in the Process Setup box, then click OK in the Queue Entry dialog box to return to the Video Post Editor.

Your final Video Post settings should look like figure 8.13.

Figure 8.13
The final Video Post settings.

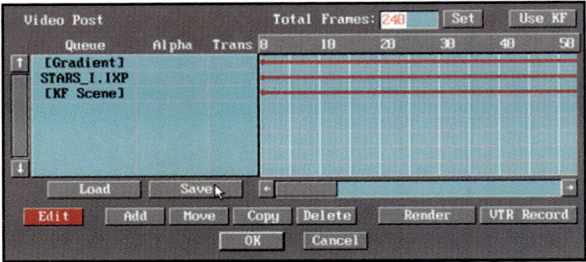

8. Click on the Render button near the bottom of the box, and render the animation.

> **NOTE:** If you are planning to end working after this effect, or to render this effect later, you should save your Video Post settings to a *.vp file now, as they will also be used in the next effect.

Conclusion

A variation on the warp tube used, and one that is almost as common, is the streaking stars warp, which will be seen in Effect 9.

Warp Star Field

Effect 9

by Ken Allen Robertson
San Francisco, California

Equipment and Software Used

- Pentium 90 with 32 MB RAM
- 3D Studio Release 4
- Scatter IPAS from Yost Groups Disk 6
- Starts IPAS in the Video Post Module
- Animator Studio (for the texture maps)

Artist Biography

Ken Robertson began his career as an actor/director for theater and film. He holds an MFA from the National Theatre Conservatory and appeared in many professional shows around the country. While studying future production methods, he discovered 3D Studio and became enthralled with it.

> "Orson Welles once said that a Hollywood Soundstage was the best toy train set a boy could ever have—Obviously, poor Uncle Orson never got to see this!"

Ken lives and works in San Francisco, where he is developing next-generation 3D games for computer, set-top systems, and possible Internet use. He also teaches classes in 3D Studio effects at the Computer Arts Institute in San Francisco.

Effect Overview

A variation on the tube type of warp (seen in Effect 8), and one that is almost as common, is the streaking stars warp.

> **NOTE:** For this effect, you must own the Yost Group's IPAS disk 6 for the scatter procedural modeling process.

Procedure

Select **File/New** from the top pull-down menu, and click on the All button in the dialog box. You will start by making the basic star materials. Press F5 to go into the Materials Editor.

Materials

1. Click on **Library/New** in the top pull-down menu.

2. Set the basic material attributes to the settings in table 9.1.

Table 9.1 Basic Star Material Settings

Attribute	Setting
Shading	Phong
2-Sided	On
Shininess	0
Shin. Strength	0
Transparency	11 (Sub)
Trans. Falloff	74 (Out)
Reflect. Blur	0
Self Illum.	100

3. From there, press the L buttons between the Specular, Diffuse, and Ambient color settings, so all three will be locked to the same color.

4. Create the following five materials with RGB color settings as listed in table 9.2.

5. Put all the materials into your new library, and go into the 3D Editor. (You can do this by pressing F3.)

Table 9.2	Color Settings for Star Materials		
Material Name	*Red*	*Green*	*Blue*
Star-blue	0	0	255
Star-red	255	0	0
Star-yelo	255	255	0
Star-purple	255	0	255
Star-white	255	255	255

*Note: All Ambient/Diffuse/Specular settings are the same and should be locked.

Construction

1. Click on **Create/Lsphere/Properties**, and drag the slider all the way to the left to create the lowest face count l-sphere possible.

2. Now click on Smoothed underneath the **Lsphere** submenu, and make a very small sphere, between 5 and 10 units. Name this object **Star-blue**, and assign the star-blue material to it.

3. Clone this object by clicking on **Modify/Object/Move**, holding down the Shift key, clicking on the object, and moving it to a new position a short distance from the original object. Name this object **Star-red**, and assign the corresponding material to it. Clone the Star object three more times, naming these objects **Star-yelo**, **Star-whit**, and **Star-prpl**. Assign the corresponding materials to each.

Now create a 16-sided cylinder that will act as a template to create our star field.

4. Click on **Create\Cylinder** and then on **Properties**. Move the Number of Sides slider until it is set to 16. Set the Segments slider to 1 and click OK.

5. Now click on Smoothed in the **Cylinder** submenu. Click in the Front viewport to make it active, then click and hold down the left mouse button at a point near the center of your star objects. Drag the mouse until you have circle about 6000 units in radius, then release the mouse button. Immediately click in the Left viewport to make it active. Click and hold the left mouse button at a position near the farthest right of your star objects. Drag the mouse left until you have a line almost 30,000 units long. Name the cylinder **Template** and click OK.

6. Leave the Left viewport active and click on **Select/Vertex/Quad**. Select the vertices at the far left end of the cylinder. Click on **Modify/Vertex/3D Scale**, and then click on Selected in the lower right button panel. Scale the left end of the cylinder down to about 50% (see fig. 9.1).

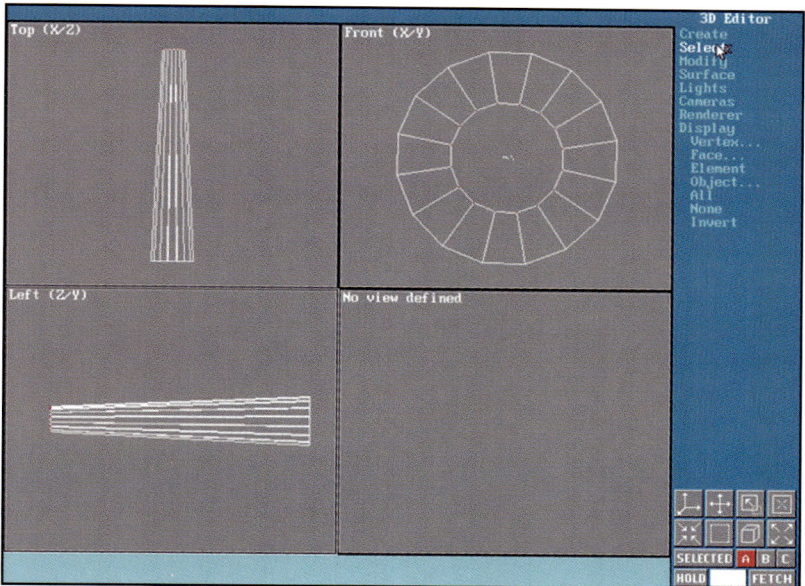

Figure 9.1
Scaling the left end of the cylinder.

You should now have a conic shape pointing away from you (in the Front viewport) and five small stars.

7. Press F12 to pull down the IPAS loader menu. Move the slider bar down until you see SCATTR and click on it (see fig. 9.2).

Figure 9.2
The IPAS loader menu.

8. When the Scatter dialog box appears, click on Pick object in the Source Object Options box, and select Star-blue. Set the number of objects to **50**, and the relative scale to **100**.

9. Now go down to the Distribution Object Options box. Click on the Distribute to Object button and select Template from the menu. Make sure the Random button (next to the spacing options) is active, and that the Perpendicular and Selected Faces buttons are inactive.

10. In the Morph Objects box, set the Number of Morphs to **50** and the Prefix to **St-blue**.

11. In the Transform box, make sure all of the Rotate and Scale WHD displays are set to **0**, and that the Aspect button is inactive. In the Translate WHD displays, enter any combination of numbers between **1** and **30**, then click on the Preview button to see the results in the preview display. What you are looking for is a good random distribution of stars along the template object (see fig. 9.3).

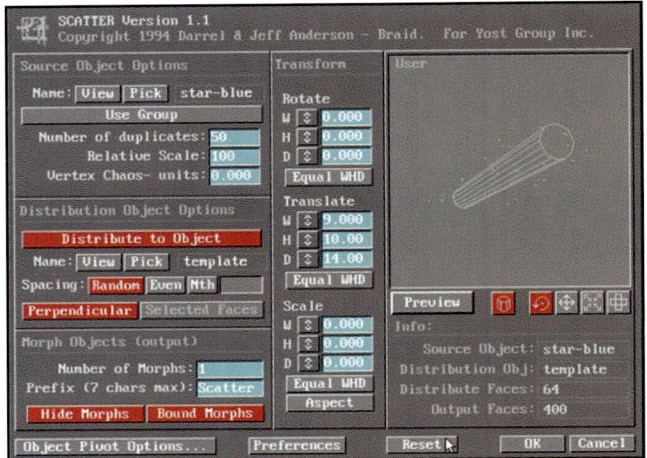

Figure 9.3
The Scatter dialog box.

12. When you are satisfied that your star field distribution is random enough, click OK at the bottom of the display.

13. Back in the 3D Editor, click on **Modify/Object/2D Scale**, and make the Left viewport active. Press the Tab key until the cursor arrows are pointing left-to-right. Press H to call up the Object Hit-List menu, and select the original Star-blue object. Stretch this object to **400**%, and then repeat the process until you have a log streak about 1/5th the size of the template cylinder (see fig. 9.4).

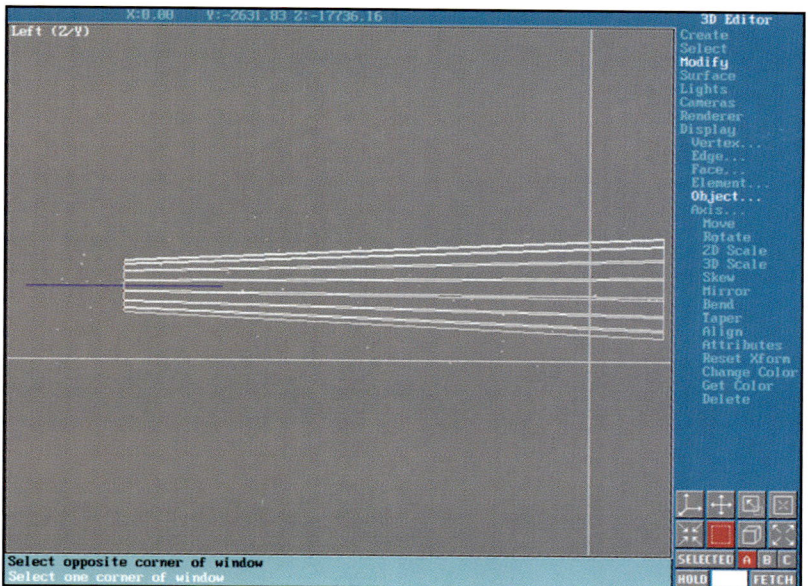

Figure 9.4
Stretching an object.

14. Press F12 again to call up the IPAS loader menu. SCATTR should still appear in the bottom button, so just hit return.

15. The Scatter dialog box should come up with the same settings you created last time. Press the Preview button and watch the preview screen (see fig. 9.5).

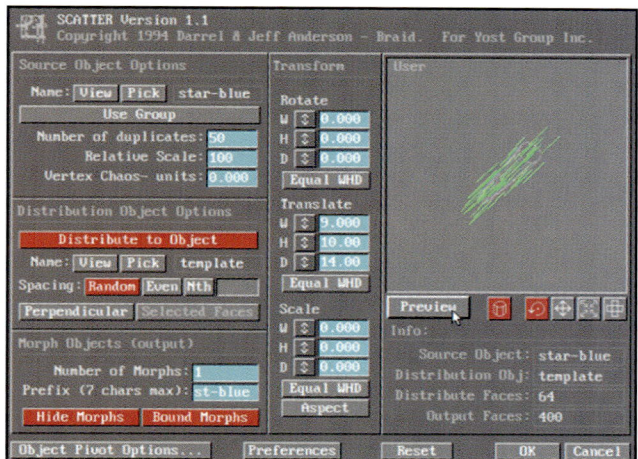

Figure 9.5
Star streaks in the preview screen.

Effect 9: Warp Star Field   169

You should now have a field of star streaks created from your stretched Star-blue object.

16. In the Morph Objects box, enter **Warp-bl** in the prefix field, then click OK.

> **STOP:** The prefix name is the only thing that should have changed from your previous Scatter settings.

17. Repeat this entire process (scatter, stretch, scatter the stretched object) with the four remaining star objects, varying the Translate WHD settings for the original star objects each time, but leaving them the same for the stretched stars. Name the new star fields and stretched star fields as shown in table 9.3.

Table 9.3 Naming for Star Fields and Warp Fields

Original Object Name	Star Field Name	Warp Field Name
Star-blue	St-blu	Warp-bl
Star-red	St-red	Warp-rd
Star-yelo	St-yelo	Warp-yl
Star-purpl	St-prpl	Warp-pl
Star-white	St-whit	Warp-wt

18. In the 3D Editor, select the original objects (now stretched) that you created, and select the template cylinder. Click on **Modify/Object/Delete**, then on the selected button in the bottom right, and then click once in the active window. When the dialog box pops up and asks if you wish to delete the selected objects, click on Yes.

You should now have 500 objects, 250 stars, and 250 star streaks (see fig. 9.6).

Now go into the Keyframer by pressing F4.

Animation

1. Set the total number of keyframes to 120, and click in the Left viewport to make it active.

2. Click on **Hierarchy/Create Dummy** and create a dummy object in the middle of your star fields. Make it large enough to be seen above your stars, and name the object **Master**.

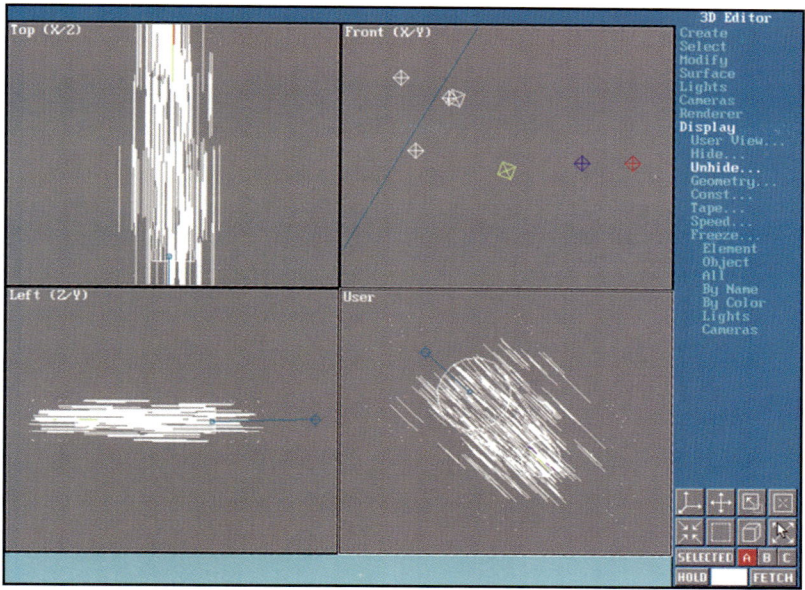

Figure 9.6
The viewports with the original objects deleted.

3. Now click on **Hierarchy/Link** and press H to call up your hit list. In the field next to Tag, type **St-*** and click on the Tag button. An asterisk will appear next to all of your star objects identifying them as child objects. Click OK, and then click on the Master dummy object. This will link all your star objects to the Master.

4. Create another dummy object at the farthest left end of your star streaks. Make this one big enough to encompass the tapered end of the entire field, and name it **Marker**. We will use it later to make sure the warp field animates the way it should.

5. Create a camera at the farthest right star streak so it is looking down the middle of the star field, and move the target to about 100 units in front of the end of the nearest star streak.

> **TIP:** Your "warp" will not begin until Frame 30. If you want, create and import a spline path from the Shaper/Lofter to create a curved flight path to this point before frame thirty. This will definitely enhance the overall effect.

Effect 9: Warp Star Field

Figure 9.7
The viewports showing the dummy objects.

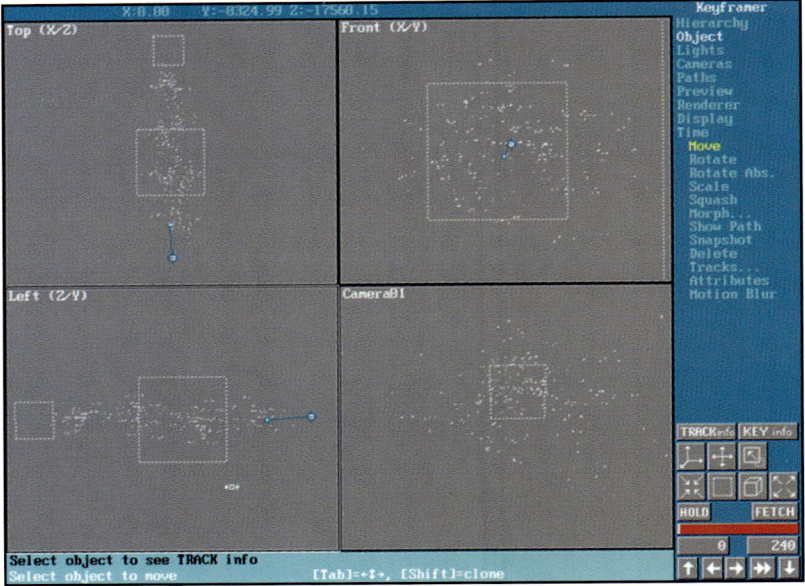

6. Click on the Track Info button, and click on one of the star streaks. In the Object field, make sure one of your warp objects' names is displayed. If not, move the slider until one appears.

7. Click on the Add button at the bottom of the Track Info display, and click on Frame 0 in the Hide column. Make sure the entire Hide column turns gray, indicating that the object will not render during the entire animation. Move the object slider to all the other warp objects, and add Hide keys at Frame 0 for them as well.

8. Now move the slider until St-blue is displayed. Add a key in the morph column at Frame 0, Frame 30, and at Frame 60. Do the same for the remaining St-* objects, but vary the second and third morph keys within about 15 Frames after those for St-blue.

9. Now click on the Key Info button in the lower left, and click on the last morph key for whichever object you are currently working on.

10. Make sure the Morph button is active in the Key Info box. Click on the morph Object entry field for this object, and when the selection menu comes up, choose the corresponding warp-* object.

11. Click on the minus sign by the Key# box, and move back to morph keyframe 2. Set the From slider (under the EaseTo slider) to about 45 for this key (see fig. 9.8).

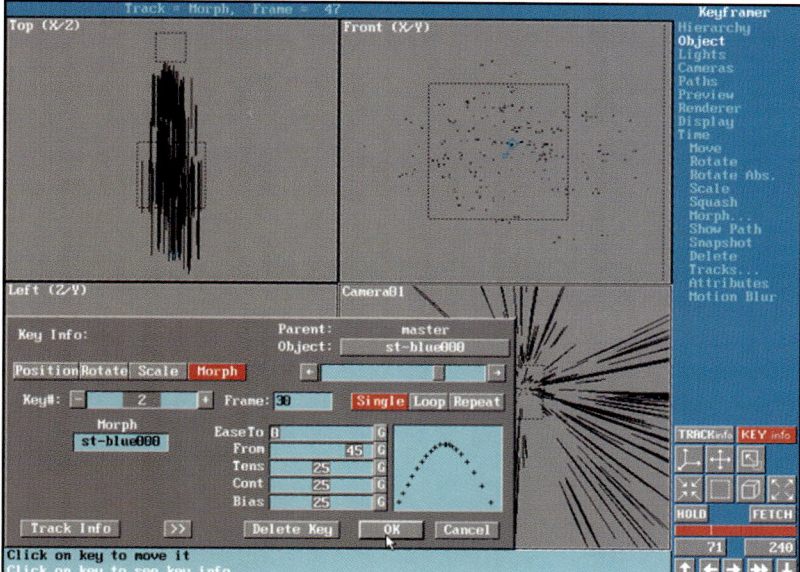

Figure 9.8
The Key Info dialog box.

12. Move the Object slider in the upper right to display the next St- object.

13. Repeat the procedure for the other St- objects, assign them to their corresponding warp- partners, and adjust the previous morph keyframes Ease From values.

14. When you have completed this process for all the St- objects, click OK.

15. Click on the lower right viewport to make it active, and press C to make this the Camera viewport.

16. Click on the Left viewport and play the animation for the meshes.

Your star objects should stay the same until about Frame 30, and then they should stretch out into the cosmos. The only problem is that they are not streaking forward (towards the camera), but stretching out from their centers in both directions.

17. To correct this, go to the keyframe in which the last morph is completed and take a look at the streaks' ends. Click on **Object/Move** and go into the Left viewport. Press the Tab key until the cursor arrows are left-to-right, and click on the Master dummy. Move the Master forward until the end of the last star streak is at the approximate same position to the Marker dummy as it was when you started.

18. Click on the Track Info button again, and then on the Master dummy. Make sure the Self button is active in the Track Info box. Click on the Copy button, and click on the key-dot at Frame 0 in the Position column. Move this dot forward to Frame 30, then click again to place it.

19. Then click OK. This will make sure the streaking motion forward doesn't begin before the morphing, so you don't have 250 stars flying toward you before you "warp."

Preview the animation from Camera viewport, and make sure the effect is animating properly.

20. Go into the Video Post module to render the animation. If you saved your settings from the preceding effect (Effect 8), you can reload them for use here (just reset the total number of frames). If not, go to the Video Post section in Effect 8 and follow the instructions. After these settings are complete, render the animation.

Conclusion

High-impact special effects don't always require the most powerful or expensive hardware and software available, but they do require a great deal of creativity and reverse engineering. Many effects have the same principles at their core. Familiarize yourself with traditional special-effects methodology, and whenever you see an effect that thrills you, start breaking it down into its simplest components. Often, a clear, effective way of recreating it on your computer will appear.

Then dress it up with lights, image processing routines, or custom maps to make a professional-quality scene.

Particle Cannon

Effect 10

by Greg Phillips
Indianapolis, Indiana

Equipment and Software Used

- IBM PC compatible Pentium 90 with 64 MB of RAM and 1 gig drive
- Video output to DPS Personal Animation Recorder
- Iomega ZIP 100 MB drive
- 3D Studio Release 4.0
- Yost Group SPURT_I.AXP
- Fractal Design Painter 3.0

Artist Biography

Greg Phillips is an award-winning 3D computer graphic artist and President of the Multimedia Group for Phillips Design Group, Inc. in Indianapolis, Indiana. He works with many types of software, including 3D Studio, Animator Studio, Fractal Design Painter, Photoshop, CorelDRAW!, Premiere, Alias Power Animator, and many more. He is coauthor of the book *3D Studio Special Effects* and contributed to *Inside 3D Studio 3.0*. His 3D designs have appeared in New York, San Francisco, and all around the world in design publications, books, cover art, art galleries, animations, exhibits, and many published articles. He is currently working on design and development of interactive CD-ROMs, kiosks, and the Internet WWW design for many national companies. He can be reached via CompuServe at 102363,372 or via the Internet at greg@dgs.com.

Effect Overview

The techniques described in this chapter show the 3D Studio user how to create a Particle Cannon effect using the IPAS plug-in SPURT_I.AXP. This effect simulates a particle blast from the laser cannon's barrels as it rotates and fires. You will use other software such as Fractal Design Painter to create color texture maps for this Particle Cannon effect. The models created in this chapter are from 3D Studio 4.0, and the texture maps are from 3D Studio and Autodesk Texture Universe CD. The final result is a particle cannon on a platform deep in space firing purple blasts of energy at attacking enemies.

Procedure

Start 3D Studio and choose **File/Load Project** and select file PARTICLE.PRJ from the \PARTICLE\PROJECT directory on the 3D Studio Hollywood and Gaming Effects CD (see fig. 10.1).

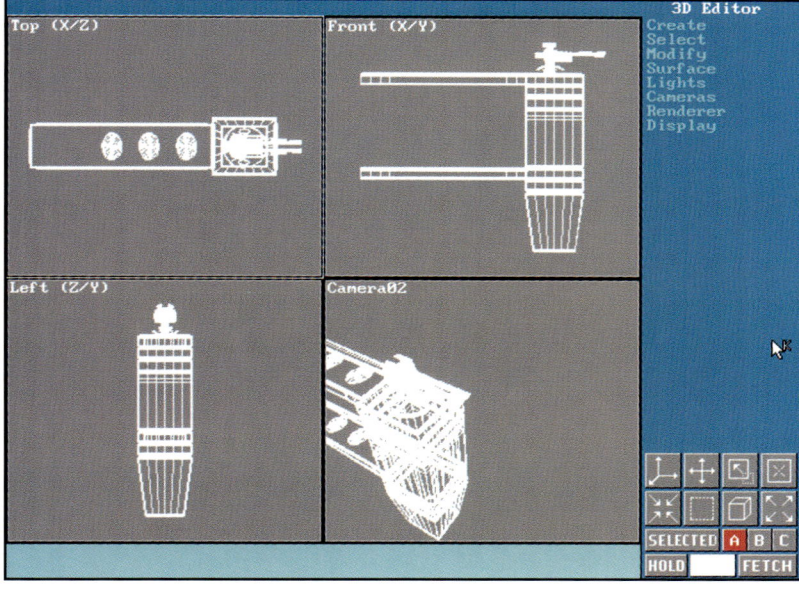

Figure 10.1
A view of the project file used to create the particle cannon.

Then choose **Info/Configure**, click on Maps Paths in the Program Configuration menu, and add the CD-ROM directory \PARTICLE\MAPS to access the images and maps necessary for this chapter. Table 10.1 lists the objects and assigned materials for this project.

Table 10.1 Objects, Materials, and Mappings for the Particle Cannon Effect

Objects	Material	Mapping
Base Rotor	Green Ice	Applied
Cannon	Bronze	Applied
Planet	Planet	Applied
Pod	Green Ice	Applied
Walk1	Green Ice	Applied
Walk2	Green Ice Laser	Applied

NOTE: If you need to access these materials at any time, choose **Surface/Material/Get Library** from the 3D Editor and select PARTICLE.MLI from the \PARTICLE\MATLIBS directory on the CD-ROM.

The file PARTICLE.PRJ contains the 3D models to complete this effect. Begin by creating the spotlight.

1. Choose **Lights/Spot/Create** and create a spotlight in the Top viewport. Create a spotlight with the name **LIGHT** and the settings RGB 227,227,227. Turn on Cast Shadows and Show Cone, Hotspot:**73.75**, Falloff:**152.00**. Figure 10.2 shows the location and direction of the spotlight.

Figure 10.2
Spotlight location and direction.

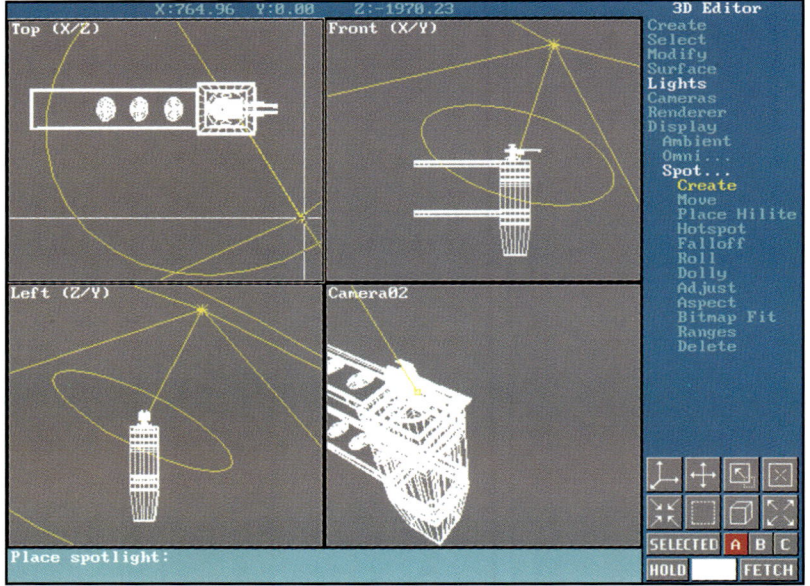

> **TIP:** Try a combination of different color lighting to create moon and sun flare effects. For example, try using **Spotlight Definition/Projector** to project different texture maps over the scene.

2. Go to 3D Studio's Material Editor, and choose **Material/Get Material from Scene** to view the material used in this scene. Take some time and view the materials used for this project. Then return to the 3D Editor to begin the next exercise.

3. Next, choose **Create/Cylinder**, select **Values**, and set values to Sides:**26**, Segments:**6**. Next choose **Smoothed** and create the cylinder named Particle1 in the Right viewport, making the diameter smaller than the cannon barrel size. Make the length of the cylinder longer than the cannon (see fig. 10.3).

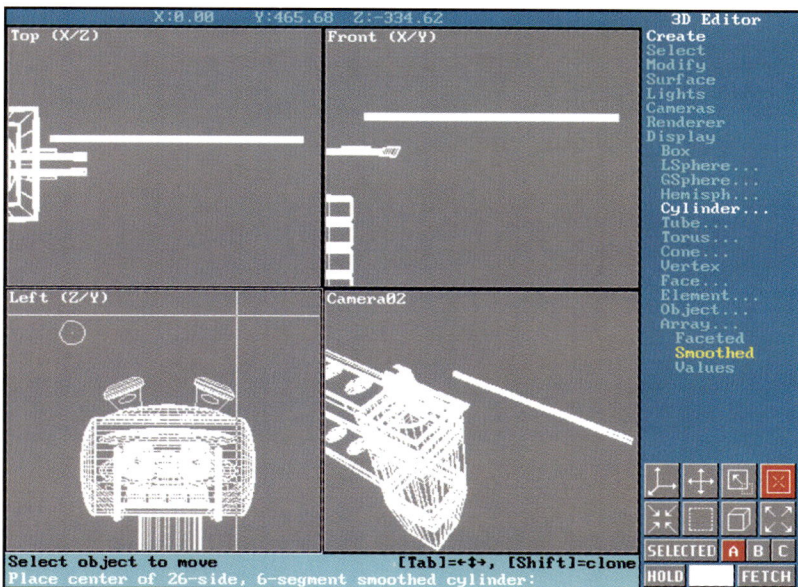

Figure 10.3
Cylinder modifications for the Particle Cannon effect.

4. Choose **Modify/Object/Taper** and use the Tab key in the Front viewport to change taper direction to horizontal and toward the left facing the cannon. Start tapering the cylinder down to a point (see fig. 10.4).

5. Continue to use **Modify/Object/Taper** in the Front viewport, and use the Tab key to change direction to the right and taper out the other side of the cylinder to give it the funnel look (see fig. 10.4).

Effect 10: Particle Cannon   179

Figure 10.4
Cylinder taper modifications for the object Particle1.

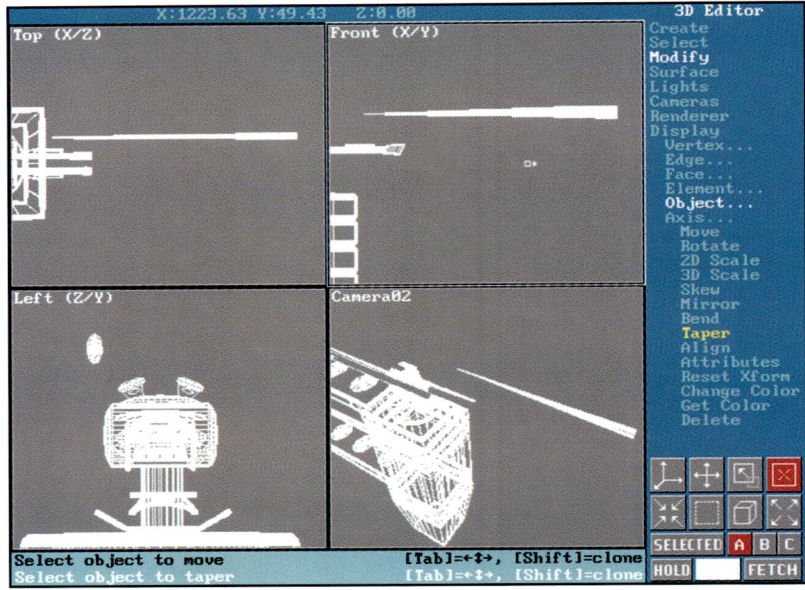

6. Choose **Modify/Object/Move** and align the cylinder object, Particle1, with the barrel of the cannon opening (see fig. 10.5).

Figure 10.5
Aligning the Particle 1 object with the cannon.

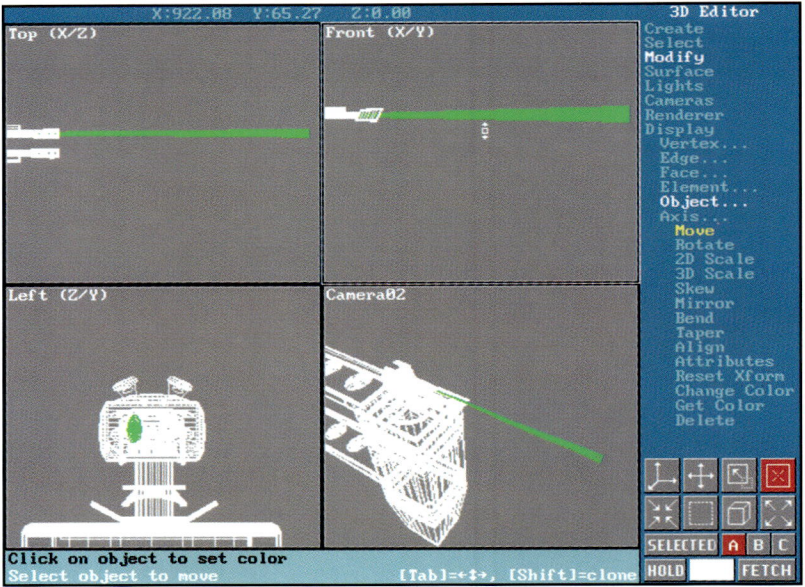

7. Choose **Modify/Object/Move** and in the Top viewport hold down the Shift key to clone the cylinder named Particle1, move it to the cannon opening next to the original, and name it Particle2 (see fig. 10.6).

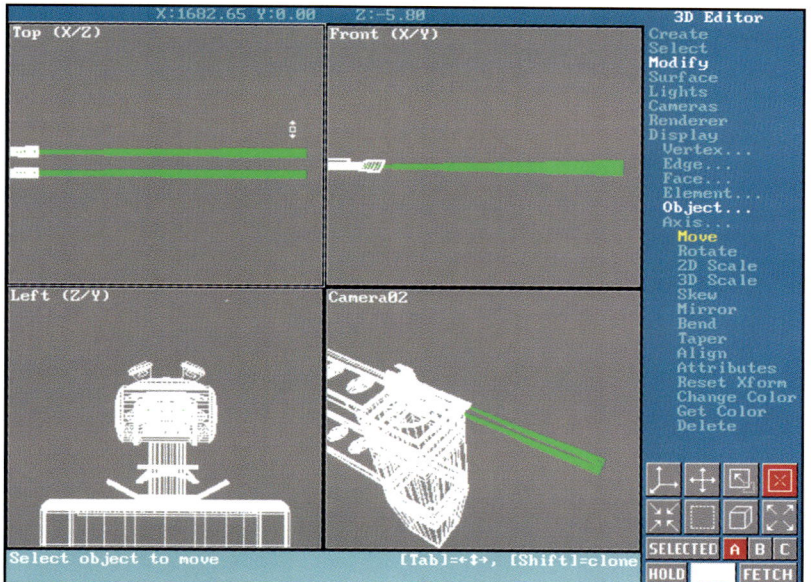

Figure 10.6
The location of new object Particle2.

8. Click in the Top viewport and choose **Surface/Mapping/Type**. Use planer or cylinder mapping and align using **Mapping/Adjust/Scale**, hold down the Alt key and select cylinder object Particle1. Next, select **Mapping/Apply Obj** and apply mapping to both objects Particle1 and Particle2.

9. Next, choose **Surface/Material/Choose** and select the material LASER. Choose **Surface/Material/Assign/Object** and select objects Particle1 and Particle2.

NOTE: If you need to access these materials, choose **Surface/Material/Get Library** and select PARTICLE.MLI from the CD-ROM directory Particle/Matlibs.

The material LASER was created in Fractal Design Painter 3.0 using the air brush and painting tools. LASER uses bright colors in random areas to help create the particle blast effect. The plug-in, SPURT_I.AXP, uses UV mapping to determine the particle's color and trail color for each frame. The cylinder object's body color and tail color are determined by samples taken from the image map LASER pixel by pixel. For each frame of the cylinder's animation, the particle's color changes. Try using gradations of color from Fractal Design Painter's lighting effects and textures to create different color particle effects. Fractal Design Painter has extensive creation tools for color, texture, and map creation (see fig. 10.7).

Figure 10.7
Fractal Design Painter's particle color creation.

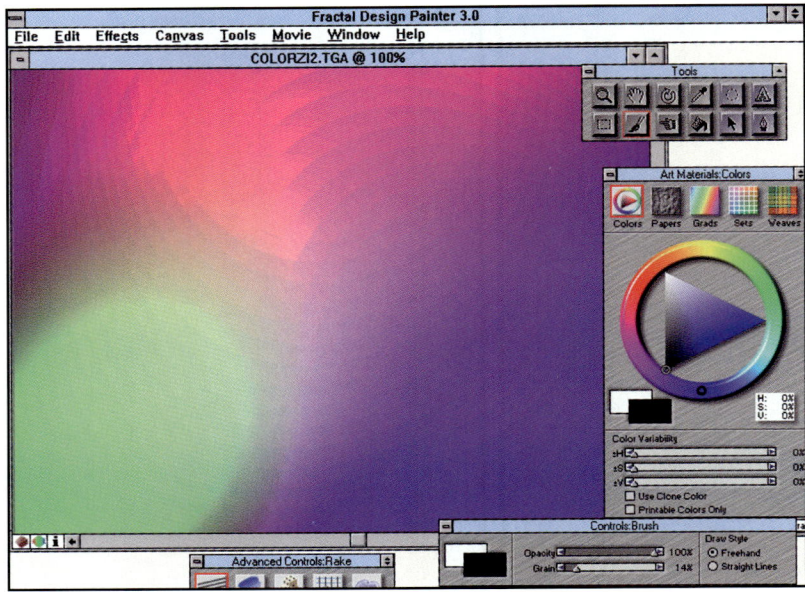

10. Choose **Modify/Object/Attributes** to open the Object Attributes dialog box, then select the cylinder object Particle1 (see fig. 10.8).

Figure 10.8
The Object Attributes dialog box with the Particle1 cylinder object selected.

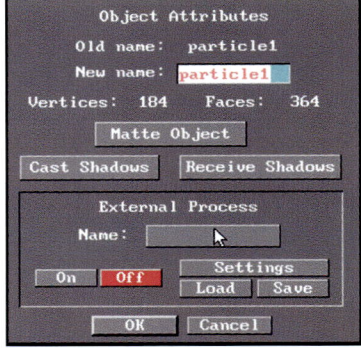

11. Select the External Process area on the menu and load SPURT.AXP (see fig. 10.9).

Figure 10.9
The External Process menu.

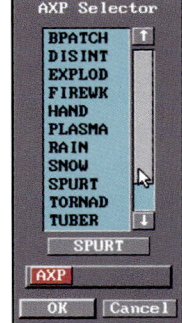

12. From the External Process menu, select Settings to access the Spurt dialog box.

13. Next, you modify the parameters to create the effect in this chapter. The following list shows the changes made in the Spurt dialog box.

    # of Particles: **40**
    Gravity: **0**
    Particle Life Span: **30**
    Object/Spark ratio: **0.09**
    Spark/Trail ratio: **6**
    Particle per point: **9**
    Random # Seed: **12345**

    Absolute Frame   Relative Frames
    Start:**0**   Peak:**10**   Hold:**5**   End:**60**

    Particle Flow: **Radial**
    Parallel Axis: **Horiz**
    Shape: **Object**
    Initial Velocity: **62**
    Deceleration: **34**
    Chaos: **0**

14. Modify attribute settings and external process SPURT.AXP perimeters for Particle2 the same as for Particle1.

> **TIP:** Try changing the parameters of Particle1 and Particle2 settings in the Spurt dialog box to vary particle flow, velocity, and other parameters in order to create different effects of particle flow and emission.
>
> Also, try moving the objects Particle1 and Particle2 to different positions to create alternative cannon ignitions. Move one cannon barrel back, for example, and alternate the cannons along with the objects Particle1 and Particle2 to create the animation of cannon recoil from a particle blast.

> **NOTE:** Now would be a good time to save your project file to your hard drive. Save as **PARTEST.PRJ**.

15. Go to the Keyframer and set the number of frames to **60** and select OK.

16. In the Keyframer, choose **Renderer/Render view** and render in the Camera viewport. After you finish, play back the 60-frame FLC file and see your results.

To view the final animation and images for this project, access the directories PARTICLE\FLICS and \PARTICLE\IMAGES on the CD-ROM.

Conclusion

Try different variations of lighting colors and IPAS settings to the animation. Build and design good 3D models, because without good 3D models your effect will be less dynamic and real. Visualize your effect when you design in 3D Studio. Try different IPAS plug-in particle effects and your animation will come alive. If you need more examples of IPAS plug-ins, see *3D Studio IPAS Plug-In Reference* from New Riders Publishing.

Search Light

Effect 11

by Richard Sher in conjuction with Eric Peterson

Los Angeles California

Equipment and Software Used

- Micron P90 with two 1.2 Gigabyte EIDE drives, Diamond Stealth 64 PCI 4 MB VRAM, 64 MB of RAM, 4X CD-ROM drive
- 3D Studio Release 4

Artist Biography

Richard Sher started as an artist creating abstract paintings with water color and acrylic media. Upon entering college, photography became his medium of choice. After discovering the television studio, he began working with analog video processing.

Richard began creating computer animations with 3D Studio in 1991. His first job using 3D Studio was creating animations for a children's TV show called *Chip and Pepper's Cartoon Madness*. This first job paid for the equipment to run 3D Studio. He later went on to do the opening for a Lucas film pilot called *Defenders of Dynatron City*. In 1993, Richard's company 3SPACE was able to purchase a Beta SP video tape recorder, three Silicon Graphics computers, Alias, Prisms, Wavefront Composer, and Pandemonium. With a group of five very dedicated employees and his partner, Alberto Menache, he has created animations for a number of CD-ROM projects including *3D Body Adventure*, *Windows Animation Festival*, and *Mathimagics*. Having sold his interest in 3SPACE, Richard is now working with Metrolite Studios producing interactive media.

Effect Overview

Creating special effects for motion pictures requires an all-out effort on the part of the production team. Whether the project is a big-name feature with an equally big budget or a TV movie, the viewers see and critique the special effects first. There is often computer animation for show openings, and the compositing—the combining of video or film footage over or within other footage—of live action with separate backgrounds, and with computer-generated objects, is now a staple effect in the repertoire of production teams. The effect that I will describe is useful in both cases, primarily because it focuses on using controlled transparency to merge the computer-generated elements over the rest of the images.

I call this effect visible light because it presents a method for simulating the projection of light through a space. Real light isn't visible unless it strikes something, and light projecting from a source through a space defines itself by the objects it hits. A sunbeam projecting through a stained-glass window into a dusty chapel is altered first by the colors of the window, and then becomes visible falling upon the dust motes. The "beam" we see is the reflection of the light from those motes and the pool of light it draped over the pews. Likewise, a film projector's beam in a pre-no-smoking theater was defined by the smoke through which it passed, reflecting a little of the light along its way to the screen.

Working in 3D Studio, our job is even more difficult than that of the director or photographer because simulating smoke or dust is not so simple a matter as shaking a nearby old rug or putting out a smoldering ashtray. Worse, there is no "beam of light" projecting through space because 3D Studio considers neither ray-traced nor volume-lighting effects.

Because we can't readily simulate either smoke or dust in 3D Studio without plug-ins, and because we don't have volume lighting, we need to provide the illusion of a projected light beam intersecting either smoke or dust. We do this with geometry mimicking the shape of the projected beam and through careful choice of materials applied to that geometry.

Using objects extruded from the same shapes used to create the light source, we have the ability to apply a variety of surface treatments and degrees of transparencies in order to fine-tune how the imaginary light beam appears. In this chapter, I will offer some of the techniques for applying materials and lighting that have worked well for me, and I hope to show you how to create your own as well.

Procedure

In beginning any project, the first step is to compose some preliminary storyboards, or at least to lay out some sort of simple plan defining the animation. On the most fundamental level, the animator needs to plan camera placement and motion. Other considerations include ways to maximize the impact of the planned effect. Often, the considerations are intertwined. We want to make the key elements of the animation appear in center stage, so the camera should move around them, tracking the elements of the animation as the center of attention. The image at the beginning of this chapter, taken from the animation described here, follows that guideline.

This exercise involves a title sequence for an imaginary Hollywood movie called *Search Light*. The words of the title will be the light itself, projecting visible, dynamic, animated beams towards the camera—towards the point of view. The effect will employ animated procedural surface textures, gradient opacity maps, both mesh and material morphs, and camera motion to achieve the final result.

In support of this effect, the animator's 3D Studio MAPS subdirectory should include these files:

- ★ NOISE_I.SXP
- ★ GRADLIN.TIF
- ★ CHECKERS.CEL

Of these, only GRADLIN.TIF is new. The animator will find it on the CD-ROM accompanying this book in the \LIGHTS directory.

Creating the Geometry

1. Start by entering 3D Studio from the DOS prompt, or by saving your existing work, if any, and executing a **File/Reset** from the **File** pull-down menu.

2. From the **View** pull-down menu, choose the **Drawing Aids** entry and define snap distances of **1** drawing unit in all three principle directions. Click on OK. Verify that Snap is on in all three principle viewports by activating each in turn and hitting the S key if the "S" is not displayed in the upper right corner of the screen.

3. Enter the 2D Shaper by choosing that module from the **Program** pull-down menu or by using the keystroke shortcut F1.

4. Verify that Snap is also active in the Shaper. Toggle Snap on if necessary.

5. Choose **Create/Text/Font** from the **Shaper** menu. When the dialog box pops up, hit the *.* button to bring up all installed fonts. The default is for Studio to recognize only the FNT format fonts, and some users never realize that a larger set is available.

> **NOTE:** 3D Studio can't read TrueType fonts, a feature that has caused no end of consternation to some users. Studio reads Autodesk's own font format, but it also reads PostScript Type 1 fonts.
>
> Those "2000 Fonts" CDs that show up in combination packages for $20 or $30 often include both TrueType and PostScript Type 1 fonts. Thus, these inexpensive CDs are an excellent source for hundreds of fonts that are compatible with Studio.

6. Select BENFRANK.PFB from the now-expanded list and click on OK. This is a solid, stable, and simple font that will make the exercise more error-tolerant.

7. Choose **Create/Text/Enter** and enter the words **SEARCH LIGHT** in uppercase letters.

8. Choose **Create/Text/Place** and click at the coordinates 0,0. Place the other corner of the box at 12,2. Execute a Zoom All using the icon panel button.

9. Choose **Shape/Steps** from the menu and experiment with various settings between zero and 10. A value of zero is clearly unacceptable, resulting in angular, deformed letters. Values between 5 and 10 result in very little improvement at each step. A value of 3 or 4 is recommended. The supplied project file uses a value of 3. Figure 11.1 illustrates the text with a shape setting of 3.

> **NOTE:** While it is true that 3D Studio reads all PostScript Type 1 fonts, those fonts not designed for use with Studio might exhibit aberrant behavior in the Studio environment. Some fonts, particularly very "arty" or cursive fonts have very complex geometry. Some shape settings will simplify the polygons forming the letters to the point that the polygons cross, leading to self-intersecting, impossible-to-loft geometry. Worse, the SHAPE-MAX parameter in Studio's 3DS.SET file limits the number of vertices available in the 2D Shaper. Some fonts—especially the ones noted here—might require in excess of the maximum allowed vertex count for only a few words. Using these fonts leads to complex, memory-hungry text.

Figure 11.1
Text in Shaper.

10. Choose **Select/Polygon/Quad/*Window** from the menu and draw a selection box around the text. The text should turn red.

11. Choose **Shape/Assign/Selected** (using the spacebar) and click in the viewport. The text should turn yellow with red vertices. Use the keystroke shortcut Alt+N to deselect the polygons. The text should uniformly be yellow.

> **TIP:** A common mistake among animators is to select portions of text without selecting entire letters for loft. Clicking on individual letters is prone to error and tedious, because many letters consist of multiple polygons. Even in the simple block text of "BENFRANK" the letter "B" is three polygons. In more complex fonts, it is not uncommon for a letter to consist of eight or 10 polygons. Hence, using Shape/Assign/ Selected with selection sets is the method of choice for assigning text for loft.

12. Choose **Shape/Check** to verify the loft-worthiness of the assigned polygons. This is always a good thing to do when working with fonts—especially fonts that didn't come packaged with Studio.

13. Move to the 3D Lofter by choosing that module from the **Program** pull-down menu or by using the keystroke shortcut F2. Choose **Shapes/Get/Shaper** from the menu.

14. Set path steps to zero using **Path/Steps**.

15. Using **Path/Move Vertex** with Snap on, move the ends of the path until the Lofter contents resemble figure 11.2. The path is 2 units long.

Figure 11.2
Text in Lofter.

16. Choose **Objects/Make** from the menu to display the Object Lofting Controls dialog box, and configure the dialog box per figure 11.3. Note that Cap End is off, that Optimization is on, and that Weld Vertices is on. Click on OK and name the object **Light**.

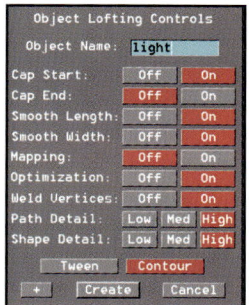

Figure 11.3
Lofting parameters.

17. Press F3 to move into the 3D Editor. Choose **Cameras/Create** from the menu and place a camera with a 50 mm focal length in front of and centered on the text object Light, as illustrated in figure 11.4. Activate the User viewport and hit C to convert it to the Camera viewport.

Figure 11.4

Light, camera, and text object positions.

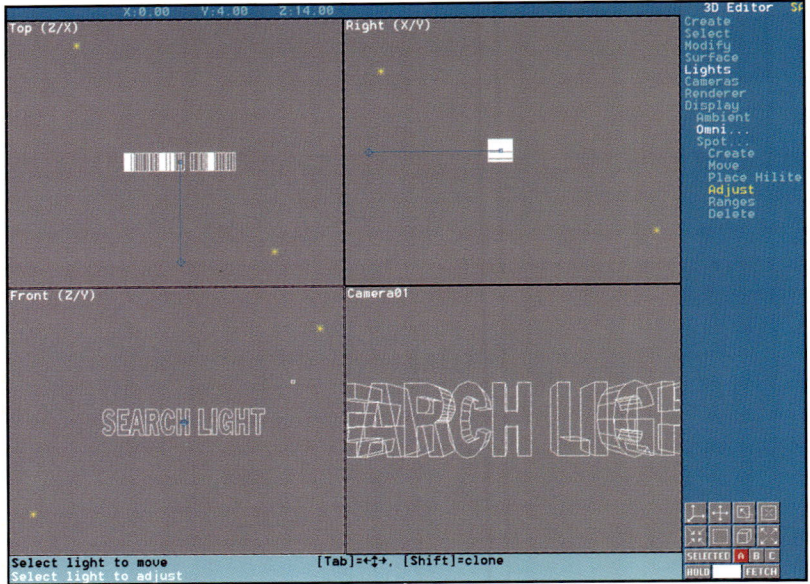

18. Use **Lights/Omni/Create** to place a very bright omni—with a luminosity of 255—above and in front of the text object. The purpose of this light is to illuminate the non-self-illuminated materials in the scene—the sides of the letters—with quite a lot of brightness to simulate light washback from the beams. Use **Lights/Omni/Move** as necessary to place the forward omni according to the placement depicted in figure 11.4.

19. Use **Lights/Omni/Move** with the Shift key to clone the main omni and to make a copy behind and below the text objects, as in figure 11.4. Use **Lights/Omni/Adjust** to move the luminosity of this fill light down to **25** or **30**. This is quite bright for a fill omni, but the scene should be bright.

20. Press F2 to reenter the Lofter. Using **Path/Move Vertex**, set the length of the path at **6** units—three times the length of the letters themselves—and choose **Objects/Make**. Turn off both caps, turn mapping on, and change the object name to **Long Beam**, as shown in figure 11.5. Click on OK. When the mapping parameter box pops up, click on OK again.

21. Press F3 to move back to the 3D Editor. Use the keystroke shortcuts Alt+C, Alt+L, and Alt+B to hide the camera and lights, and to switch the geometry to box mode. In the Top viewport, use **Modify/Object/Move** with the cursor toggled to vertical and with Snap on to align the back edge of the Long Beam object to the front edge of the Light object. Choose **Modify/Object/Change Color** to change the color of the Long Beam to something other than the white of the Light object (see fig. 11.6).

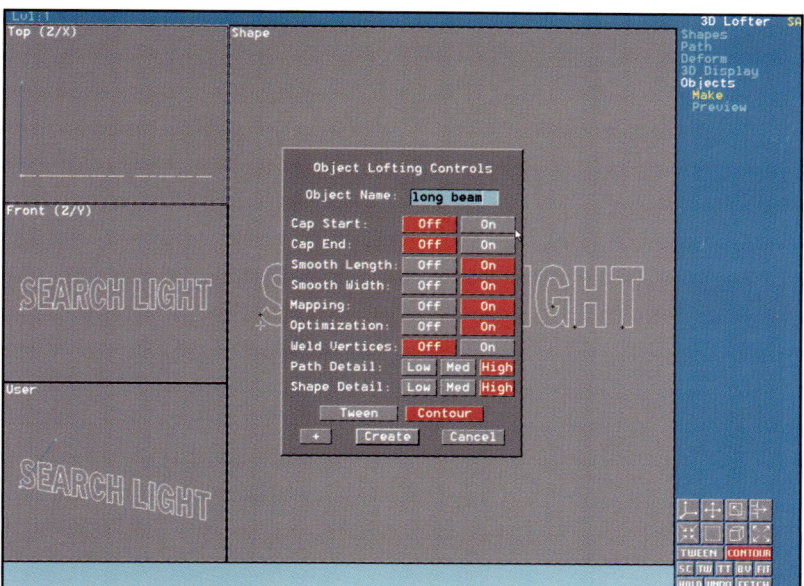

Figure 11.5
Light beam lofting parameters.

> **TIP:** I like to change the color of the objects I am working with for the added convenience. Giving objects unique colors also reduces the eye strain for some people.

22. Choose **Select/Face/Quad/*Window** and in the Top viewport draw a selection box around the interface between the two objects. This will select only those faces at the front end of the Light object. Choose **Create/Face/Detach/Selected** using the spacebar, and click in the viewport. Name the detached front faces **Light Face**.

23. While still in the Top viewport, choose **Surface/Mapping/Type/*Cylindrical**. Then use **Surface/Mapping/Adjust/Scale** and click on the Light object while holding the Alt key. Use **Surface/Mapping/Apply** to fix the mapping coordinates to the Light object.

24. Activate the Top viewport and choose **Modify/Axis/Show** to display the home position of the construction axes. Use **Modify/Axis/Place** to put the little "x" denoting home somewhere along the interface between the Light and Long Beam objects.

25. Use **Modify/Object/2D Scale/shift+select** with Local Axis off and with the cursor toggled vertical in the Top viewport to create a copy of

Long Beam somewhat shorter than the original object. Call this object, whose length should be about half that of Long Beam, **Middl Beam**. Use **Modify/Object/Change Color** to give Middl Beam its own unique color. If Box Mode is still active, the animator can pick the individual beam objects without handicap. If Box Mode is off, however, then using hit lists—hitting H after choosing **Modify/Object/Change Color**—will simplify selecting the correct object. See figure 11.7.

Figure 11.6
Light and Long Beam objects in Editor.

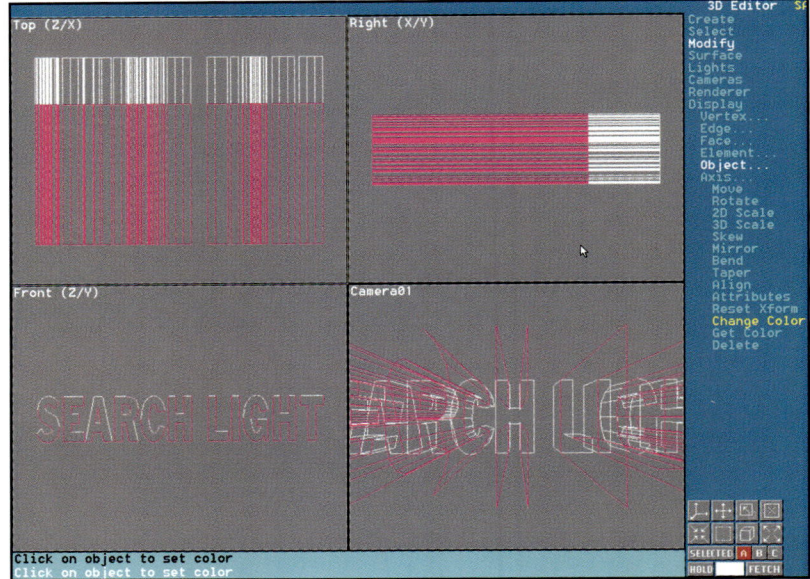

26. Use **Modify/Object/2D Scale/shift+select** again in the Top viewport to create another copy of Long Beam. This one should be shorter even than Middl Beam, perhaps 1/4 to 1/3 the length of Long Beam itself. Change the color of this object—**Min Beam**—as well. See figure 11.8.

Creating the Project Materials

1. Press F5 to switch to the Materials Editor.

2. Create a material matching the parameters depicted in figure 11.9. This is a plain, white, very bright, self-illuminated material. Choose **Material/Put To Current** to transfer the material to the 3D Editor.

3. Press F3 to return to the 3D Editor, and then choose **Surface/Material/Assign/Object**, and hit the H key. When the object selection box pops up, select the Light Face object. Click on OK.

4. Press F5 to return to the Materials Editor. In the second sample window, configure a material duplicating the parameters shown in figure 11.10.

Click on the Cube button to change the sample window appearance, and turn on Pattern background as well. Note the settings of NOISE_I.SXP in figure 11.11. Transfer the material to the 3D Editor using **Material/Put To Current**.

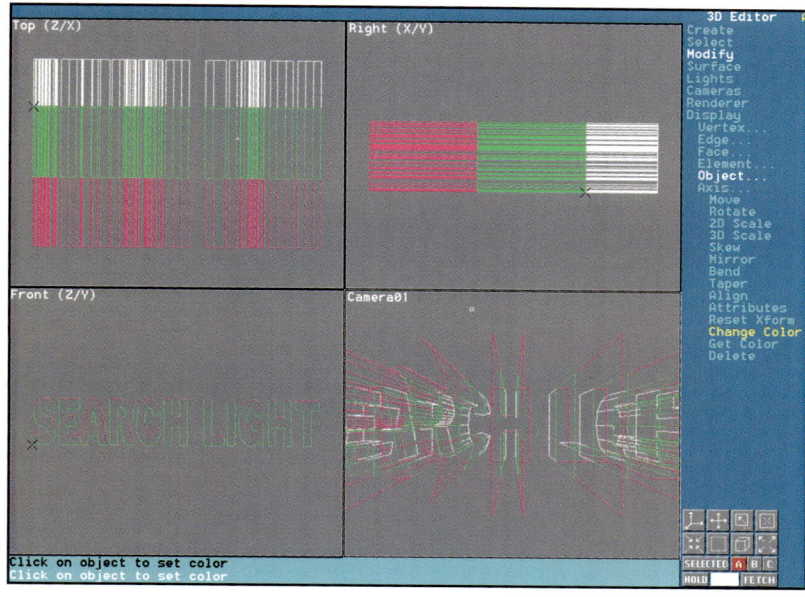

Figure 11.7
Building light beam morph targets.

Figure 11.8
All beams are in place.

Figure 11.9
Light face material.

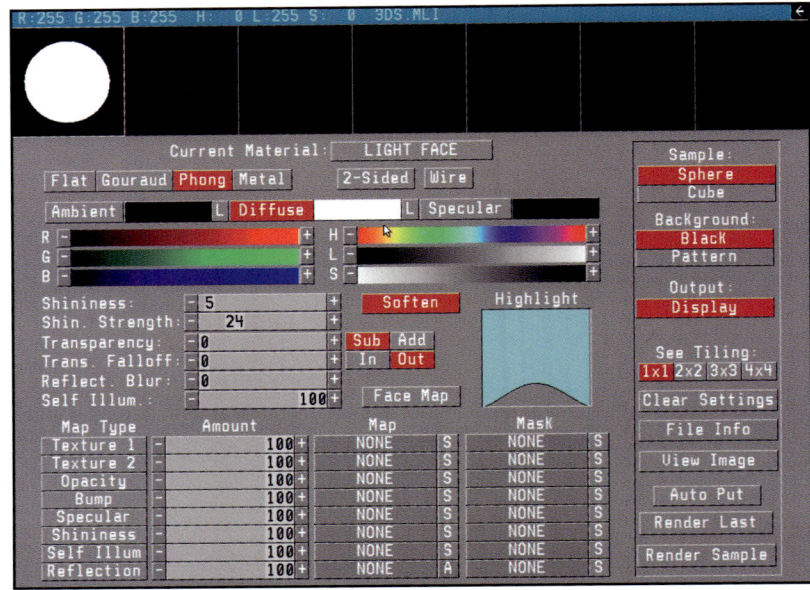

Here's how the material of step 4 works: The noise SXP provides a black/white mottling effect not unlike the effect of light passing through smoke. Applying the SXP as a texture map provides for a swirling, changing texture everywhere in the object that varies with position, independent of the mapping coordinates. Using the black/white gradient in the opacity slot forces the object to fade out toward one end—the end where the map is totally black. The opacity map uses the applied lofted mapping coordinates. Applying the identical map in the shininess field kills any reflections from the transparent portions of the material.

5. Press F3 to switch back to the 3D Editor. Apply the material to the objects Min Beam and Long Beam using hit lists.

6. Return once again to the Materials Editor. Click-drag a copy of the Beam Dim material to the third sample window and rename it **Beam Bright**. Change the parameters as shown in figure 11.12. Transfer this material to the current Editor material as well.

7. Return to the 3D Editor and apply Beam Bright to the object Middl Beam.

8. Return to the Materials Editor and, in the fourth sample window, choose **Material/Get Material** from the pull-down. Scroll through the default material library until Checker texture appears. Click on that material, click on OK, and transfer the material to the 3D Editor's current material. See figure 11.13.

9. Press F3 to return to the 3D Editor. Assign Checker texture to the object Light.

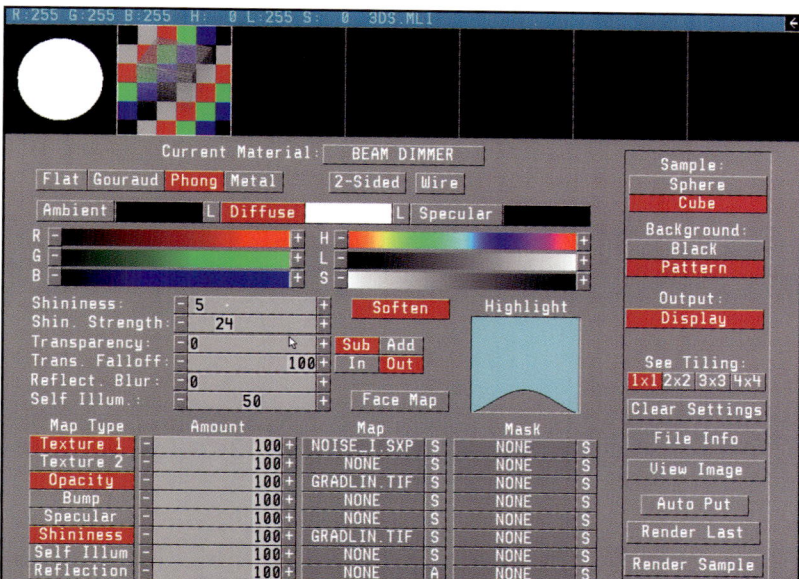

Figure 11.10
Dim beam material.

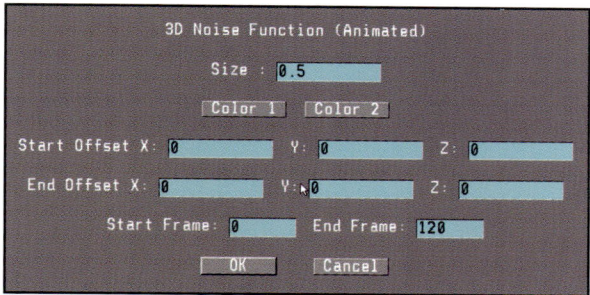

Figure 11.11
Noise__I.SXP settings.

Setting Up the Animation

Using the three versions of the light beam, the goal here is to set up a sequence of morph targets so that the beam appears to grow in both length and brightness over an interval while moving the camera through the beam. Note that it would be possible to simply stretch or scale the beam to get the effect of the geometry changing, but for the brightness and other material properties to change over time—examine figures 11.10 and 11.12 closely—only a morph will work.

1. Press F4 to enter the Keyframer. Execute a Zoom All from the icon panel. Choose **Display/Hide/By Name** and select from the list both Min Beam and Middl Beam. Convert the User viewport to a camera viewport by activating it and hitting C.

2. Define the total length of the animation using **Time/Total** frames or by clicking on the total frame counter in the icon panel. Set the total number of frames to **120**. This will play back to 4 seconds at 30 frames per second, which will provide smooth, jerk-free animation.

Figure 11.12
Beam Bright material.

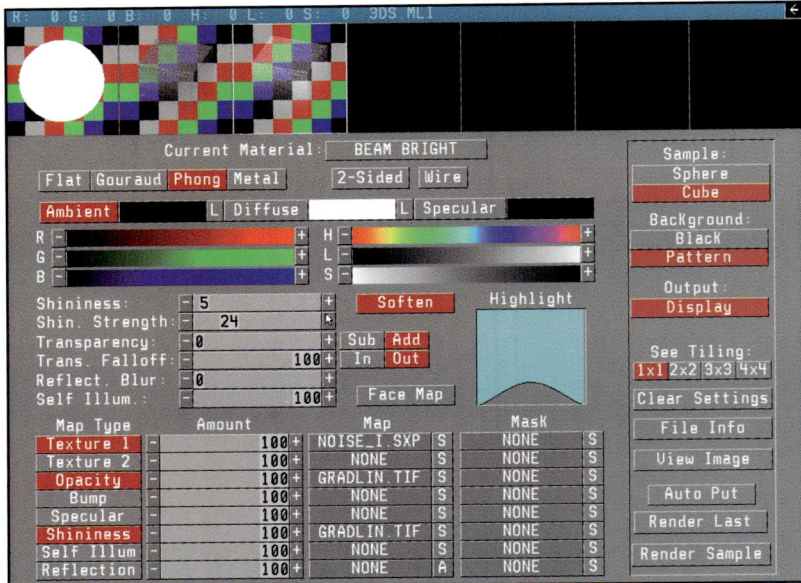

Figure 11.13
Retrieved Checker material.

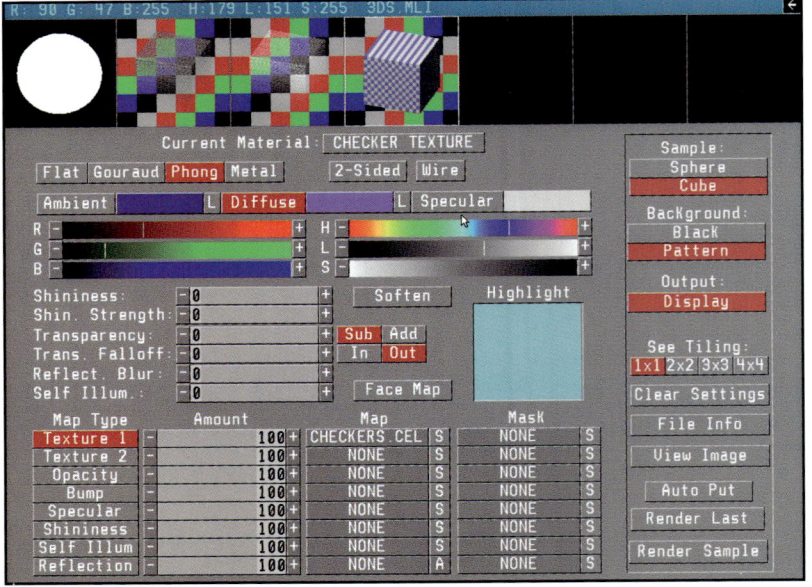

3. Click on the Track Info button in the icon panel and click anywhere in the camera viewport. When the Track Info dialog box pops up, use the object slider in the upper right corner to scroll all the way back to the World keys. Use the Copy button to copy All Keys from Frame 0 to Frame 1. Use **Time/Define Segment** and enter values of **1** and **120**. This will protect the Editor configuration in precisely the original configuration.

4. Use the keyboard shortcut Alt+C to turn the camera back on. At Frame 1, move the camera to a position below and to the left of the text. Also, set a zero-angle camera roll key at Frame 1, and set a position key for the camera target without actually moving it anywhere. See figure 11.14.

5. Go to Frame 120 and move the camera to a position above and to the right of the text. Move the camera target as necessary to center the objects, and roll the camera slightly to maximize the coverage of the text. See figure 11.15.

6. Go to Frame 1. Choose **Object/Morph/Assign** and click on the Long Beam object. When the Morph Target dialog box comes up, pick the Min Beam object and then click on OK. Choose **Object/Morph/Options** and once again select the Long Beam object. Turn the Morph Materials button On.

7. Go to Frame 30 and assign Middl Beam as a morph target for Long beam. Go to Frame 75 and assign Long Beam as its own morph target. Go to Frame 120 and assign Min Beam again.

8. In the Top viewport, hit the double-arrow Play Forward icon and note that although the geometry morphs correctly, it also moves to retain the center of the original object. It will be necessary to adjust the position of the Long Beam object as it morphs. Go to Frame 1 and using **Object/Move** with Snap on and with the cursor toggled vertical, realign the edge of the morphed beam with the edge of the Light and Light Face objects. When moving the Long Beam object, pick on any vertex at the back edge. This will force the back edge to align with the Snap grid, to which the Light Face and Light objects are also aligned.

9. Go to frames 30, 75, and 120 and repeat the procedure of step 8. After position keys are in place at all the major keyframe events, go back to intermediate frames and place position keys as required to fix the back edge of the morphing beam against the face of the light assembly.

Figure 11.14
Setting a position key for the camera target.

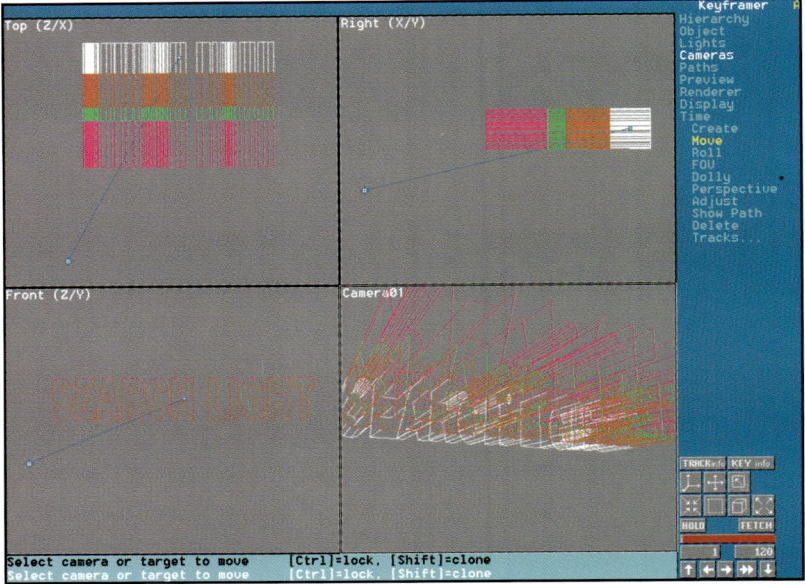

Figure 11.15
Camera position at Frame 120.

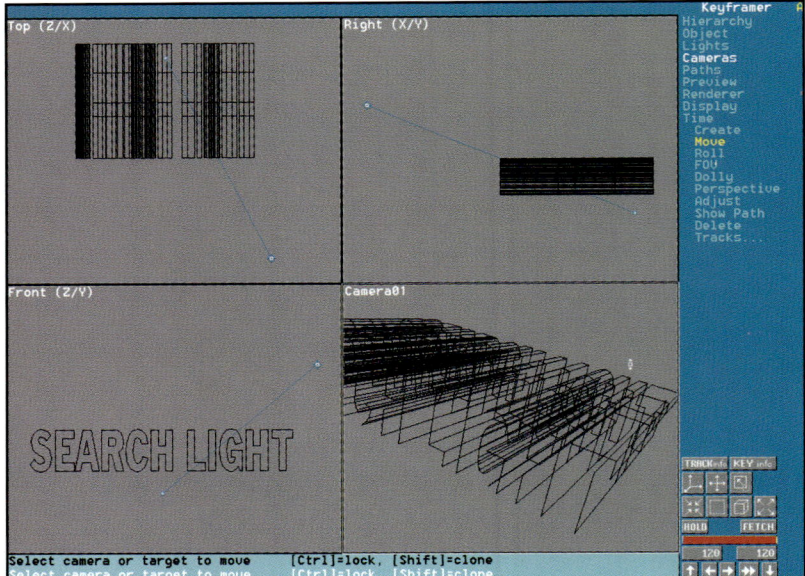

Conclusion

This is only a preliminary exercise! It's possible to combine this type of effect with IPAS plug-in dust, with animated beams that sweep through space, or with moving hierarchically linked objects to get searchlight effects. By combining this type of effect—the use of geometry to simulate light beams—with actual spotlight beams, it is possible to create very powerful illusions of volume lighting. Using geometry beams in conjunction with projector lights provides the most powerful illusions of all.

The KPT Gradient Designer

Effect 12

by Brandon McDougall
Ojai, California

Equipment and Software Used

- Banyan 90 with 64 MB memory, scuzzy controller cards, and 2 gig drives.
- Targa 32 Video card running on a 486/50 single frame output to GVR S950 single frame recording deck
- 3D Studio
- Photoshop
- Animator Pro
- Imagine 3D

Artist Biography

Brandon MacDougall works as a 3D artist for Interplay Productions. He has helped pioneer the acceptance of 3D tools for the gaming industry. He also owns Vision Graphics, which specializes in 3D models and rendering for digital backdrops for the entertainment business. He has worked on games such as *CyberRace*, *Video Speedway*, *SimCity Enhanced*, *Net Runner*, *Conquest of the New World*, and *SimAnt Enhanced*.

Effects Overview

Far too many times, what we see in our mind's eye—the colors, the lighting effects, and the motion—never really materializes in the finished renderings. 3D tools, although very powerful, still can lack some of the ease and power of traditional tools that 2D artists take for granted.

Smoke, fog, and rays of light can be added by 2D art programs very quickly. The 3D artist must be able to use 2D processing tools to enhance his or her renderings. The addition of effects can make or break a final rendering. Just try to imagine the demise of the Emperor in the Star Wars movie *Return of the Jedi* without the blue smoke and lighting as he is thrown down the power shaft.

HSC has helped integrate this concept with the creation of the Gradient Designer for 3D Studio. The Gradient Designer for 3D Studio is a very powerful tool for making complex lighting effects. And thanks to a well-thought-out interface and the real-time preview window, it has become easy to make changes to enhance your artwork. You will take a somewhat dull rendering, and add color and lighting effects to generate that eerie look and feel by building up multiple composites of color from gradient GRD files.

Procedure

Before you start 3D Studio, be sure to run 3D Studio in a high-color video mode, which is necessary for the Gradient Designer's interface. If you generally run the 3D Editor in 256-color mode, you can make an alternative 3DS.SET file with high-color video selected.

In DOS, in your \3DS4 directory, copy 3DS.SET to 3DS.OLD. Invoke 3D Studio with the Vibrant loadable module option, using 3DS VIBCFG at the command line. Select a TrueColor main display, save the settings, and exit 3D Studio. In DOS, copy 3DS.SET to 3DSG.SET. Rename 3DS.OLD back to 3DS.SET.

You can now run 3D Studio by typing **3DS set=3DSG.SET** at the DOS prompt. This enables 3D Studio to run in TrueColor mode, which enables the Gradient Designer to operate properly.

You can also set up a batch file to run 3D Studio with the TrueColor settings.

In DOS, run the Edit program and type **3DS set=\3DS4\3DSG.SET**. Save the file as **true.bat** in the 3D Studio directory and type **True**.

1. If you have not installed Gradient Designer, please do so now. Refer to the Explorer Guide if you have any questions about doing this. You will need to add the path of the CD-ROM containing the sample images to the 3DS Map Path.

Run 3D Studio in TrueColor mode. Under the **Info** menu select **Configure**, then click on the Map Paths button. This command window is where you tell 3D Studio where to find your maps. Locate your CD-ROM directory and Gradient Designer sample files, and click OK.

You should also copy my sample *.GRD files from the CD-ROM to your hard drive. Copy the sample *.GRD files from the CD-ROM to the Gradient directory made by the Gradient Designer's install program (C:\3ds4\GRADIENT). You are now ready to start.

Launch the Gradient Designer. You can find the Gradient Designer under the **Program** menu or by pressing the F12 key and selecting Gradient.

You should now have the Gradient Designer's interface in front of you. Clear any previous projects in the Gradient Designer. You can do this by clicking on the Clear button located in the lower left hand side of the interface.

2. Click the Generate Proxy toggle in the dialog box. This should be checked in order for the proxy to generate. Under the **Options** menu, select **Load Background...** (see fig. 12.1).

Figure 12.1
Gradient Designer's Load Background requester.

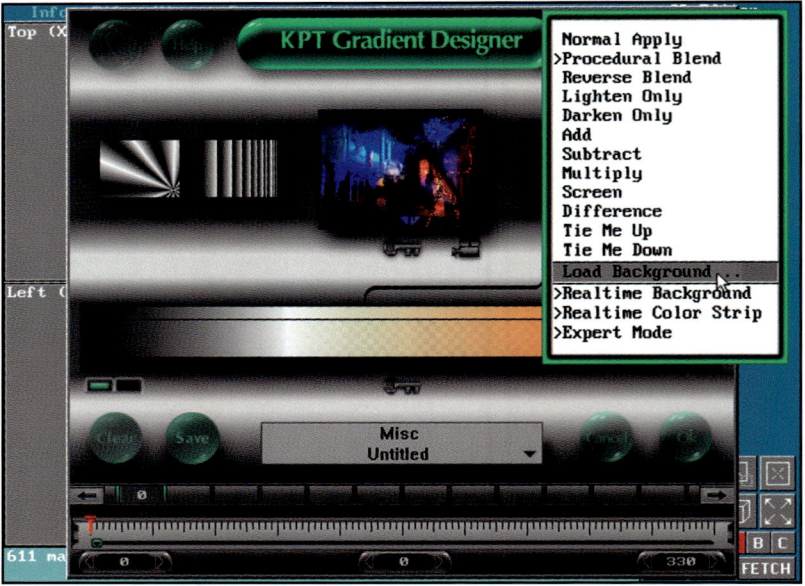

3. In the file requester, click on the *.TGA file extension, then go to the CD-ROM directory in which the skeleton images are located, and select SKEL00.TGA.

204 3D Studio Hollywood and Gaming Effects

4. After you select SKEL00.TGA, a proxy image will be generated. This proxy image enables the Gradient Designer to work quickly by putting your updates on a very small postage-stamp representation of your original loaded image.

   Go back to the **Options** menu and select **Procedural Blend**. Procedural Blend looks at your backdrop image and its luminance value at a pixel level. After sorting this level, Procedural Blend overlays your selected color in a value determined by the luminance of the backdrop image. Another way to look at it is this: The brighter portions of the back drop image will get more of the color that you have selected from the color bars.

   Next, go down to the color bar and select a dark blue color. This is located in the center of your screen. You will also see an update to your image in the preview window. If you would like to see a larger image of the real-time preview window, right-clicking on the real-time preview window brings up a small wire box that enables you to increase the size of the view for a single frame.

   Click in the window and drag until the numerical readout matches the screen size you wish to view. After adjusting for size, release the mouse and the window renders at the size you requested (see fig. 12.2).

Figure 12.2
Full-size rendering from the preview window.

5. You now need to add a Radial Sweep (see fig. 12.3). Radial Sweep is located in the small window to the far left of the real-time preview window. This is the Algorithm Control box. After you select **Radial Sweep**, tell the Radial Sweep to repeat eight times. You will find this command in the Looping Control box, which is located just to the left of the preview window. The looping amounts are at the bottom of this menu.

Figure 12.3
Selecting Radial Sweep in the Gradient Designer.

We now must save out the image in order to composite the next level of Procedural Blend.

Click on the Save button. Save this image in your Gradient directory with the *.GRD extension. Name it **TEMP01.GRD**. Make sure that you have 640×480 selected. Gradient Designer will default the saved image to the size of the dragged out real-time preview window, so make sure you check this when saving.

Now let's go ahead and add more colors to this image. Under the **Options** menu (see fig. 13.1), select **Load Background** and load TEMP01.GRD. This can be the file you just saved to your Gradient directory, or you can load the LEVEL01.GRD image from the CD-ROM.

6. Above the color selection bar you see a bracket (see fig. 12.4). You use this bar to divide the gradient into separate segments so you can add different colors along the selection bar. Slide the bracket so it encompasses only half of the color selection, then select a new color—let's use a bright yellow/orange color. This will give more of the effect of light streaming across the image.

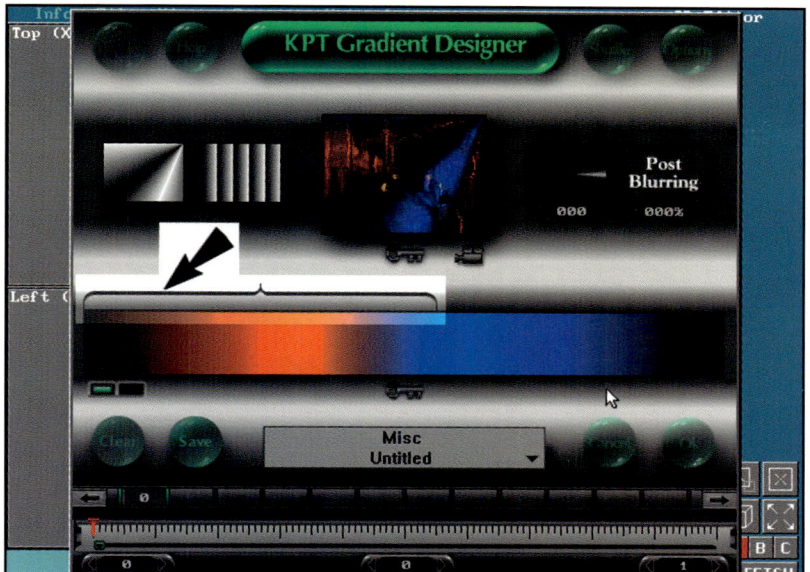

Figure 12.4
Gradient Designer's moveable bracket to divide color selection.

7. After you make a color selection, click on the preview window with mouse button 2 (the right button for right-handers), and drag a bounding box out to full screen so you can preview the image. Press Esc to return to the Gradient Designer.

8. Now fine tune your image. To the right of the preview window is the Direction Control box. Moving the mouse in this box enables you to control the direction or angle of the Radial Sweep, which enables you to control dark and light hues on top of the image. Also to the right of the Direction Control box is the Post Blurring control. I use blurring to soften the hit between the two gradient colors I select. Generally a numeric value of **20** works well.

9. Save the file as **TEMP02.GRD**.

The Gradient Designer works best when you combine different gradient color effects with a single backdrop. I have supplied four levels, from LEVEL000.GRD to LEVEL003.GRD. You can access the demo files by clicking in the Preset Menu box (see fig. 12.5). After you review all four levels, you can see how I have made several changes to each—moving the radial sweep, adding new colors, working with opacity, and changing the blur features. You can review all your changes nearly in real time, thanks to the real-time preview window.

Figure 12.5
Gradient Designer's load Preset Menu.

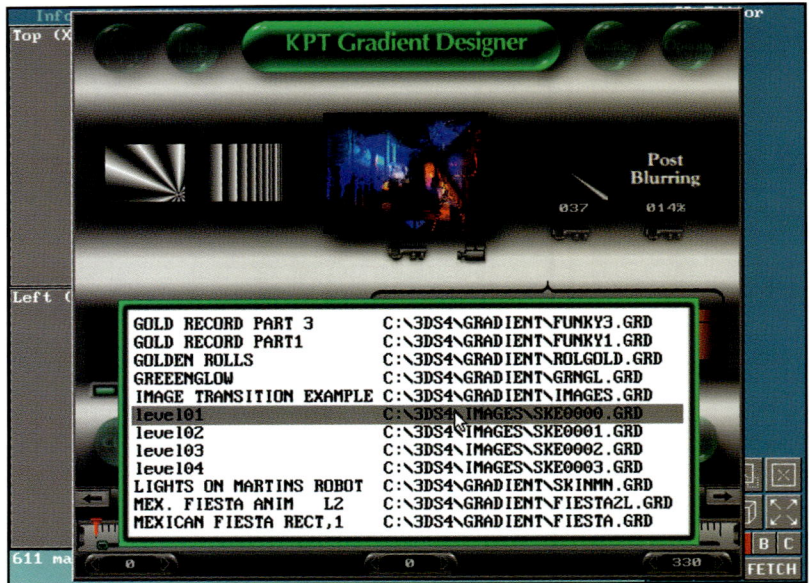

Remember to save each major change you do with a new file name and reload it as the new backdrop. I would keep the Procedural Blend selection active as it should not washout the image.

You now are almost ready to add the composite of the lightning bolt. When you save a GRD file, you are actually saving a set of parameters created in the gradient design process. Upon rendering, 3D Studio uses another IPAS routine known as BXP (Bitmap External Process) to interpret the GRD file and render your design to a predetermined resolution.

10. To use Video Post from the Keyframer, go to Render Video Post and select a viewport.

11. In the Video Post dialog box, select the Add button, then click underneath the word Queue in the blue column area. This creates a generic Video Post queue entry called KF Scene. Next, select the Edit button and click on the KF Scene queue entry to bring up the Queue Parameters dialog box. Select the Bitmap button, then click on the square next to the Bitmap button to select your gradient design (GRD) file. You will also need to click on the *.* file button to see the *.GRD file. Select level003.grd, located on the CD-ROM or in your Gradient directory, then click OK.

12. Click on OK again in the Queue Entry dialog box, which you use to select and load grid files into the queue.

13. You now want to add your composite of the lightning bolt. In the Video Post dialog box, select the Add button, then click underneath the word Queue in the blue column area. Next, select the Edit button and click on the second line in the KF Scene queue entry to bring up the Queue Parameters dialog box. Select the Bitmap button, then click on the square next to the Bitmap button to select your lightning bolt image LIGHTBLT.TGA from the CD-ROM, then click OK.

14. After you load the lightning bolt image into the second line of the queue, click on the Alpha window beside LIGHTBT.TGA. The Alpha dialog box appears.

15. Input the Alpha information you need to composite the image correctly. Select Queue RGB (see fig. 12.6), make sure Intensity is selected, and leave everything else the same. Click on OK to exit.

    Click on Render to see your image.

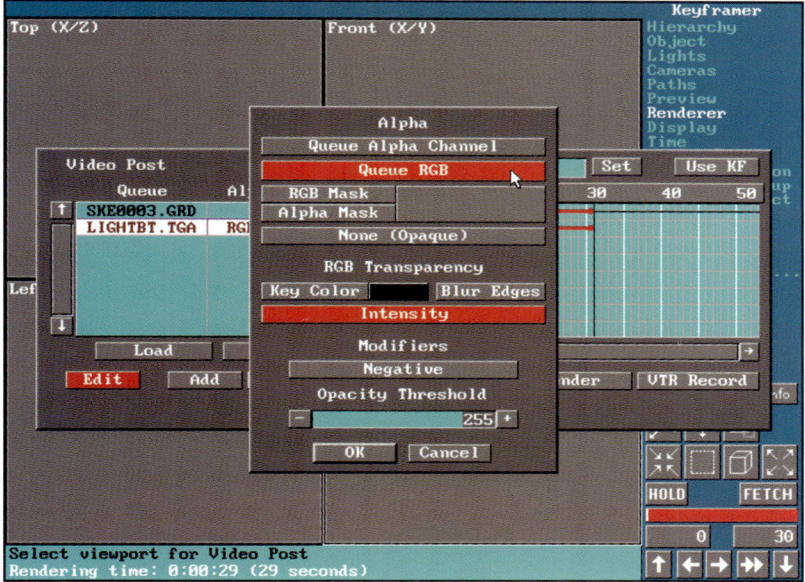

Figure 12.6
3D Studio's composite control window.

Conclusion

Artists need to be familiar with many 3D and 2D tools in order accomplish artwork that has a sense of quality and interest. Too many times, we do not use 2D art programs because we are not familiar with the tools or we have the impression that, unless it is 3D, it is not powerful.

You have taken a somewhat dull-looking image and used the Gradient Designer to add some very interesting lighting effects. You have done this by building up *.GRD files, loading the files as a new backdrop, and adding to this by changing colors and settings. You also have composited a lightning bolt onto the image to add more dramatic effect.

After you save the final image, you can load it into Photoshop and add lens flares and fog. Or try using LEVEL003.GRD as a bitmap in the Material Editor, saving it as a new material and mapping on one of your objects. Also, you could make animations of the Radial Sweep by making key frames in the Gradient Designer, saving out the *.GRD file, and loading the file as a backdrop in 3D Studio's Keyframer.

Combining 2D and 3D effects provides that sought after Hollywood visual effect look and adds more interest visually to your artwork.

Organic Modeling with Metaballs

Effect 13

by Kyle McKisic
Burke, Virginia

Equipment and Software Used

- Pentium 90 with 128 MB RAM
- 3D Studio Release 4
- Schreiber Instruments MetaREYES Metaballs or Digimation's Metaballs Modeler
- KUB's The Script Extensions (TSE)
- Digimation's Bones Pro 1.5

Artist Biography

Kyle McKisic is an undergraduate student at The Ohio State University. First introduced to 3D Studio while still in high school, Kyle began working on animation for multimedia products in the summer immediately following his graduation. He has since contributed graphics and animation to 13 different titles published on Philips CD-I, PC CD-ROM, and Mac CD-ROM. Kyle is a contributing writer for *Planet Studio*, has been published in *Computer Graphics World*, and was the only student to have animation featured in Autodesk's 1994 SIGGRAPH reel. He is a very active member of CompuServe's AAMEDIA forum and can be reached at 75542.363@compuserve.com.

Effect Overview

Modeling and animation programs are inherently adept at making cubes, spheres, cylinders, and other objects easily created using mathematical conventions. But organic models such as people, animals, and alien monsters become a little trickier. This chapter examines constructing two different characters, which you use metaballs to model, employing a slightly different method for each.

Metaballs modeling is a process by which you create reference objects, or spheres, that the computer interprets to form one smooth geometric mesh. You never render these spheres; you use them only as a means to create the rendered geometry. The advantage of using reference objects rather than some conventional modeling processes is that it enables you to create seamless, organic forms with relative ease.

You can use metaballs technology in several different ways. In the 3D Editor, you can use it to create a single, static mesh that you can scale, rotate, and squash just like a regular mesh object. You also can use it to animate reference spheres in the Keyframer and have metaballs modeling create a new mesh for each frame of the animation to yield an effect that resembles the way liquid mercury reacts. This chapter deals only with creating a static mesh as a means for character generation.

NOTE: Using metaballs as a modeling technique will give you single element, fully welded surfaces. Therefore, Digimation's Bones Pro is needed to articulate the mesh object.

Each metaballs program offers the capability to assign various degrees of positive or negative fusion values to its reference spheres. Positive values cause metaballs to join together when they get close, whereas negative fusion values cause a dent or hole in the resulting mesh object. Both programs (MetaREYES Metaballs and Digimation's Metaballs Modeler) use a system of object colors to let you easily see the difference between the various fusion values.

NOTE: Whereas the created surface tends to wrap around the outside of the positive reference spheres, it does not wrap around the negative spheres. Instead, the surface will tend to pass "inside" the negative spheres, or between the negative spheres and the positive ones. This is how negative spheres are used—to influence the geometry created over the positive spheres, and to create definite concavities beneath the negative spheres.

Table 13.1 presents the color values the MetaREYES modeler uses to define its fusion values.

Table 13.1	MetaREYES Metaballs Fusion Color Assignments	
Color	Color Numbers	
	Positive Fusion	Negative Fusion
Soft	6	11
Medium Soft	17	14
Medium Hard	25	27
Hard	37	45

Soft color values cause a smoother resultant metaball mesh, with very few creases or definite edges, whereas harder color values cause the mesh to follow the form of the reference spheres more closely, often creating harder edges.

Table 13.2 shows you the default color values the Metaball Modeler uses to define *its* fusion values.

Table 13.2	Metaball Modeler Default Fusion Color Assignments	
Color	Color Numbers	
	Positive Fusion	Negative Fusion
Soft	31	15
Medium Soft	27	11
Medium Hard	23	7
Hard	19	3

During the exercises for this chapter, you use the MetaREYES color set for the reference spheres. Digimation's Metaball Modeler uses a configuration file named BLOB.SET, located in the 3D Studio home directory. This file enables you to change the color values it uses. You can load BLOB.SET in a text editor and change the color values under the Color Set heading.

TIP: The level of detail that you use for a reference sphere doesn't matter. You use each sphere only for reference data; the modeler only needs to find the sphere's center point and radius. So, a reference sphere that has 100 segments versus one that has 10 or 8 segments yields the same results.

It is important to understand how each modeler determines the detail level of the mesh created over and around the reference spheres, and how the available controls affect the detail level.

★ MetaREYES generates its geometry based on the size, in units, of your reference spheres. The values on the detail slider bar represent tenths of a unit. So with a detail value of 100, for example, the modeler would create a mesh with polygons that measure 10 units in size.

★ Digimation's Metaball Modeler generates its geometry based on the number of detail sections you want to create over the object. When you have a group of reference spheres, for example, the program creates a bounding box around the extents of all the spheres. Then it divides each side into the number of sections that you specify through the user interface and uses the size of the sections to create faces over the spheres. This process doesn't depend on the size, in units of your spheres, because the detail setting is based on a proportion of your object.

Procedure: Character 1

Before we get started on the first character, you need to understand how Bones Pro works and why you need to keep the animation process in mind as you model. Bones Pro is a skeletal deformation program. Skeletal deformation is a tool that enables you to animate lower-detail reference objects, or "bones," to influence a much higher-resolution mesh object. As you can imagine, each bone has a certain influence over vertices in the mesh object. Because of these influences, it is best to create your mesh in a very open stance, or as extended as possible, so that your bone influences will affect only the areas you want.

Imagine creating a human character with its arms hanging down by its sides. You would have bones in both the arms and legs, and because their influences would be very close or overlapping, you would likely run into problems when you moved either of them, as they would move vertices in the other part of the mesh. When you moved the arm, part of the leg would travel with it! So, with this in mind, let's get on to our first character—which, I might add, is much simpler than what was just discussed because it doesn't have any arms or legs.

Creating the Mesh Object

Because this chapter deals with two modelers that are very similar in form and function but differ significantly in the specifics, each step is split into two substeps: one for each modeler. Each substep is labeled FUSION or BLOB, as you will either be using FUSION.PXP or BLOB.PXP.

1. Choose **File/Load** from the menu and load the metaballs source file BMONS_1.3DS (see fig 13.1).

2. Run the Metaballs plug-in program you have—FUSION.PXP or BLOB.PXP. You can access PXP IPAS routines by selecting the **PXP Loader** from the **Program** menu or by pressing F12.

Figure 13.1
The metaball reference spheres that will make the creature. Note the extended posture of the character, keeping Bones Pro animation in mind.

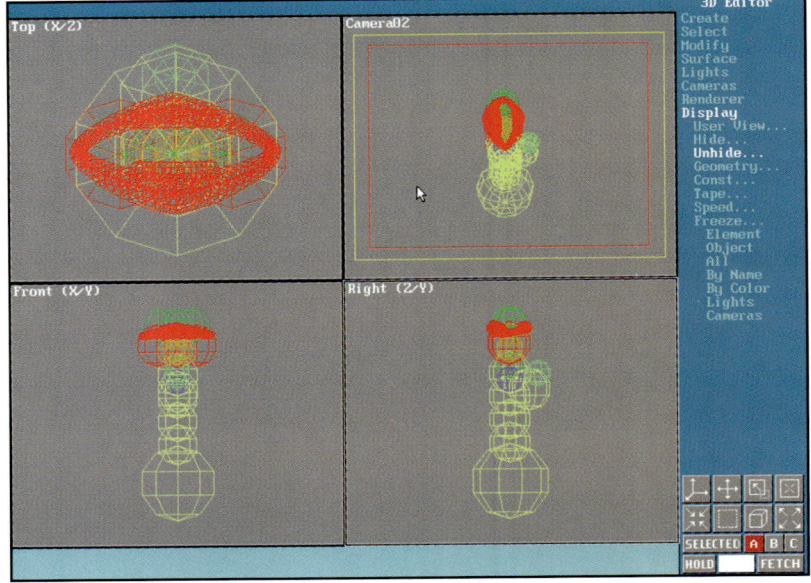

3a. FUSION. In the Grouping Options portion of the dialog box, choose ALL GROUP, and set the Polygon Size slider to 80. Enter the name **BMONS** in the Mesh Name field in the Generation Parameters dialog box (see fig 13.2).

Figure 13.2
The MetaREYES Metaballs 2.0 dialog box. Note the Polygon Size slider bar.

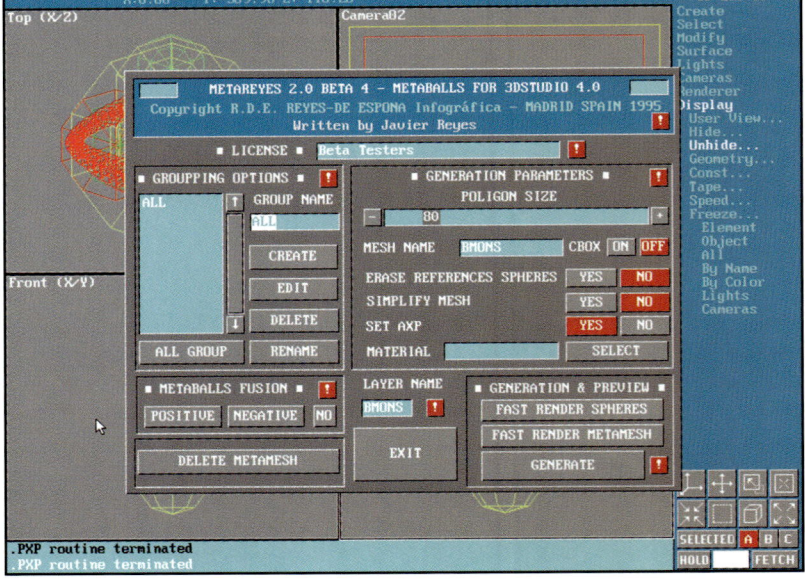

3b. BLOB. Set the Source Prefix to BMONS, the Threshold Level to 30, and the Detail Level to 50. Set the Primary Reference Object to BMONS0000 (see fig 13.3).

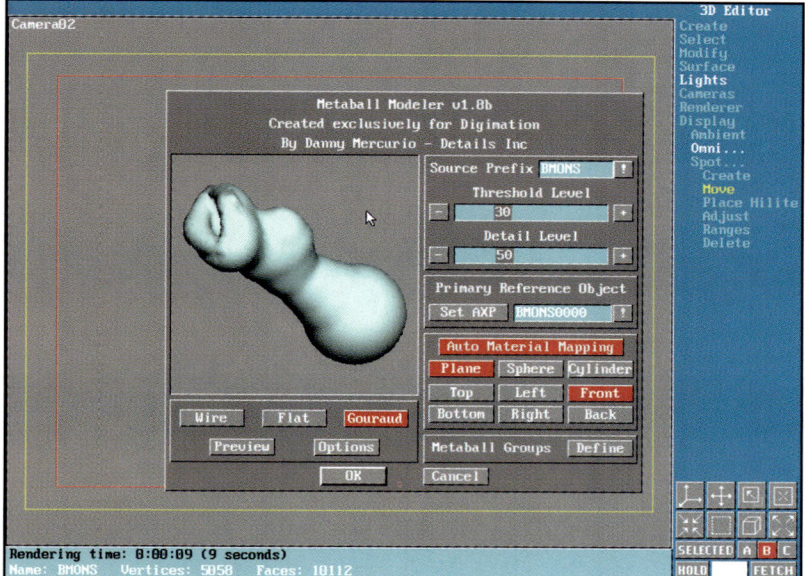

Figure 13.3
Digimation's Metaball Modeler dialog box. Note the large preview window and the Threshold Level and Detail Level parameters.

4a. FUSION. Choose Generate to create the mesh object.

4b. BLOB. Choose OK to create the mesh object.

> **TIP:** Both MetaREYES and Digimation's Metaballs Modeler enable you to preview the mesh before you write it out to the 3D Editor, which can prove quite helpful when you test the mesh's detail levels.

Processing the Mesh Object

SMOOTH.PXP is an IPAS plug-in included with Digimation's Bones Pro 1.5. Smooth enables you to process your mesh object so it works better with Bones Pro deformation, eliminating hard edges and keeping the polygons in the mesh uniform. And, it's especially useful for dealing with Metaball mesh objects.

1. Use the **PXP Loader** from the **Program** menu to run SMOOTH.PXP, or press F12 and select Smooth from the menu.

2. Click on BMONS to bring up the SMOOTH interface.

3. Choose Smooth from the menu and set the Tension to 2. Choose Do.

4. Choose Save&Exit to make the changes to your mesh.

You can see the difference Smooth makes in your mesh (see figs. 13.4 and 13.5).

Figure 13.4
The mesh before smoothing. Notice how you can see the hard polygon edges in the area of the mouth.

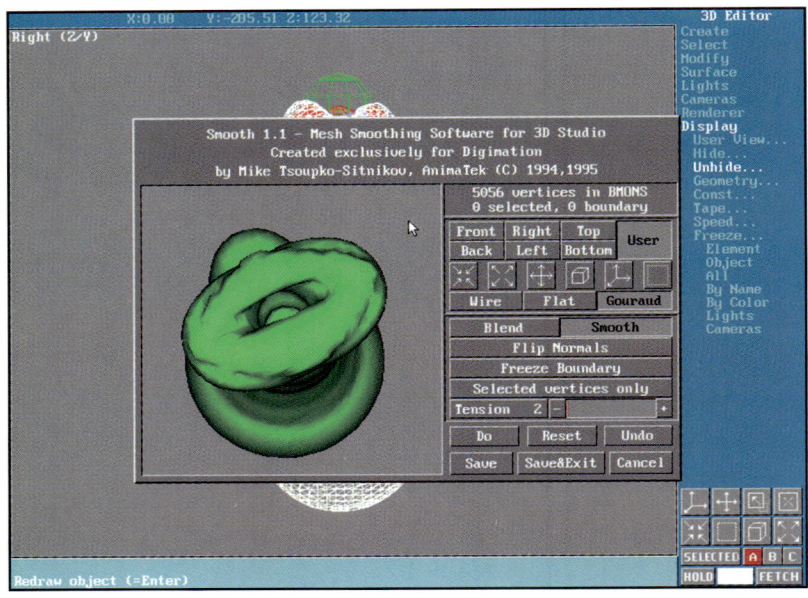

Figure 13.5
The mesh after smoothing. No edges!

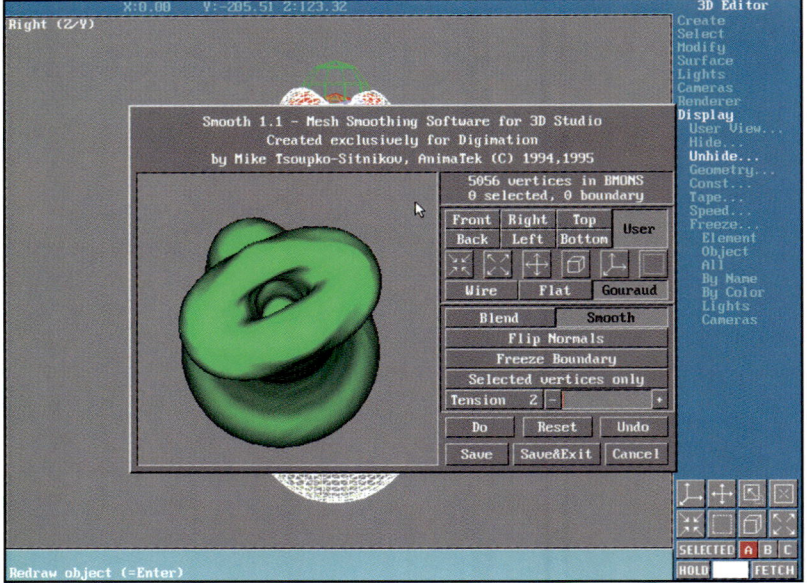

After you generate the mesh object, you can add the organic materials that bring it to life.

1. Go into the Materials Editor by pressing F5.

2. Add the <*n*:\METACHAR\MAPS> directory to your map paths by pressing * on the keyboard and selecting Map Paths from the dialog box.

3. Choose **File** then **Load** to load the material library METAMONS.MLI from the CD-ROM. The material library is located in <*n*:\METACHAR\MATLIBS> where *n* is the letter of your CD-ROM drive.

When 3D Studio renders an object whose material contains a bump map, it inverts the values of the bump map on the polygons that lie on the opposite side of the object from which the mapping coordinates were applied. One way to solve this potential problem is to select all those polygons that lie on the opposite side of the mesh, create a new material identical to the original, invert its bump map, and apply the material to the set of faces. For a simple object with uniform polygons, such as a sphere or a cylinder, you can do this with relative ease—just select the polygons on the opposite side. But when you deal with a mesh similar to our character, you face a much more difficult situation. The Script Extensions (TSE) from KUB, however, offers a solution. A freeware script, named SELECT.P3D, enables you to select polygons from a mesh based on their orientation or the vector direction of their normals.

1. Go into the 3D Editor by pressing F3 and use the **PXP Loader** from the **Program** menu to run SCRIPT.PXP, or press F12 and select SCRIPT from the menu (see fig 13.6).

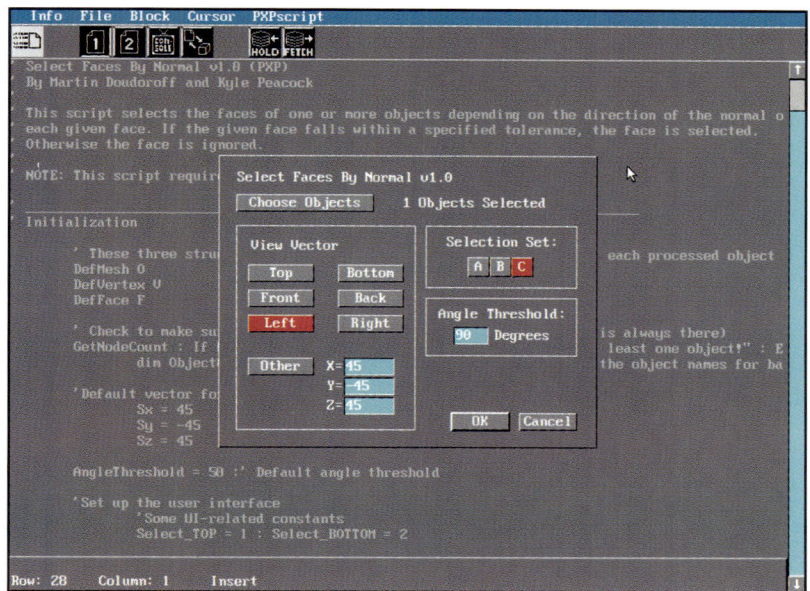

Figure 13.6
The Script Extensions, running SELECT.P3D. Notice the selection set variables where you can specify whether you want the selected set of polygons to be in the A, B, or C selection set in the 3D Editor.

Effect 13: Organic Modeling with Metaballs

2. Choose **File/Load** to load SELECT.P3D.

3. Press F1 to run the script.

4. Choose Choose Objects and select the object BMONS from the list. Choose OK.

5. Choose Left as the View Vector and change the Angle Threshold Value to 90 degrees. Choose OK to select the faces.

6. Exit TSE and return to the 3D Editor.

Now that you have a properly selected set of faces (see fig 13.7), you need to apply mapping coordinates and materials to the object.

Figure 13.7
See how complex the selection set is after selecting the polygons?

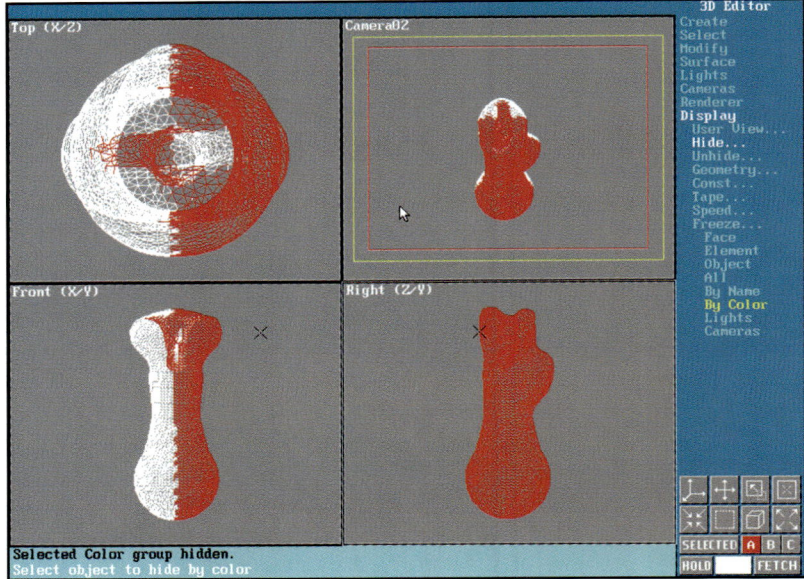

Applying Mapping Coordinates and Materials

1. In the Materials Editor, press G and select BMONS1 POS from the dialog box. Render the sample, and then select **Put the Material to Current** from the **Material** pull-down menu.

2. Go back to the 3D Editor by pressing F3 and select **Surface/Material/Apply/Face**. Press the spacebar and click in the active viewport.

3. Choose the material BMONS1 POS and apply it to the selected set of faces by selecting **Surface/Materials/Apply/Face**, pressing the spacebar, and clicking in an active viewport.

4. Hide all the objects in your scene except BMONS, and choose **Select/Invert**.

5. Choose the material BMONS1 NEG from the library and apply it to the selected set of faces.

6. Look at the mesh in the Left viewport and display the geometry in box mode by pressing Alt+B.

7. Choose **Surface/Mapping/Type** and make sure that PLANAR is active.

8. Choose **Surface/Mapping/Adjust/Region Fit** and click in the Left viewport on the upper left corner of the object BMONS; then drag down to the lower right corner and click, defining an area for the mapping coordinates.

9. Choose **Surface/Mapping/Apply/Object** and click on the object BMONS.

Now that you have created the basic body mesh, go ahead and add some of the extras that help bring your character to life.

1. Choose **Display/Unhide/By Name** and select **teeth/eye** from the list.

2. Choose **Create/Object/Attach**, choose **teeth/eye,** and choose BMONS.

You might be wondering why you had to use **Create/Object/Attach** rather than **Create/Object/Boolean**. If you perform a Boolean operation between two objects, they weld together and lose the mapping coordinates. If you attach an object to another, the attached object becomes an element and still can carry its own set of mapping coordinates, which is what you want because the eyes and teeth have their own set of mapping coordinates, separate from the body.

Now, your mesh is done and ready to render. Choose **File/Save** in the File menu and save your mesh to the hard drive.

Introducing Snapshot Modeling

Now that you have created a fairly simple model, you are ready to move on to another design that utilizes the Snapshot command in the Keyframer to help you generate reference spheres. The Snapshot command lets you animate an object in the Keyframer, then create one or more instance objects at any frame during your animation. You can create single objects of many objects over a range of frames. The easiest way to understand the Snapshot command is to see it in action.

1. Choose **File/Load** and load the file SNAPSHOT.3DS from the CD-ROM.

2. Enter the Keyframer by pressing F4 and drag the frame slider at the bottom of the screen back and forth so you can see how the sphere moves and scales at the same time.

3. Choose **Object/Snapshot** from the menu.

4. Choose the sphere; a dialog box pops up.

5. Choose Range, and set the number of copies to 30. Click on OK.

Note how it creates many uniformly spaced copies of the object that carry with them the position and scale of the object at each frame. This built-in tool enables you, as a metaballs modeler, to create very complex, freeform shapes with relative ease.

NOTE: When you create Snapshot copies of your objects, you are **allowed to specify more copies than you have frames. Snapshot simply creates more interpolations along the path.**

Now, on to the next character.

Procedure: Character 2

1. Choose **File/Load** and load the file MONS2.3DS from the CD-ROM (see fig 13.8).

Figure 13.8
The creature's initial reference spheres. Note the animation paths that will be used to create snapshot instance objects.

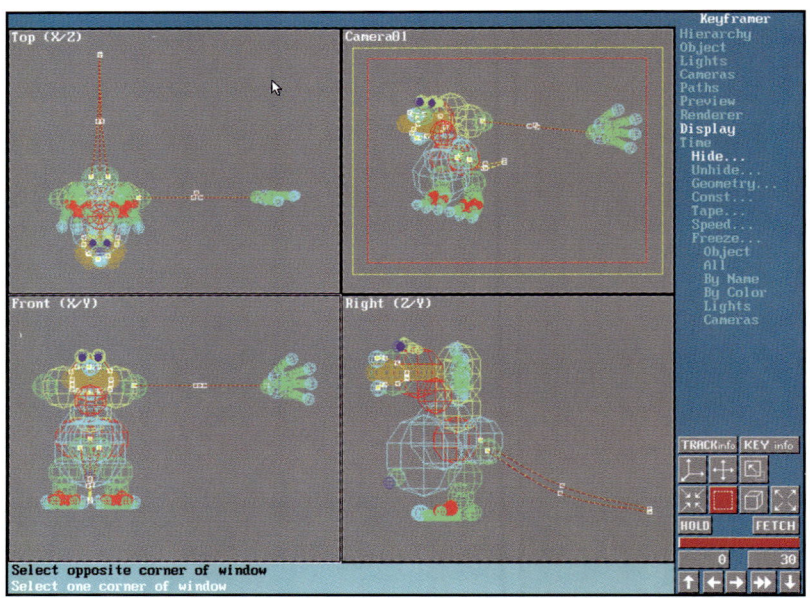

2. Enter the Keyframer. You see part of the character and some reference spheres' animated paths.

3. Choose **Object/Snapshot** from the menu at the right. Choose the sphere that is animated to connect the shoulder to the hand. Create 15 copies for this object.

4. Create snapshot copies for the following objects. You can select objects by their names by pressing H and choosing the object from the list.

Note that the range for each of these is 0–30 frames.

Object	# of Copies
LAYER10193	15
LAYER10507	30
LAYER10508	30
LAYER10509	30
LAYER10070	12
LAYER10071	12
LAYER10072	12
LAYER10073	12

After you create the snapshot copies, press F3 to return to the 3D Editor so you can add another arm.

1. Activate your Front viewport, choose **Select/Object/Quad**, and select the group of objects that defines the arm. Be careful not to select the yellow reference sphere that defines the shoulder (see fig 13.9).

2. Choose **Modify/Object/Mirror** and press the spacebar.

3. Activate the Front viewport and press Tab until your cursor changes to the horizontal arrows.

4. Hold down Shift and click in the viewport. Move the box so that its right side edge splits the shoulder reference sphere in half.

> **TIP:** Holding Shift down while performing a transformation on an object clones the object, which is easier and faster than going through the two-step process of creating the object copies and then mirroring them.

5. Choose **Select/None,** or press Alt+N on the keyboard.

Figure 13.9
The proper selection set for copying the arm reference spheres.

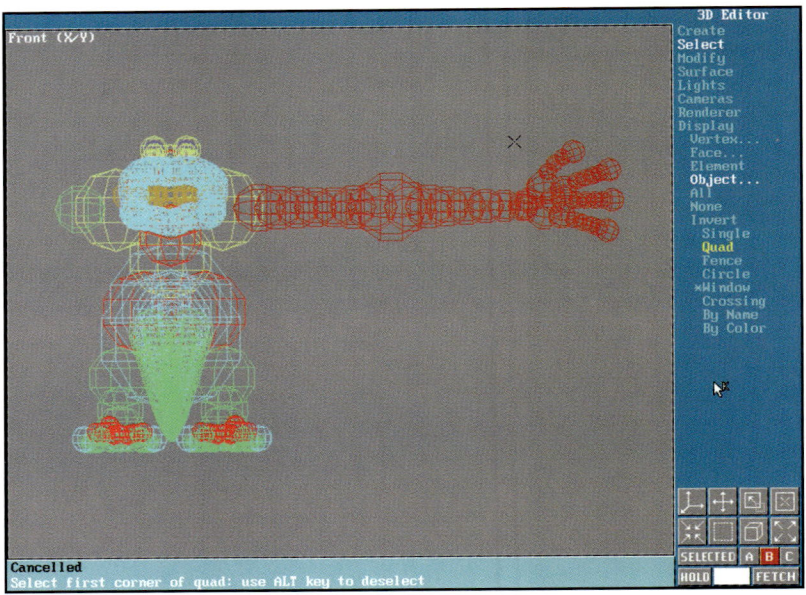

Generating the Mesh Object

Again, these steps are split up between the two modelers.

1. Run the Metaballs plug-in program you have. You can access PXP IPAS routines by selecting the **PXP Loader** from the **Program** menu or by pressing F12.

2a. FUSION. In the Grouping Options portion of the dialog, choose ALL GROUP, and set the Polygon Size slider to 16. Enter the name **BMONS2** in the Mesh Name field.

2b. BLOB. Set the Source Prefix to LAYER, the Threshold Level to 30, and the Detail level to 50. Set the Primary Reference Object to LAYER0000.

3a. FUSION. Choose Generate to create the mesh object.

3b. BLOB. Choose OK to create the mesh object.

Next, you will again use SMOOTH.PXP to eliminate hard edges and keep the polygons in the mesh uniform.

1. Use the **PXP Loader** from the **Program** menu, or press F12 and select Smooth from the menu to run SMOOTH.PXP (see fig. 13.10).

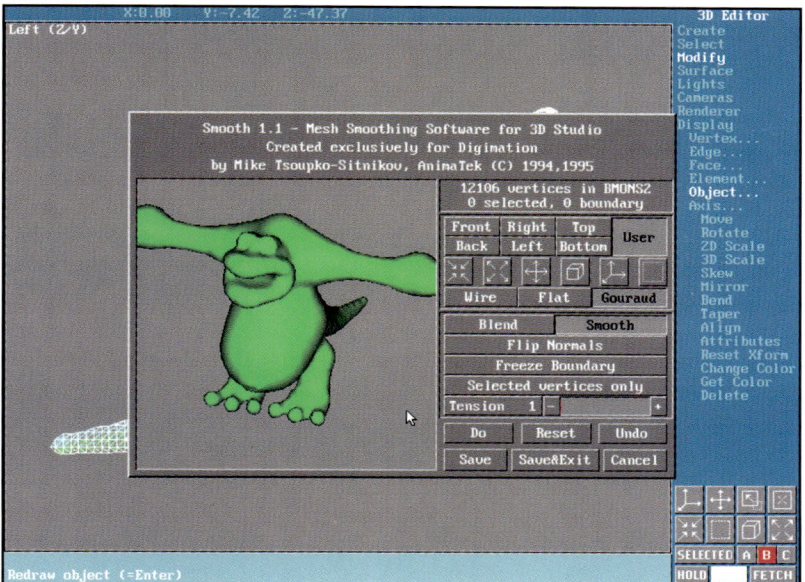

Figure 13.10
The mesh after smoothing. No hard edges!

2. Click on BMONS2 to bring up the SMOOTH interface.

3. Choose Smooth from the menu and set the tension to 2. Choose Do.

4. Choose Save&Exit to make the changes to your mesh.

We need to apply a reversed bump map to some faces of this mesh as well. Just as we selected the back surface faces for the other mesh, we'll do the same here.

Selecting the Polygons

1. Use the **PXP Loader** in the **Program** menu or press F12 and select SCRIPT from the menu to run SCRIPT.PXP.

2. Choose **File/Load** and load SELECT.P3D.

3. Press F1 to run the script.

4. Choose Choose Objects, and select the object BMONS2 from the list, then choose OK.

5. Choose Left as the View Vector and change the Angle Threshold Value to 90 degrees. Choose OK to select the faces.

6. Exit TSE and return to the 3D Editor.

Applying Mapping Coordinates and Materials

Now that you have a properly selected set of faces, you need to apply mapping coordinates and materials to the object.

1. Choose the material BMONS2 POS and apply it to the selected set of faces by choosing **Surface/Materials/Apply/Face**, pressing the spacebar, and clicking in an active viewport.

2. Hide all the objects in your scene except for BMONS2 and choose **Select/Invert**.

3. Choose the material BMONS 2 NEG from the library and apply it to the selected set of faces.

4. Look at the mesh in the Left viewport and press Alt+B to display the geometry in box mode.

5. Choose **Surface/Mapping/Type** and make sure that PLANAR is active.

6. Choose **Surface/Mapping/Adjust/Region Fit** and click in the Left viewport on the upper left corner of the object BMONS, then drag down to the lower right corner and click, defining an area for the mapping coordinates.

7. Choose **Surface/Mapping/Apply/Object** and click on the object BMONS.

8. Hide all the objects except for BMONS2 and choose **Select/Invert** to invert your selection set.

9. Choose the material BMONS 2 POS from the library and apply it to the selected set of faces.

Now that you have the basic body mesh created, go ahead and add some of the extras that help bring the character to life.

1. Choose **Display/Unhide/By Name** and select **teeth/eyes** from the list.

2. Choose **Create/Object/Attach**, choose **teeth/eyes,** and choose BMONS2.

Conclusion

When you pursue your own modeling tasks, keep in mind that metaballs is a modeling and animation tool, very similar in many respects to using a B-spline modeler or the 2D Shaper and 3D Lofter to create a mesh object. Metaballs is not the end-all solution to all your needs, but used in proper conjunction with other modeling and animation tools, it can yield some amazing results.

The most important aspect of any modeling process is to understand what is really going on. Try to understand how a certain process affects the geometry. Ask yourself what the program is really doing, not what the program is intended to do or seems to do. Only when you understand a routine or tool at the base level does the true power come to you. Take a paper clip for instance. How many times have you bent it out of shape to use it for something besides holding paper together? Well, once you bend the paper clip, it becomes a piece of wire metal—a *tool*. Once you see past what the tool is meant to do, it opens doors to techniques you otherwise could never dream of.

Appendix

Textures on the CD-ROM—Maps and AniMaps

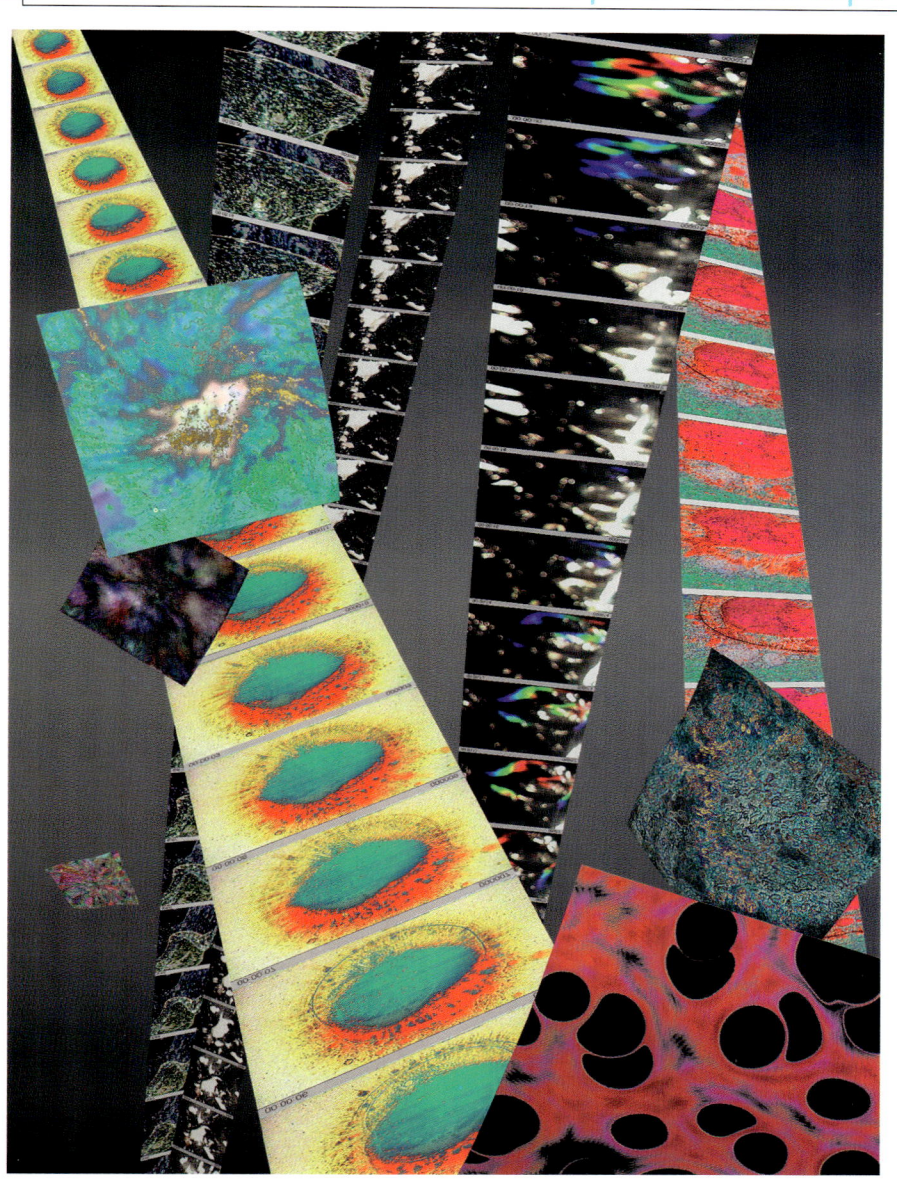

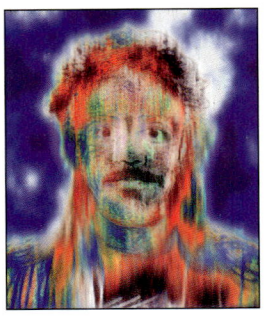

by Tim Forcade
Lawrence, Kansas

Equipment and Software Used

- LANtastic networked IBM PC and Macintosh computers
- Panasonic S-VHS camcorder
- Macintosh ColorOne Scanner
- VideoVision Studio
- Adobe Photoshop
- Kai's Power Tools
- Aldus Gallery Effects
- Xaos Paint Alchemy
- 3D Studio Release 4.0
- Animator Pro
- Adobe Premiere 4.0
- DeBabelizer
- Image Alchemy

Artist Biography

Building on an education in traditional fine arts that stressed drawing, painting, sculpture, and graphic design, Tim Forcade's artwork has advanced through optical, kinetic, and digital electronic media. This has resulted in numerous works utilizing photography, electronics, and video as well as the invention of electronic image processing systems of his own design.

Concurrent with his art work, Tim has over two decades of practice as a commercial artist, designer, and photographer. In 1978, Tim formed Forcade & Associates as a graphic resource to the commercial and professional communities. His project experience extends from illustration and publication design, through photography and 3D visualization, to computer animation & multimedia.

Tim's work has been exhibited in the U.S., Canada, Europe, and Japan. He has written and presented extensively on the subjects of applied 2D and 3D computer graphics and animation. He is a contributing editor to *Computer Graphics World* and *Computer Artist* magazines and is the author of the book *3D Studio IPAS Plug-in Reference* from New Riders Publishing. He can be reached via Compuserve at 72007,2742 or via Internet at tforcade@falcon.cc.ukans.edu

Working with Tim at Forcade & Associates is Terry Gilbert and Guy Stephens (see above group portrait: rastermonkey.tractorcity2) who provided invaluable assistance to Tim in creating these maps.

Overview

For a number of years as a painter, I worked long hours in the studio creating monumental abstract canvases in mixed media, including charcoal, oil, collage, enamel, and encaustic. The media were applied to stretched canvases and paper using a combination of application techniques ranging from carefully drawn or brushed to thrown, dripped, rolled, and splattered. The results were paintings that combined two-dimensional geometric and organic forms into eccentric pictures of three-dimensional images and patterns.

During that time, I also did a considerable amount of experimenting with mixed media including electronics, kinetics, and projected light. This included some travel around the U.S and Canada doing light shows for a rock/R&B band.

The light shows consisted of a pulsing montage of projected abstract patterns and images. I used an array of slide projectors, movie projectors, overhead projectors, and multiple strobe lights along with various homemade motorized gadgets and optical gizmos. I also used a number of techniques such as multicolored oil, water and chemical mixtures, miniature painted glass slides, and motorized projection screens to create a rhythmic accompaniment to the music.

Many of these techniques share compelling similarities with those we used to create the images and animations you will find on the CD-ROM. Here the brushes, overhead projectors, and liquid-filled bowls were enhanced with a video camera, scanner, non-linear editing software, and numerous image processing programs.

In spite of a reliance on applied automata such as arithmetic difference or edge detection filters, much of what went into these map images and animations was created using manual techniques—the computer-aided equivalent of brushing, dripping, and spattering.

The objective was to create rich and detailed images that rely as little as possible on real-world surfaces or objects. For those instances where a map was created using an object, any visual cues that might suggest the source object or objects have been minimized. We wanted to create a series of nonobjective images with the intent of exploring the use of color, texture, and space for optical special effects.

This is what this collection attempts to provide you—some unusual images and animation clips. These are static and moving pictures that are useful for either direct application as any of 3D Studio's maps, masks, or projection lights, or as points of departure to create your own custom effects. Furthermore, many of these will work well along with the special effects described elsewhere in this book.

The CD-ROM contains some 90 MB (107 images) of static maps and 150 MB (18 animations) of animated maps. The static maps are all 24-bit color or 8-bit grayscale at an average resolution of 600×600 (see table A.1).

Table A.1 A Complete List of the Static Maps Located on the CD-ROM in the \NRPMAPS Directory

File Name	Specifications	File Name	Specifications
BLOBBUMP.TIF	512x512 grayscale	CLOUDZ5.TIF	512x512 color
BLOBS.TIF	512x512 color	CLOUDZ6.TIF	512x512 color
CLOUDZ.TIF	512x512 color alpha	CRMWRM1.TIF	600x600 color
CLOUDZ2.TIF	512x512 color alpha	CRMWRM2.TIF	600x600 color
CLOUDZ4.TIF	512x512 color	CSMOOGE.TIF	512x512 color

File Name	Specifications	File Name	Specifications
CURDS.TIF	600x600 grayscale	**FACEPAT1.TIF**	380x380 color tile
EMBOSS.TIF	600x600 color tile alpha	**FACEPAT2.TIF**	290x290 color tile
EMBOSS2.TIF	600x600 color	**FACEPAT3.TIF**	380x380 color tile
EXPLO1.TIF	600x600 color	**FACEPAT4.TIF**	380x380 color
EXPLO2.TIF	600x600 grayscale	**FISH.TIF**	750x742 color tile alpha

continues

Table A.1 Continued

File Name	Specifications	File Name	Specifications
FISH2.TIF	750x742 color tile alpha	GLOBULAR.TIF	600x600 color
FISH3.TIF	750x742 color tile alpha	HELIUM1.TIF	600x600 color
FISH4.TIF	750x742 color tile alpha	HELIUM2.TIF	600x600 color
FISH5.TIF	750x742 grayscale tile	HELIUM3.TIF	600x600 color
FLOWER1.TIF	600x600 color	JUPITER1.TIF	600x600 color

File Name	Specifications	File Name	Specifications
JUPITER2.TIF	600x600 color	**LINES.TIF**	512x512 color
JUPITER3.TIF	600x600 color	**LINES2.TIF**	512x512 color
JUPITER5.TIF	600x600 color	**LINES3.TIF**	512x512 color
JUPITER6.TIF	600x600 color	**LOOPS01.TIF**	600x600 color
KELPOID.TIF	600x600 color	**MARSFACE.TIF**	300x300 grayscale tile

continues

Table A.1 Continued

File Name	Specifications	File Name	Specifications
MURKY1.TIF	600x600 color tile	NETCOLOR.TIF	600x600 color alpha
MURKY2.TIF	600x600 color	NODULES1.TIF	600x600 color tile
NEBULA1.TIF	600x600 color	NODULES2.TIF	600x600 color tile
NEBULA2.TIF	600x600 color	NODULES3.TIF	600x600 color tile
NETBLUR.TIF	600x600 color alpha	NODULES4.TIF	600x600 color

File Name	Specifications	File Name	Specifications
OILY.TIF	512x512 color	**OILY6.TIF**	512x512 color
OILY2.TIF	512x512 color	**OILY7.TIF**	512x512 color
OILY3.TIF	512x512 color	**OILY8.TIF**	512x512 color
OILY4.TIF	512x512 color	**PANELS.TIF**	600x600 grayscale tile
OILY5.TIF	512x512 color	**PAPER.TIF**	600x600 color

continues

Table A.1 Continued

File Name	Specifications	File Name	Specifications
PAPER2.TIF	600x600 color	PLANET01.TIF	600x600 color alpha
PAPER3.TIF	600x600 color	PLANET02.TIF	600x600 color
PAT01.TIF	600x600 color tile	PLANETS1.TIF	600x600 color
PHOTO1.TIF	610x930 color alpha	RAW1.TIF	600x600 color
PHOTO2.TIF	836x610 color alpha	RAW2.TIF	600x600 color alpha

File Name	Specifications	File Name	Specifications
RAW3.TIF	600x600 color alpha	RIPPLES1.TIF	600x600 color
RAW4.TIF	600x600 grayscale	SAT01.TIF	600x600 color
RAW5.TIF	600x600 color	SAT02.TIF	600x600 color
RAW6.TIF	600x600 color	SAT03.TIF	600x600 color
RAW7.TIF	600x600 color	SAT04.TIF	600x600 color alpha

continues

Table A.1   Continued

File Name	Specifications	File Name	Specifications
SCRNCOLR.TIF	595x595 color alpha	SMOOGE2.TIF	512x512 color
SCRNMSK.TIF	595x595 grayscale	SMOOGE3.TIF	512x512 color
SCRTCH3.TIF	756x512 color	SMOOGE4.TIF	512x512 color
SEGMENT.TIF	600x600 color tile	SMOOGE5.TIF	512x512 color
SMOOGE.TIF	512x512 color	SMOOGE6.TIF	512x512 color

File Name	Specifications	File Name	Specifications
SPECS.TIF	600x600 grayscale	STREAKS.TIF	512x512 color
SPLATCLD.TIF	600x600 color alpha	SWIRL1.TIF	600x600 color tile alpha
SPLOTCH1.TIF	489x489 color	SWIRL2.TIF	600x600 grayscale tile
SPLOTCH2.TIF	489x489 color	SYMET1.TIF	600x600 color tile
SPLOTCH3.TIF	489x489 color	WATERY.TIF	512x512 color

continues

Table A.1 Continued

File Name	Specifications	File Name	Specifications
WATERY2.TIF	512x512 color alpha	YEL3MSK.TIF	756x512 grayscale tile
WATERY3.TIF	512x512 color alpha	YELPEEL3.TIF	756x512 color tile
WATERY4.TIF	512x512 color alpha		
WRMMASS.TIF	600x600 color		
WRMMSK1.TIF	600x600 grayscale		

Procedure

1. From either the 3D Editor or Keyframer, using **Renderer/View/Flic**, load CATALOG1.FLC from the \NRPMAPS directory on the CD-ROM. Press the spacebar immediately after clicking on the file name to stop the FLIC and display the first frame of the FLC file. Each frame of the FLIC displays 12 map images. The corresponding file name for each map is printed at the upper left of each sample image.

2. Press the right arrow to step through the FLC file and view the remaining images. Some of the images have three or more variations in characteristics such as the color palette. You can use any of the static maps in the Materials Editor as any map type or any mask. You can also use them as background images using **Renderer/Setup/Background** or projector spotlights.

> **NOTE:** If you intend to use a static map image directly off the CD-ROM, be sure to add \NRPMAPS to 3D Studio's Map Paths so 3D Studio can find the map images at render time.

The animated maps are 320×240, 24-bit JPEG or 400×400 FLIC format. There are two categories of animated maps (or animaps) on the CD-ROM: videotaped and constructed. The former originated as real-world phenomena that were first videotaped on location or in our studio, and then captured to a hard disk for editing and image processing. They are designed to be used with their accompanying IFL files as maps in 3D Studio's Materials Editor, as background sequences, or with projector spotlights for lighting effects. These maps average approximately 10 seconds or 300 frames each.

Examples of the video type include DEDHED\DED*.JPG, which depicts continuously varying liquid blobs, or BULBBLAP\BULB*.JPG, an exploding light bulb.

The constructed animaps were created as animations in 3D Studio and rendered to disk in FLIC format. These are designed primarily for use in transition effects or as wipes. However, they are also suitable for use as maps, masks, or in projector spotlights.

Examples of the constructed animaps include CHANGE\BATIK.FLC a color batik pattern transition or CHANGE\SPECS.FLC, a blob pattern transition. These animaps are mostly grayscale pattern transitions from black to white, also suitable for use anywhere you might use a static image map.

Each animated map is located in the directory listed in Table A.2 on the CD-ROM. For each videotaped animation map (AniMap Texture), you will find a corresponding IFL file and preview FLIC file in the same CD-ROM directory.

The IFL files are text files that list the file names of each JPG texture sequence. These IFL file names should be substituted for the file name of any background image or projector light image that you wish to use. This will automatically substitute each AniMap frame, in order, as that background or projected image is animated.

The FLIC files that accompany the JPEG AniMap Textures are provided at a lower resolution of 160×120. These files contain every frame of each AniMap sequence and, as such, are suitable for previews.

Table A.2 A Complete List of the Animated Maps on the CD-ROM in the \NRPMAPS Directory

File Name	Total Frames	Resolution	Directory	Description
AniMap Textures				
BULB*.JPG BULBLAP.IFL & .FLC	244	320×240	\NRPMAPS\BULBBLAP	exploding light bulb
DEDHED*.JPG DEDHED.IFL & .FLC	178	320×240	\NPRMAPS\DEDHED	psychedelic oil & dye
POUR*.JPG LIQUID.IFL & .FLC	238	320×240	\NPRMAPS\LIQUID	flowing viscous liquid

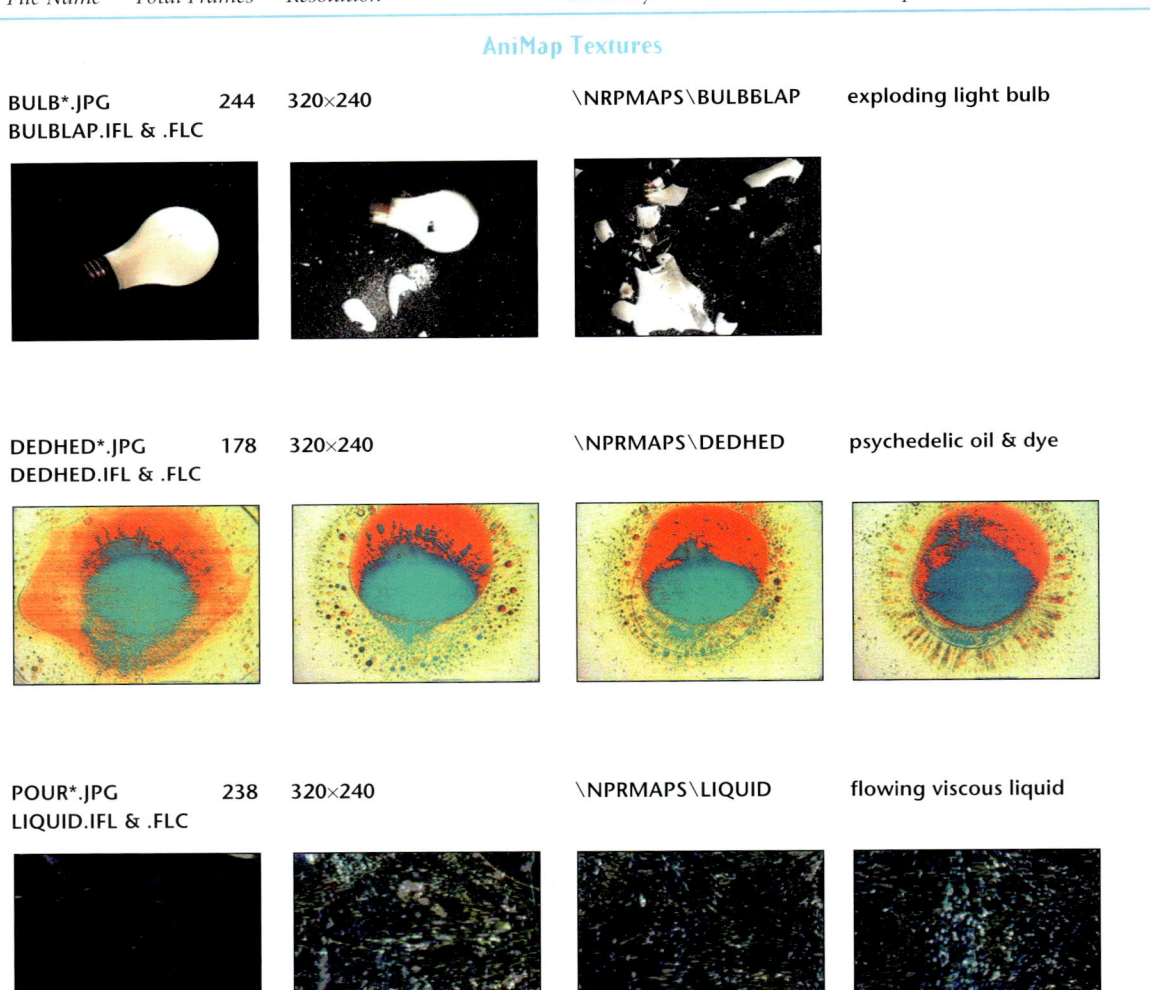

File Name	Total Frames	Resolution	Directory	Description
PLAS*.JPG PLAS.IFL & .FLC	421	320×240	\NPRMAPS\PLAS	shifting film
PLA*.JPG PLASTIC.IFL & .FLC	317	320×240	\NPRMAPS\PLASTIC	slatted shifting film
PSYC*.JPG PSYCHA.IFL & .FLC	741	320×240	\NPRMAPS\PSYCHA	more psychedelia
RBOW*.JPG RAINBOW.IFL & .FLC	314	320×240	\NPRMAPS\RAINBOW	shifting opticals

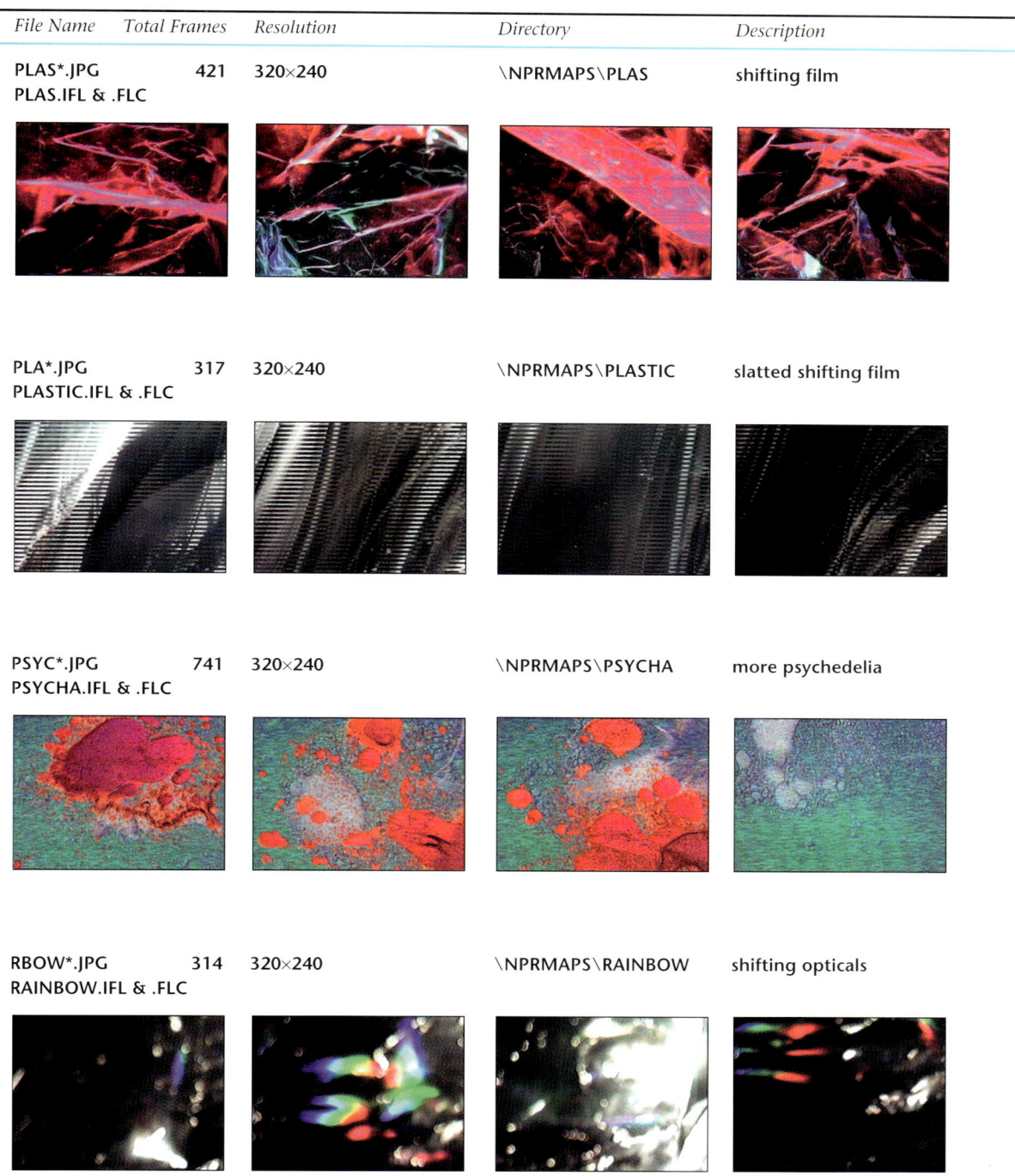

continues

Table A.2 Continued

File Name	Total Frames	Resolution	Directory	Description
SPTR*.JPG SPATR1.IFL & .FLC	276	320×240	\NPRMAPS\SPATR1	foamy spray
SPAT*.JPG SPATR2.IFL & .FLC	276	320×240	\NPRMAPS\SPATR2	processed spray
SYMT*.JPG SYMSPRAY.IFL & .FLC	267	320×240	\NPRMAPS\SYMSPRAY	symmetrical spray

AniMap Transitions & Wipes

File Name	Total Frames	Resolution	Directory	Description
BATIK.FLC	120	400×400	\NRPMAPS\CHANGE	expanding reticulation

246 3D Studio Hollywood and Gaming Effects

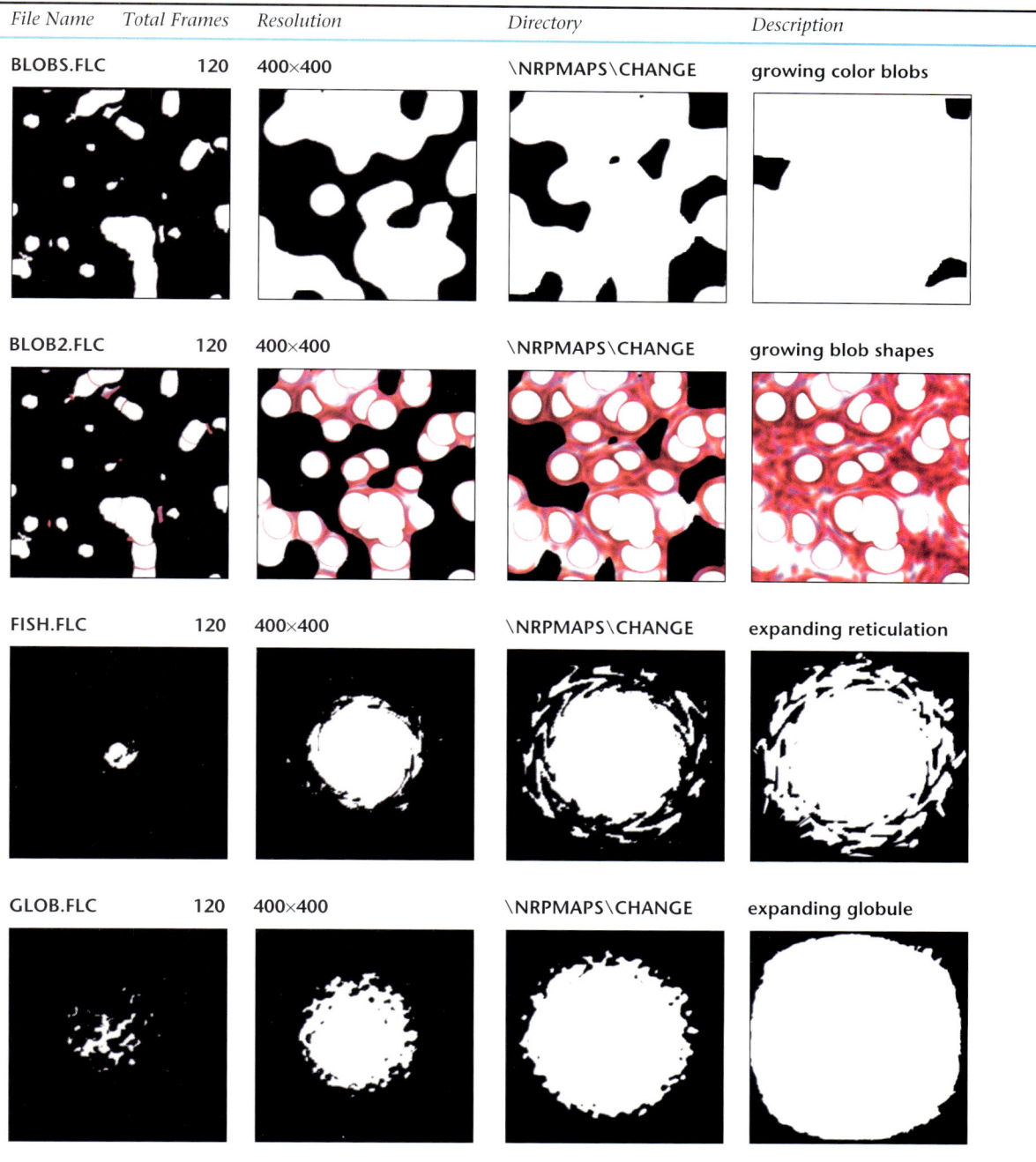

File Name	Total Frames	Resolution	Directory	Description
BLOBS.FLC	120	400×400	\NRPMAPS\CHANGE	growing color blobs
BLOB2.FLC	120	400×400	\NRPMAPS\CHANGE	growing blob shapes
FISH.FLC	120	400×400	\NRPMAPS\CHANGE	expanding reticulation
GLOB.FLC	120	400×400	\NRPMAPS\CHANGE	expanding globule

continues

Table A.2 Continued

File name	Total Frames	Resolution	Directory	Description
SPECS.FLC	120	400×400	\NRPMAPS\CHANGE	growing specs
STREAK.FLC	120	400×400	\NRPMAPS\CHANGE	growing streaks
SWIRL.FLC	120	400×400	\NRPMAPS\CHANGE	expanding reticulation

Procedure

1. From either the 3D Editor or Keyframer, choose **Renderer/View/Flic**, and load BULBBLAP.FLC from the \NRPMAPS\BULBBLAP directory on the CD-ROM. This will run the FLIC preview animation.

2. The BULBBLAP.FLC is provided as a quick reference to the higher resolution JPEG version located in the same directory. You can view each individual animation frame using **Renderer/View/Image**, changing to the animap directory you want and clicking on the frame number.

3. You can view any AniMap Transition or Wipe in the same way, with **Renderer/View/Flic**. In this case, however, you are viewing the finished form of the animation. All AniMap transitions and wipes are provided in FLIC format only.

Any of the animaps can be used in the Material Editor as any map or mask type to create animated materials. They can also be used as background images by choosing **Renderer/Setup/Background** dialog or using the animated map with projector spotlights.

> **NOTE:** If you use the animated maps directly off of the CD-ROM, be sure to add the \NRPMAPS to 3D Studio's Map Paths so 3D Studio can access these images and IFL files at render time.

Conclusion

As you would expect, the key to getting the most from these maps is taking the time to experiment with them. Although they are certainly suitable for use singly as texture or opacity maps, try various combinations of still maps or still and animation maps on the same material. Also try using the maps, particularly the animaps, as starting points to create unique moving textures with your paint or special effects programs.

Remember that editing the animation maps' IFL files in your text editor can produce some remarkable variations in the animaps. This technique makes it simple to produce ramps, rhythmic variations, reverses, and loops from those sequences.

Talk to Me

I am very curious to know what you think of these textures and animaps. Are they applicable and useful to you for your animations and illustrations? Is the subject matter useful? Would you like to see more explosive or gooey or spatter effects? Should they be softer or sharper? Do you want more color, less color, or maybe higher resolution? How about the proportion of static to moving maps—more static maps or more animaps? Do you prefer a wider variety of textures or "suites" of similar images that are tuned to each Material Editor map type?

Finally, I would like to know how you are using the textures and animaps on the *3D Studio Hollywood and Gaming Effects* CD-ROM or the previous textures and animaps that we did for either *3D Studio Special Effects* or *Inside 3D Studio* books. Please e-mail your comments or examples to me.

Thanks for your input and I hope you enjoy these images.

Index

SYMBOLS

2D Shaper commands
  Create
    N-gon/# Sides, 14, 151
    N-gon/Circular, 14
    Quad, 64
    Text, 189
  Display
    3D Display/Choose, 14
    3D Display/On, 14, 63
    Choose, 63
  Select/Polygon/Quad/*Window, 190
  Shape
    Assign, 83, 117-118
    Assign/None, 118
    Assign/Selected, 190
    Check, 190
    Steps, 189

3D Editor commands
  Cameras
    Adjust,Move,FOV.., 75
    Create, 191
  Create
    Box, 124
    Cylinder, 166, 179
    Element/Tessellate, 89
    Face/Detach/Selected, 193
    Lsphere, 166
    Object/Attach, 88, 121, 221, 226
    Object/Boolean, 221
    Object/Copy, 102-103
    Object/Get Shape, 14, 64
    Torus, 101
  Display
    Construction/Show, 153
    Freeze/By Name, 124
    Geometry/Box, 30
    Hide/All, 91
    Hide/By Name, 76
    Hide/Object, 86, 124
    Hide/Object/By Name, 86, 120
    Speed/By Name, 124
    Speed/Set Fast, 124
    Unhide/All, 69, 77
    Unhide/By Name, 77, 124, 221, 226
    Unhide/Object/By Name, 86, 92-93, 121

  Lights
    Omni, 192
    Spot/Create, 76-77, 178
  Modify
    Axis/Place, 36, 101, 193
    Axis/Show, 193
    Object/2D Scale, 15, 102-103, 156, 168
    Object/2D Scale/shift-select, 193-194
    Object/3D Scale, 102, 156
    Object/Attributes, 69, 75, 86, 88, 92, 122, 124, 182
    Object/Change Color, 104, 192, 194
    Object/Delete, 170
    Object/Mirror, 223
    Object/Move, 15, 102, 119, 166, 180, 192
    Object/Reset Xform, 14
    Object/Rotate, 14, 85, 88, 119
    Object/Taper, 179
    Vertex/3D Scale, 166
  Renderer
    Render View, 122
    View/Flic, 243, 248
  Select
    Face/Quad/*Window, 193
    Invert, 85, 221, 226
    None, 223
    Object/By Color, 105
    Object/By Name, 88, 119
    Object/Quad, 103, 223
    Vertex/Quad, 166
  Surface
    Apply/By Name, 93
    Mapping/Adjust, 101
    Mapping/Adjust/Acquire, 120
    Mapping/Adjust/Region Fit, 221, 226
    Mapping/Adjust/Scale, 14, 16, 68, 75, 181, 193
    Mapping/Apply, 193
    Mapping/Apply/Object, 75, 121, 181, 221, 226
    Mapping/Assign/Object, 101
    Mapping/Type, 101, 181, 193, 221, 226
    Mapping/Type/Cylindrical, 75, 120
    Mapping/Type/Planar, 14
    Mapping/Type/Spherical, 16
    Material/Apply/Face, 220, 226
    Material/Assign, 69, 155
    Material/Assign/By Name, 93
    Material/Assign/Object, 121, 181, 194
    Material/Choose, 69, 75, 93, 121, 181
    Material/Get Library, 93, 121
    Normals/Object Flip, 16

3D Lofter commands
    Objects
        Make, 84, 117-118, 191-192
        Preview, 117, 152
    Path
        2D Scale, 151
        Move Vertex, 152, 191-192
        Refine, 151
        Steps, 191
        SurfRev, 117
    Shapes
        Align, 117-118
        Center, 118
        Get/Shaper, 84, 117-118, 151, 190
        Rotate, 118
        Scale, 151

A

Alpha dialog box, 209
animated maps
    on CD-ROM, 243-249
    texture maps, 73-80
animated textures, 102-111, 188-197, 199
animation
    human/computer-character interaction effect, 124-144
    Inverse Kinematics (Muscle Bot effect), legs, 48-51
    keyframing test animations (Muscle Bot effect), 45-48
    lighting (Gizmo Lighting effect), 65-67
    particles, 83-86, 88-97
    Search Light effect, 197, 199
    Solar Flares effect, 23-24
    Warp Star Field effect, 170-172, 174
    Warp Tube effect, 155-160
APX stand-in objects (Tail of the Comet effect), 84-86, 88-91
arms (Muscle Bot effect), 34-36
autoscaling, Cylindrical mapping, 75
AVI files (exporting/editing) software requirements, 75
AXP Selector dialog box, 86

B

BATIK.FLC, 246
BLOB.PXP IPAS plug-in (Metaball Modeler), 215, 217, 224
BLOB2.FLC, 247
Blobbump.tif, 232
BLOBS.FLC, 247
Blobs.tif, 232
BMONS_1.3DS file, loading, 215
bodies (Muscle Bot effect), 30-33
bones (Muscle Bot effect)
    arms, 34-36
    bodies, 30-33
    heads, 37
    legs, 33-34
    linking, 43-44
    modification effects on bounding boxes, 30
    muscles, 38-39
    retaining bones, 40-42
    setting influence, 51-57
Bones Pro (Digimation)
    Human/Computer-Character Interaction effect, 122-124
    Muscle Bot effect, 29-30, 39, 42, 51-57
Bones Pro dialog box, 51-57, 143
bounding boxes
    attaching stand-in objects, 88
    modification effects of bones (Muscle Bot effect), 30
BRIGHT material, 21
BULB*.JPG, 244
BULBLAP.IFL & .FLC, 244
bump maps, 219

C

camera motion, 188-197, 199
Cameras commands
    Adjust,Move,FOV.., 75
    Create, 159, 191
Carter, David, 28
Chadwick, Eric, 6
Click on Object Name dialog box, 88
clones, 223
    geometry, 32
    Tail of the Comet effect, 84-85
CLOUD material, 21
CLOUD2 material, 21
clouds (Solar Flares effect), 9-13
Cloudz.tif, 232
Cloudz2.tif, 232
Cloudz4.tif, 232
Cloudz5.tif, 232
Cloudz6.tif, 232
color texture maps, 177-184
comet (Tail of the Comet effect), 92-94
commands
    Cameras
        Adjust,Move,FOV.., 75
        Create, 159, 191
    Create
        Box, 124
        Cylinder, 166, 179
        Element/Tessellate, 89
        Face/Detach/Selected, 193
        Gsphere, 9
        Lsphere, 166
        N-gon/# Sides, 14, 151
        N-gon/Circular, 14
        Object/Attach, 88, 121, 221, 226
        Object/Boolean, 221
        Object/Copy, 102-103
        Object/Get Shape, 14, 64

    Quad, 64
    Text, 189
    Torus, 101
Display
    3D Display, 14, 63
    Choose, 63
    Construction/Show, 8, 153
    Freeze, 124-125
    Geometry/Box, 30
    Hide, 159
    Hide/All, 91
    Hide/By Color, 108-110
    Hide/By Name, 76, 135, 197
    Hide/Object, 86, 124-125
    Hide/Object/By Name, 86, 120
    Speed, 124
    Unhide/All, 69, 77
    Unhide/By Color, 109
    Unhide/By Name, 77, 124, 128, 143, 221, 226
    Unhide/Object/By Name, 86, 92-93, 121
Edit (Photoshop 3.0), 67
File
    Clone (Fractal Design Painter), 144
    Clone Source (Fractal Design Painter), 144
    Load, 215, 222, 225
    Load Project, 73, 83, 116, 177
    New, 165
    Open, 65
    Open (Fractal Design Painter), 144
    Reset, 188
    Save, 221
Hierarchy
    Center Pivot, 16, 125
    Create Dummy, 45, 107, 156, 170
    Link, 16, 94, 107, 125, 171
    Object Pivot, 125
    Show Tree, 125
Info
    Configure, 18, 73, 154, 177, 204
    Scene Info, 51
Library
    Load Library, 18
    New, 165
Lights
    Omni, 192
    Spot/Create, 76-77, 178
Material
    Get from Scene, 74, 179
    Get Material, 75, 196
    Put To Current, 194-195, 220
Modify
    Axis/Place, 36, 101, 193
    Axis/Show, 193
    Object/2D Scale, 15, 102-103, 156, 168, 193-194
    Object/3D Scale, 9, 13, 102, 156
    Object/Attributes, 69, 75, 86, 88, 92, 122, 124, 182
    Object/Change Color, 104, 192, 194
    Object/Delete, 170
    Object/Mirror, 223
    Object/Move, 13, 15, 64, 102, 119, 166, 180, 192
    Object/Reset Xform, 14
    Object/Rotate, 14, 17, 85, 88, 119
    Object/Taper, 179
    Vertex/3D Scale, 166
Object
    Attributes, 51, 135, 143
    Morph, 199
    Move, 107, 109-110, 160, 173, 199
    Preview, 152
    Rotate, 109
    Rotate Abs., 79-80
    Snapshot, 222-223
    Tracks/Copy, 93
    Tracks/Loop, 48
Objects
    Make, 84, 117-118, 191-192
    Preview, 117
Options (KPT Gradient Designer), 204-206
Path
    2D Scale, 151
    Move Vertex, 152, 191-192
    Refine, 151
    Steps, 191
    SurfRev, 117
Preview/Make, 159
Program
    DOS Window, 18
    KXP Loader, 51
    PXP Loader, 215, 219, 224-225
Renderer
    Output/Coords, 96
    Render View, 13, 111, 122, 148, 184
    Setup/Background, 136, 147, 243, 249
    Setup/Configure, 10, 13
    Video Post, 24, 95, 97, 160
    View/Flic, 115, 243, 248
Select
    Face/Quad/*Window, 193
    Invert, 85, 221, 226
    None, 223
    Object/By Color, 105
    Object/By Name, 88, 119
    Object/Quad, 103, 223
    Polygon/Quad/*Window, 190
    Save Selection (Photoshop 3.0), 67
    Vertex/Quad, 166
Shape
    Assign, 83, 117-118
    Assign/None, 118
    Assign/Selected, 190
    Check, 190
    Steps, 189
Shapes
    Align, 117-118
    Center, 118
    Get/Shaper, 84, 117-118, 151, 190
    Rotate, 118
    Scale, 151
Surface
    Apply/By Name, 93

Mapping/Adjust, 101
Mapping/Adjust/Acquire, 120
Mapping/Adjust/Region Fit, 221, 226
Mapping/Adjust/Scale, 11, 14, 16, 68, 75, 181, 193
Mapping/Apply, 193
Mapping/Apply/Object, 75, 121, 181, 221, 226
Mapping/Assign/Object, 101
Mapping/Type, 101, 181, 193, 221, 226
Mapping/Type/Cylindrical, 75, 120
Mapping/Type/Planar, 11, 14
Mapping/Type/Spherical, 16
Material/Apply/Face, 220, 226
Material/Assign, 69, 155
Material/Assign/By Name, 93
Material/Assign/Object, 121, 181, 194
Material/Choose, 69, 75, 93, 121, 181
Material/Get Library, 74, 93, 121
Normals/Object Flip, 16

Time
    Define Segment, 17, 199
    Total, 198

Views
    Angle Snap, 14
    Drawing Aids, 188
    Unit Setup, 8

Window/Palettes/Show Layers (Photoshop 3.0), 66

Configuration dialog box, 154
Copy Tracks dialog box, 93
Create commands
    Box, 124
    Cylinder, 166, 179
    Element/Tessellate, 89
    Face/Detach/Selected, 193
    Gsphere, 9
    Lsphere, 166
    N-gon
        # Sides, 14, 151
        Circular, 14
    Object
        Attach, 88, 121, 221, 226
        Boolean, 221
        Copy, 102-103
        Get Shape, 14, 64
    Quad, 64
    Text, 189
    Torus, 101

Crmwrm1.tif, 232
Crmwrm2.tif, 232
Csmooge.tif, 232
Curds.tif, 233
cylinders, creating, 166-167
cylinrical mapping, autoscaling, 75

D

The Daedalus Encounter, see **Solar Flare effect**
DEDHED*.JPG, 244
DEDHED.IFL & .FLC, 244

Define Gradient Colors dialog box, 95, 161
dialog boxes
    Alpha, 209
    AXP Selector, 86
    Bones Pro, 51-57, 143
    Click on Object Name, 88
    Configuration, 154
    Copy Tracks, 93
    Define Gradient Colors, 95, 161
    Get Shape, 14
    Glow Filter, 95
    Key Info, 17, 158, 172
    Metaballs Modeler, 217
    MetaREYES Metaballs 2.0, 216
    Object Attachment Tree, 125
    Object Attributes, 124, 182
    Object Lofting Controls, 152-153
    Queue Entry, 95, 160-161, 208
    Queue Parameters, 208-209
    Scatter, 167-170
    Surface of Revolution, 117
    Track Info, 90-91, 156-157, 172, 174, 199
    Unhide, 86
    Video Post, 208-209
    Video Post Queue, 95-96

Digimation
    Bones Pro, 29-30, 39, 42, 51-57, 122-124
    Metaballs Modeler, 214-215, 217, 224

Disintegrate IPAS, 86, 88-91
Display commands
    3D Display, 14, 63
    Choose, 63
    Construction/Show, 8, 153
    Freeze, 124-125
    Geometry/Box, 30
    Hide, 159
        All, 91
        By Color, 108-110
        By Name, 76, 135, 197
        Object, 86, 120, 124-125
    Speed, 124
    Unhide
        All, 69, 77
        By Color, 109
        By Name, 77, 124, 128, 143, 221, 226
        Object/By Name, 86, 92-93, 121

DSPLAC_I.PXP, 11-13
dummy objects, creating, 107

E

Edit commands (Photoshop 3.0), 67
editing AVI files, software requirements, 75
Emboss.tif, 233
Emboss2.tif, 233
Explo1.tif, 233
Explo2.tif, 233
exporting AVI files, software requirements, 75

F

Facepat1.tif, 233
Facepat2.tif, 233
Facepat3.tif, 233
Facepat4.tif, 233
Fast Preview mode, 136
File commands
    Clone (Fractal Design Painter), 144
    Clone Source (Fractal Design Painter), 144
    Load, 215, 222, 225
    Load Project, 73, 83, 116, 177
    New, 165
    Open, 65, 144
    Reset, 188
    Save, 221
files
    BMONS_1.3DS, loading, 215
    IFL extension, 116
    MONS2.3DS, loading, 222
    Muscle Bot effect, 29
    SELECT.P3D, loading, 225
    sequential TGA, creating FLICs from, 147-148
    SNAPSHOT.3DS, loading, 222
    Solar Flares effect, 8
FISH.FLC, 247
Fish.tif, 233
Fish2.tif, 234
Fish3.tif, 234
Fish4.tif, 234
Fish5.tif, 234
Flare IPAS, 96
FLARE1 material, 21-22
FLARE2 material, 22
FLARE3 material, 22
FLARELOW material, 22
FLICs, creating from sequential TGA files, 147-148
Flower1.tif, 234
fonts, 189
Forcade, Tim, 230
Fractal Design Painter, 144-147
FUSION.PXP IPAS plug-in (MetaREYES Metaballs), 215-217, 224

G-H

geometry, clones, 32
Get Shape dialog box, 14
Gizmo Lighting effect, 60-69
GLOB.FLC, 247
Globular.tif, 234
Glow Filter dialog box, 95
gradient opacity maps, 188-197, 199
GRIDS_I.PXP, 9-10
hammer (computer-created), interacting with humans
    animation, 124-144
    creating, 116-122
    retouching images, 144-147
    skeleton, 122-124
hardware requirements
    Gizmo Lighting effect, 60
    Human/Computer-Character Interaction effect, 114
    KPT Gradient Designer, 202
    maps, 230
    Muscle Bot effect, 28
    Organic Modeling with Metaballs effect, 212
    Particle Cannon effect, 176
    Search Light effect, 186
    Solar Flares effect, 6
    Tail of the Comet effect, 82
    Time Machine effect, 72
    Tornado effect, 100
    Warp Star Field effect, 164
    Warp Tube effect, 150
heads (Muscle Bot effect), 37
Helium1.tif, 234
Helium2.tif, 234
Helium3.tif, 234
Hierarchy commands
    Center Pivot, 16, 125
    Create Dummy, 45, 107, 156, 170
    Link, 16, 94, 107, 125, 171
    Object Pivot, 125
    Show Tree, 125
Human/Computer-Character Interaction effect
    animation, 124-144
    FLICs, creating from sequential TGA files, 147-148
    hammer, creating, 116-124
    hardware/software requirements, 114
    image file lists, creating, 116
    overview, 115
    retouching images, 144-147

I-J

IFL file extension, 116
image file lists, creating, 116
image processing, 83-86, 88-97
images, retouching (Human/Computer-Character Interaction effect), 144-147
Info commands
    Configure, 18, 73, 154, 177, 204
    Scene Info, 51
Inverse Kinematics (Muscle Bot effect), 48-51
IPAS
    BLOB.PXP plug-in (Metaball Modeler), 215, 217, 224
    Disintegrate, 86, 88-91
    DSPLAC_I.PXP, 11-13
    Flare, 96
    FUSION.PXP plug-in, 215-217, 224
    GRIDS_I.PXP, 9-10
    Magic 4, 92-94

SCRIPT.PXP, 225
SMOKE_I.SXP, 7
SMOOTH.PXP plug-in, 217-218, 224-225
SPURT_I.AXP plug-in, 177-184

Jupiter1.tif, 234
Jupiter2.tif, 235
Jupiter3.tif, 235
Jupiter6.tif, 235

K

Kelpoid.tif, 235
Key Info dialog box, 17, 158, 172
keyboard shortcuts
    2D Shaper (F1), 63
    3D Editor (F3), 64
    3D Lofter (F2), 83
    Fast Preview (F7), 136
    Inverse Kinematics (F8), 48
    IPAS loader menu (F12), 167
    Keyframer (F4), 45
    Materials Editor (F5), 64
Keyframer commands
    Cameras/Create, 159
    Display
        Freeze/Object, 125
        Hide, 159
        Hide/By Color, 108-110
        Hide/By Name, 135, 197
        Hide/Object, 125
        Unhide/By Color, 109
        Unhide/By Name, 128, 143
    Hierarchy
        Center Pivot, 16, 125
        Create Dummy, 45, 107, 156, 170
        Link, 16, 94, 107, 125, 171
        Object Pivot, 125
        Show Tree, 125
    Info/Scene Info, 51
    Object
        Attributes, 51, 135, 143
        Morph/Assign, 199
        Morph/Options, 199
        Move, 107, 109-110, 160, 173, 199
        Rotate Abs., 79-80
        Rotate, 109
        Snapshot, 222-223
        Tracks/Copy, 93
        Tracks/Loop, 48
    Preview/Make, 159
    Renderer
        Render View, 111, 148, 184
        Setup/Background, 136
        Video Post, 95, 97, 160
        View/Flic, 243, 248
    Time
        Define Segment, 17, 199
        Total, 198

keyframing test animations (Muscle Bot effect), 45-48
KPT Gradient Designer, 202-209
KUB's The Script Extensions (TSE), 219-220, 225

L

Layering
    Gizmo Lighting effect, 61-69
    Solar Flares effect, 7-24
legs (Muscle Bot effect), 33-34
    Inverse Kinematics, 48-51
Library commands
    Load Library, 18
    New, 165
lighting
    Gizmo Lighting effect, 61-69
    Gradient Designer, 203-209
    Time Machine effect, 73-80
    visible light, 187-199
Lights commands
    Omni, 192
    Spot/Create, 76-77, 178
Lines.tif, 235
Lines2.tif, 235
Lines3.tif, 235
linking bones (Muscle Bot effect), 43-44
LIQUID.IFL & .FLC, 244
loading
    files
        BMONS_1.3DS, 215
        MONS2.3DS, 222
        SELECT.P3D, 225
        SNAPSHOT.3DS, 222
    projects
        COMET.PRJ, 83
        HAMMER.PRJ, 116
        PARTICLE.PRJ, 177
        TIME.PRJ, 73
lofting Tail of the Comet text, 84
Loops01.tif, 235
Lspheres, creating, 166

M

MacDougall, Brandon, 202
Maestri, George, 100
Magic 4 IPAS, 92-94
mapping coordinates, applying to metaball-modeling mesh objects, 220-221, 226
maps, 231
    animated
        on CD-ROM, 243-249
        texture, 73-80
    bump, 219
    color texture, 177-184
    hardware/software requirements, 230

opacity, 102-111
- gradient, 188-197, 199
- static, on CD-ROM, 232-243

Marsface.tif, 235
Material morphs, 188-197, 199
Material commands
- Get from Scene, 74, 179
- Get Material, 75, 196
- Put To Current, 194-195, 220

materials
- accessing, 74
- applying to metaball-modeling mesh objects, 220-221, 226
- Particle Cannon effect, 178
- Search Light effect, 194, 196, 198
- Solar Flares effect, 18-23
- Warp Star Field effect, 165-166
- Warp Tube effect, 154-155

Materials Editor commands
- Info/Configure, 18, 154
- Library
  - Load Library, 18
  - New, 165
- Material
  - Get from Scene, 179
  - Get Material, 196
  - Get Material/SKY GLASS, 75
  - Put To Current, 194-195, 220

McKisic, Kyle, 212
mesh morphs, 188-197, 199
mesh objects
- armed/legged characters
  - applying materials/mapping coordinates, 226
  - generating, 224-225
  - selecting polygons, 225
- armless/legless characters
  - applying materials/mapping coordinates, 220-221
  - creating, 215-217
  - processing, 217-220
  - snapshot modeling, 221-222

metaball modeling, 213-215
- armed/legged characters, 222-224
  - applying materials/mapping coordinates to mesh objects, 226
  - generating mesh objects, 224-225
  - selecting polygons, 225
- armless/legless characters
  - applying materials/mapping coordinates to mesh objects, 220-221
  - creating mesh objects, 215-217
  - processing mesh objects, 217-220
  - snapshot modeling, 221-222
- skeletal deformation, 215

Metaballs Modeler (Digimation)
- fusion color assignments, 214
- generating
  - geometry, 215
  - mesh objects, 217, 224
- Metaballs Modeler dialog box, 217

MetaREYES Metaballs (Schreiber Instruments)
- fusion color assignments, 214
- generating
  - geometry, 214
  - mesh objects, 217, 224
- MetaREYES Metaballs 2.0 dialog box, 216

modeling
- metaball, *see* metaball modeling
- snapshot, 221-222

Modify commands
- Axis
  - Place, 36, 101, 193
  - Show, 193
- Object
  - 2D Scale, 15, 102-103, 156, 168
  - 2D Scale/shift-select, 193-194
  - 3D Scale, 9, 13, 102, 156
  - Attributes, 69, 75, 86, 88, 92, 122, 124, 182
  - Change Color, 104, 192, 194
  - Delete, 170
  - Mirror, 223
  - Move, 13, 15, 64, 102, 119, 166, 180, 192
  - Reset Xform, 14
  - Rotate, 14, 17, 85, 88, 119
  - Taper, 179
- Vertex/3D Scale, 166

MONS2.3DS file, loading, 222
morphs, mesh/material, 188-197, 199
motion tests (Human/Computer-Character Interaction effect), 142-143
Murky1.tif, 236
Murky2.tif, 236
Muscle Bot effect
- arms, 34-36
- bodies, 30-33
- bones
  - linking, 43-44
  - modification effects on bounding boxes, 30
  - retaining bones, 40-42
  - setting influence, 51-57
- files, 29
- hardware/software requirements, 28
- heads, 37
- keyframing test animations, 45-48
- legs, 33-34, 48-51
- muscles, 38-39
- overview, 29
- rendering, 58

N-O

Nash, Kirk O., 82, 114
nebula (Solar Flares effect), 15-16
NEBULA material, 22
Nebula1.tif, 236
Nebula2.tif, 236
Netblur.tif, 236
Netcolor.tif, 236
Nodules1.tif, 236

Nodules2.tif, 236
Nodules3.tif, 236
Nodules4.tif, 236
Object Attachment Tree dialog box, 125
Object Attributes dialog box, 124, 182
Object Lofting Controls dialog box, 152-153
Object commands
    Attributes, 51, 135, 143
    Morph, 199
    Move, 107, 109-110, 160, 173, 199
    Preview, 152
    Rotate Abs., 79-80
    Rotate, 109
    Snapshot, 222-223
    Tracks
        Copy, 93
        Loop, 48
Objects commands
    Make, 84, 117-118, 191-192
    Preview, 117
Oily.tif, 237
Oily2.tif, 237
Oily3.tif, 237
Oily4.tif, 237
Oily5.tif, 237
Oily6.tif, 237
Oily7.tif, 237
Oily8.tif, 237
opacity maps, 102-111, 188-197, 199
Options command (KPT Gradient Designer), 204-206
Organic Modeling with Metaballs effect
    armed/legged characters, 222-224
        applying materials/mapping coordinates to mesh
            objects, 226
        generating mesh objects, 224-225
        selecting polygons, 225
    armless/legless characters
        applying materials/mapping coordinates to mesh
            objects, 220-221
        creating mesh objects, 215-217
        processing mesh objects, 217-220
        snapshot modeling, 221-222
    hardware/software requirements, 212
    overview, 213-215
    skeletal deformation, 215

P

Panels.tif, 237
Paper.tif, 237
Paper2.tif, 238
Paper3.tif, 238
particle animation, 83-86, 88-97
Particle Cannon effect, 176-184
Pat01.tif, 238
Path commands
    2D Scale, 151
    Move Vertex, 152, 191-192
    Refine, 151
    Steps, 191
    SurfRev, 117
Phillips, Greg, 72, 176
Photo1.tif, 238
Photo2.tif, 238
Photoshop 3.0, Gizmo Lighting effect, 65-67
PLA*.JPG, 245
Planet01.tif, 238
Planet02.tif, 238
Planets1.tif, 238
PLAS*.JPG, 245
PLAS.IFL & .FLC, 245
plasma fields, creating, 155
PLASTIC.IFL & .FLC, 245
polygons, selecting for metaball modeling, 225
POUR*.JPG, 244
Preview/Make command, 159
Procedural Blends (KPT Gradient Designer), 205
Program commands
    DOS Window, 18
    KXP Loader, 51
    PXP Loader, 215, 219, 224-225
PSYC*.JPG, 245
PSYCHA.IFL & .FLC, 245

Q-R

Queue Entry dialog box, 95, 160-161, 208
Queue Parameters dialog box, 208-209

Radial Sweeps (KPT Gradient Designer), 206
RAINBOW.IFL & .FLC, 245
Raw1.tif, 238
Raw2.tif, 238
Raw3.tif, 239
Raw4.tif, 239
Raw5.tif, 239
Raw6.tif, 239
Raw7.tif, 239
RBOW*.JPG, 245
Renderer commands
    Output/Coords, 96
    Render View, 13, 111, 122, 148, 184
    Setup
        Background, 136, 147, 243, 249
        Configure, 10, 13
    Video Post, 24, 95, 97, 160
    View/Flic, 115, 243, 248
rendering
    Muscle Bot effect, 58
    Solar Flares effect, 16-17
retaining bones (Muscle Bot effect), 40-42
retouching images (Human/Computer-Character Interaction effect), 144-147
Ripples1.tif, 239
Robertson, Ken, 150, 164

S

Safe Frame, 10
Sat01.tif, 239
Sat02.tif, 239
Sat03.tif, 239
Sat04.tif, 239
scaling shapes, 151-152
Scatter dialog box, 167-170
Schreiber Instruments' MetaREYES Metaballs
    fusion color assignments, 214
    generating geometry, 214
    generating mesh objects, 217, 224
    MetaREYES Metaballs 2.0 dialog box, 216
The Script Extensions (KUB), 219-220, 225
SCRIPT.PXP IPAS, 225
Scrncolr.tif, 240
Scrnmsk.tif, 240
Scrtch3.tif, 240
Search Light effect
    animation, 197, 199
    geometry, 188-193, 195
    hardware/software requirements, 186
    materials, 194, 196, 198
    overview, 187-188
Segment.tif, 240
SELECT.P3D script, 219-220, 225
Select commands
    Face/Quad/*Window, 193
    Invert, 85, 221, 226
    None, 223
    Object
        By Color, 105
        By Name, 88, 119
        Quad, 103, 223
    Polygon/Quad/*Window, 190
    Save Selection (Photoshop 3.0), 67
    Vertex/Quad, 166
sequential TGA files, creating FLICs from, 147-148
Shape commands
    Assign, 83, 117-118
        None, 118
        Selected, 190
    Check, 190
    Steps, 189
Shapes commands
    Align, 117-118
    Center, 118
    Get/Shaper, 84, 117-118, 151, 190
    Rotate, 118
    Scale, 151
Sher, Richard, 186
skeletal deformation, 215
skeletons
    hammer, interacting with humans, 122-124
    see also Muscle Bot effect
SKY GLASS material, 75
SMOKE_I.SXP, 7
Smooge.tif, 240
Smooge2.tif, 240
Smooge3.tif, 240
Smooge4.tif, 240
Smooge5.tif, 240
Smooge6.tif, 240
SMOOTH.PXP IPAS plug-in, 217-218, 224-225
snapshot modeling, 221-222
SNAPSHOT.3DS file, loading, 222
software requirements
    Gizmo Lighting effect, 60
    exporting/editing AVI files, 75
    Human/Computer-Character Interaction effect, 114
    KPT Gradient Designer, 202
    maps, 230
    Muscle Bot effect, 28
    Organic Modeling with Metaballs effect, 212
    Particle Cannon effect, 176
    Search Light effect, 186
    Solar Flares effect, 6-7
    Tail of the Comet effect, 82
    Time Machine effect, 72
    Tornado effect, 100
    Warp Star Field effect, 164
    Warp Tube effect, 150
Solar Flares effect
    animation, 23-24
    creating Solar Flares, 14-15
    files, 8
    hardware/software requirements, 6
    materials, 18-23
    nebula, 15-16
    overview, 7
    rendering, 16-17
    spiraling clouds, 9-13
    sun surfaces, 8-9
SPAT*.JPG, 246
SPATR1.IFL & .FLC, 246
SPATR2.IFL & .FLC, 246
SPECS.FLC, 248
Specs.tif, 241
Splatcld.tif, 241
Splotch1.tif, 241
Splotch2.tif, 241
Splotch3.tif, 241
spotlights, creating, 76-77, 178-179
SPOTS material, 22
SPTR*.JPG, 246
SPURT_I.AXP IPAS plug-in, 177-184
static maps on CD-ROM, 232-243
storyboarding animations, 128
STREAK.FLC, 248
Streaks.tif, 241
strobe effect, creating, 79-80
sun surfaces (Solar Flares effect), 8-9
SURFACE material, 22
Surface of Revolution dialog box, 117
surface textures, animated procedural, 188-197, 199

Surface commands
    Apply/By Name, 93
    Mapping
        Adjust, 101
        Adjust/Acquire, 120
        Adjust/Region Fit, 221, 226
        Adjust/Scale, 11, 14, 16, 68, 75, 181, 193
        Apply, 193
        Apply/Object, 75, 121, 181, 221, 226
        Assign/Object, 101
        Type, 101, 181, 193, 221, 226
        Type/Cylindrical, 75, 120
        Type/Planar, 11, 14
        Type/Spherical, 16
    Material
        Apply/Face, 220, 226
        Assign, 69, 155
        Assign/By Name, 93
        Assign/Object, 121, 181, 194
        Choose, 69, 75, 93, 121, 181
        Get Library, 74, 93, 121
    Normals/Object Flip, 16
SWIRL.FLC, 248
Swirl1.tif, 241
Swirl2.tif, 241
SXP animation direction, 14
Symet1.tif, 241
SYMSPRAY.IFL & .FLC, 246
SYMT*.JPG, 246

T

Tail of the Comet effect
    APX stand-in objects, 84-86, 88-91
    comet, 92-94
    hardware/software requirements, 82
    overview, 83
    text, 83-84
    Video Post Image Processing effects, 95-97
Taylor, Paul, 60
tessellating stand-in AXP objects (Tail of the Comet), 89
testing
    keyframing test animations (Muscle Bot effect), 45-48
    motion (Human/Computer-Character Interaction effect), 142-143
text (Tail of the Comet effect), 83-86, 88-91
texture maps
    animated, 73-80
    color, 177-184
textures
    AniMap on CD-ROM, 243-246, 248-249
    animated, 102-111, 188-197, 199
TGA files (sequential), creating FLICs from, 147-148
Time Machine effect, 72-80
Time commands
    Define Segment, 17, 199
    Total, 198

Tornado effect
    animating tornado, 108-109
    distorting funnel, 109-110
    funnel stacks, 101-104
    hardware/software requirements, 100
    nesting stacks, 106-108
    rendering, 110-111
    textures, 104-106
toruses, creating, 101
Track Info dialog box, 90-91, 156-157, 172, 174, 199
transitions, AniMap (on CD-ROM), 243, 246-249
transparencies (Solar Flares effect), 7-24
tweaking, 142-143

U–V

Unhide dialog box, 86

Video Post dialog box, 208-209
Video Post Image Processing effects
    Tail of the Comet effect, 95-97
    Warp Tube effect, 160-162
Video Post Queue dialog box, 95-96
Views commands
    Angle Snap, 14
    Drawing Aids, 188
    Unit Setup, 8
visible light, 187-199

W–Z

Warp Star Field effect
    animating star field, 170-172, 174
    creating star field, 166-171
    hardware/software requirements, 164
    materials, 165-166
    overview, 165
Warp Tube effect
    animating warp tube, 155-160
    creating warp tube, 151-154
    hardware/software requirements, 150
    materials, 154-155
    overview, 151
    Video Post, 160-162
Watery.tif, 241
Watery2.tif, 242
Watery3.tif, 242
Watery4.tif, 242
Window/Palettes/Show Layers command (Photoshop 3.0), 66
wipes, AniMap (on CD-ROM), 243, 246-249
Wrmmass.tif, 242
Wrmmsk1.tif, 242

Yel3msk.tif, 242
Yelpeel3.tif, 242

REGISTRATION CARD

3D Studio Hollywood and Gaming Effects

Name _____ Title _____

Company _____ Type of business _____

Address _____

City/State/ZIP _____

Have you used these types of books before?   ☐ yes   ☐ no

If yes, which ones? _____
_____

How many computer books do you purchase each year?   ☐ 1–5   ☐ 6 or more

How did you learn about this book? _____

Where did you purchase this book? _____

Which applications do you currently use? _____
_____

Which computer magazines do you subscribe to? _____
_____

What trade shows do you attend? _____
_____

Comments: _____
_____
_____

Would you like to be placed on our preferred mailing list?   ☐ yes   ☐ no

☐ **I would like to see my name in print!** You may use my name and quote me in future New Riders products and promotions. My daytime phone number is: _____

New Riders Publishing   201 West 103rd Street ♦ Indianapolis, Indiana 46290 USA

Fax to **317-581-4670**   Orders/Customer Service **1-800-653-6156**   Source Code **NRP95**

Fold Here

BUSINESS REPLY MAIL
FIRST-CLASS MAIL PERMIT NO. 9918 INDIANAPOLIS IN

POSTAGE WILL BE PAID BY THE ADDRESSEE

NO POSTAGE
NECESSARY
IF MAILED
IN THE
UNITED STATES

**NEW RIDERS PUBLISHING
201 W 103RD ST
INDIANAPOLIS IN 46290-9058**